Drawn & Described

A collection of locomotive drawings
and accompanying articles

by Ian Beattie

As published in RAILWAY MODELLER

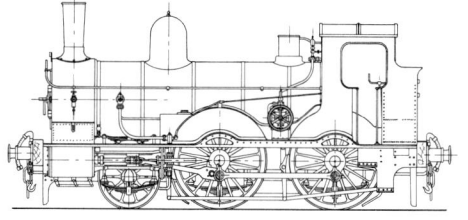

Compiled by Tim Rayner

A Peco Publication

© Peco Publications
and Publicity Ltd. 2001

Underleys, Beer, Seaton, Devon EX12 3NA.
Telephone 01297 20580.

First Published October 2001

All rights reserved. No part of this publication may be reproduced or transmitted in any form or by any means, electronic or mechanical, including photocopying, recording or by any information storage and retrieval system, without prior permission in writing from the copyright owners.
ISBN 0 900586 90 7

Printed by The Amadeus Press, Ezra House,
West 26 Business Park, Cleckheaton,
West Yorkshire BD19 4TQ.

For Anne-Marie
and Katherine

The drawings have been reproduced
to 4mm scale.
Unless credited otherwise,
the photographs are by Frank Hornby.

Preface

IAN BEATTIE was born in November 1942. He was brought up in North London and educated at Mill Hill School and afterwards studied at the Chelsea College of Aeronautical and Automobile Engineering. He then spent several years with Mercedes Benz at its London headquarters.

During the 1960s he moved to Devon where his parents were living. In 1977 his first book was published, *Automobile Body Design* – a book of detailed line drawings. His love of cars, aeroplanes and photography remained undiminished but his career path led him to concentrate on railways, writing a series of books on locomotives, line drawn to scale, published by Bradford Barton.

Apart from the love of his work Ian was very widely read with a particular interest in Scotland and the family origins. He loved the life in Devon particularly his home in Ottery St.Mary, where he lived surrounded by his books, videos and a great collection of music.

His affection for his family was enormous and especially for his nieces Anne-Marie and Katherine to whom this book is dedicated.

Jenny Critchley-Salmonson

Ian Beattie, 1942-2000.
PHOTOGRAPHED BESIDE HIS NIECE ANNE-MARIE.

Introduction

WE HAVE selected 54 drawings from Ian's published writings, illustrating a good cross-section of the 'Big Four' major railway companies, the nationalised system, plus experimental and narrow gauge machines. This mix of steam, diesel and electric subjects large and small, successful and less so depicts admirably Ian's diverse skills. Needless to say it was hard to choose which drawings to include, so it is possible that there will be a further volume in the future.

In this collection of Ian's articles, we have left the text very much as published. Occasionally the very characteristic prolix writing style will have been trimmed further than in the originals to improve clarity. Where appropriate, notes in brackets have been added to give an update to the articles. Subsequent published corrections, such as the revised 'Schools' front elevation (from the letters page of the November 1999 edition) have been incorporated here. A list of the drawings and the issues of RAILWAY MODELLER in which they appeared is given inside the rear cover.

It is a modelling axiom that drawings should be backed up by photographs of the chosen prototype – the more the better. Certainly,

having been given a subject for his next 'Drawn & Described', Ian's first move would be to phone Frank Hornby (who he had known since Bradford Barton days) to ascertain what negatives Frank had of the chosen prototype in his vast and well-ordered collection. Only once suitable pictures (from as many angles as possible) had been ordered, printed and delivered, and research carried out from both Ian's personal archive and our own at Beer, could drawing start in earnest.

We make no apology for the fact that many of the photographs within these pages, mostly by Frank Hornby and Walter Boyden, have been seen before either in the early Bradford Barton books or in the RAILWAY MODELLER articles. We have used them again because of their undoubted quality and authenticity but mainly because each one formed part of Ian's references for that particular loco, was almost certainly clipped to the edge of the drawing board as he worked, and because here, we feel, is where they belong.

All of us at Peco Publications suffered a great loss at the time of Ian's early death and so it is that this book is published in his memory.

Section 1
Great Western Railway (and constituents)

Locomotive	Page	Locomotive	Page
48xx/58xx/14xx 0-4-2T	4-5	'Large Prairie' 2-6-2T	14-15
Barry Railway Class B1 0-6-2T	6-7	Collett 2251 0-6-0	16-17
Taff Vale Railway Class A 0-6-2T	8-9	47xx fast freight 2-8-0	18-19
Churchward 'Star' 4-6-0 and 4-4-2	9-11	56xx 0-6-2T	20-21
Diesel railcars Nos.19-38	12-13	15xx 0-6-0PT	22-23

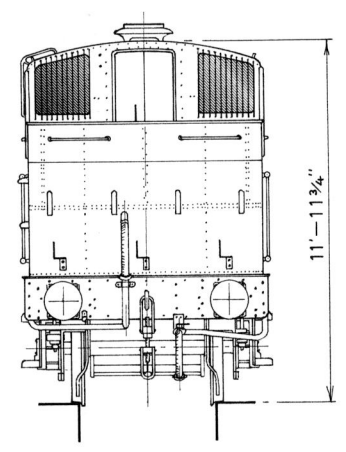
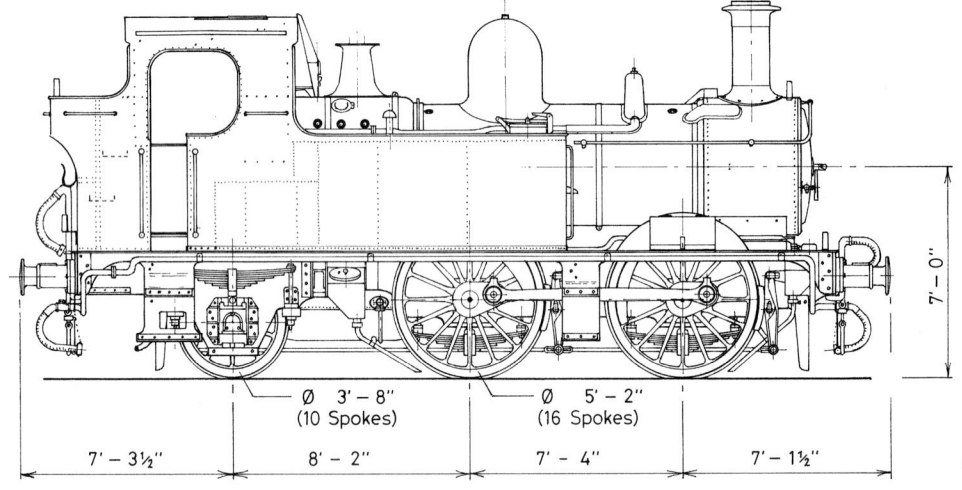
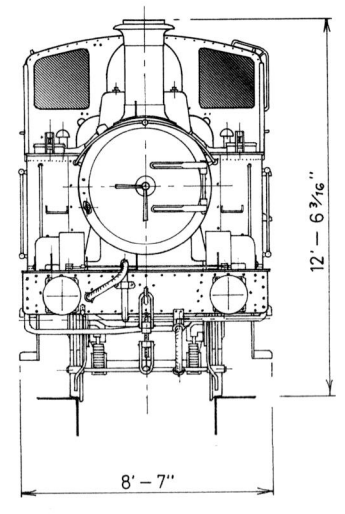
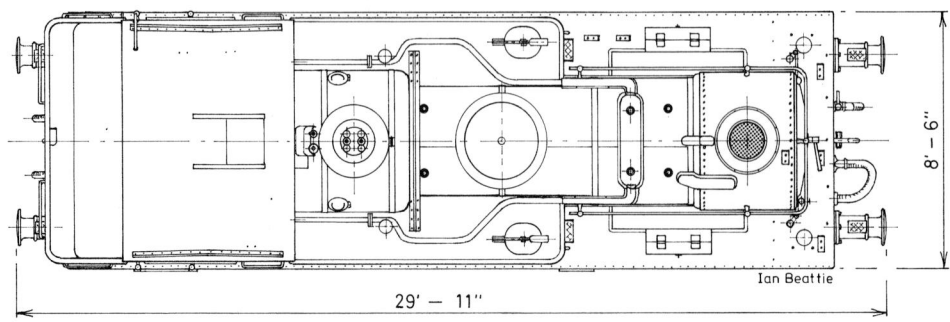

Ian Beattie

48xx/58xx/14xx 0-4-2T

WITH ITS antiquated appearance belying an eager, rip-roaring performance, the tiny Collett Auto-tank somehow epitomises the atmosphere and flavour of the erstwhile Great Western Railway, notwithstanding such epoch-making top link machinery in the 'Star'/'Castle'/'King' mould.

A product of Charles B. Collett, Chief Mechanical Engineer to the GWR between 1922 and 1941, the Auto-tank owed its outline to a precursive design of 0-4-2T, the 517 Class built from the late 1860s at Wolverhampton under the then chief engineer George Armstrong's aegis for handling branch and other light duties. The great success of these little engines in their designated tasks led to replacements being sought as age and wear inexorably overtook them.

During 1923, only a year or so into Collett's reign as CME, a singleton 517 Class 0-4-2T – No.1421 of 1877 vintage – was adapted, modernised and then tested on auto-train traffic in the Cardiff region; its fine showing ensured continuation of the species and acted as basis for the updated version.

In common with all 20th-Century GW locomotives the Collett Auto-tanks were assembled in the erecting shops at Swindon, the first batch of 30 being outshopped in 1932-33 and followed successively until a total of 75 engines completed the class in 1936. Numbered 4800-74, the tanks featured not only auto-train equipment but Automatic Train Control gear, a GW pioneer of the highly sophisticated BR Automatic Warning System.

A secondary batch of 20 0-4-2Ts with neither ATC nor push/pull connections emerged in 1933 for shunting and similar working, numbers allotted for these being 5800-19; these engines were otherwise identical to the 48xx series although they tended to serve over a less widespread area than their more ubiquitous stable-mates, being based mainly in the Worcester and Bristol regions. Unlike the latter, the 58xx 0-4-2Ts retained their original numbers throughout their existence.

Due to their deliberately light axle load there was no restriction anywhere on the GWR network to the Auto-tanks' presence and this quality combined with nimbleness (aided by tall driving wheels) and excellent boiler characteristics, ensured the Class's welcome anywhere on the Railway. Their legendary élan coupled with antique lines (albeit augmented by spacious modern, all-enclosed cabs complete with large windows, much appreciated by crews after the spartan 517s) pursued the Auto-tanks' internal reputation for efficiency.

Following World War 2 Britain's railways were subjected to politically-motivated experiments in the use of oil as fuel for steam locomotives; the Great Western was no exception and in 1946 selected 8-coupled freight engines were so modified, including number changes: the 48xx sequence was chosen and relevant plates thus removed from the Auto-tanks, which were assigned numbers 1400-74 in lieu. Although the oil-burning episode quickly sank into oblivion, the 2-8-0s involved reverting to both coal combustion and their original identities, the Auto-tanks famously retained the 14xx series thenceforward.

Long before obsolescence overcame them the 0-4-2Ts were sacrificed to a lethal cocktail of rationalisation, modernisation and the great god Diesel: as branch after branch closed during the '50s and '60s and push/pull workings were superseded by the onset of diesel railcars the little tanks disappeared inexorably onto the scrap lines. All 95 14xx/58xx 0-4-2Ts were removed from revenue-earning service between 1956 and 1964; fortunately no fewer than four of these cheerfully hard-working engines have been retained for posterity.

Notes on the drawings

Sundry alterations and modifications were applied to the Auto-tanks over time, mostly however of a minor nature; therefore in order to depict these comprehensively the drawings illustrate a typical 0-4-2T in its final manifestation before withdrawal. Most evident was the topfeed apparatus, applied to the majority of the fleet from 1944 onwards, and the effective whistle shield that diverted steam away from the windows; the twin footsteps added to the fireman's (left hand) side of the bunker – rendered in dashed lines on the side elevation here – were a comparatively late BR fitment. Also present on many Autotanks were smokebox 'chin' steps and transverse lids under the smokebox covering the sandbox operating linkage.

Not shown on the drawings is the push/pull equipment, outwardly comprising a boxlike structure beside the brake standard fore and aft, plus connecting lines running along the right-hand valance.

Liveries involved included Brunswick passenger green under GW ownership, then lined black in BR days reverting to green (both plain and lined were witnessed) from the mid-1950s.

The youngest member of the class, 1936-built No.1474 poses nicely on the boil at Southall in April 1957. Top feed was notable by its absence on this particular Auto-tank but bunker footholds are nonetheless present. PHOTOGRAPH: NORMAN BROWNE.

Type:	General-purpose tank
Cylinders:	2, 16" x 24" bore/stroke
Boiler Pressure:	165 lbs/sq in
Heating Surface:	953 sq ft
Grate Area:	12.8 sq ft
Tractive Effort:	13900 lbs
Mean Weight in Working Order:	41 tons 6 cwt
Water Capacity:	800 gallons
Number Built:	95, 1932-36
Preserved:	4

Barry Railway Class B1 0-6-2T

Editor's note. Between the October 1985 and April 1995 issues of RAILWAY MODELLER, Ian produced no fewer than 25 drawings of locomotives from the South Wales valleys – that there were so many classes from which to choose is a testament in itself to the erstwhile railway activity in this part of the Principality. The occasional series covered all manner of machines, but as the 0-6-2T was the area's signature tune two examples (plus, later in this section the GWR 56xx variety) are studied here.

PREVIOUSLY in this series three types of locomotive used by the Barry Railway have been covered, of which two were passenger types (Class J 2-4-2T, RM Oct 1985; Class G 0-4-4T, RM Jan 1987) and the third a small batch of 8-coupled goods tanks (RM Nov 1986); as with all the South Wales railway systems coal was the principal source of income, indeed the reason for the being of the Barry Railway and in concert with its competitors made much use of 0-6-2 tanks as the chief tractive means of transporting the mineral from pit to port.

The Barry system was a latecomer on the Welsh scene, opening in 1888, established to meet hugely expanded exports of coal engendered during the expansive Victorian era; the port of Barry was founded as a direct result of this expansion and the railway that served it was routed mainly in the Aberdare and Rhondda valleys as well as having important connections with other coal railways.

The initial 'coal tanks' were 0-6-0Ts, followed quite quickly by a fleet of 0-6-2Ts – classes A and B respectively – all outshopped by a number of renowned British private locomotive builders: the Barry Railway was not equipped to build its own machines, though the maintenance works at Barry always handled repairs and overhauls with expert thoroughness and despatch, as befitted an intensively worked railway. A further series of 0-6-2 tanks was commissioned whilst the Class Bs were being completed of very similar mechanical specification to the latter but incorporating larger coal and water capacities: these engines, the B1 Class, utilised 4'3" diameter coupled wheels common to the earlier locomotives, and were erected in five batches from three builders. Messrs Sharp Stewart built 9 in 1890 (Barry Nos.38-46), 6 in 1894 (Nos.73-78) and 12 in 1900 (Nos.105-116); the Vulcan Foundry supplied 10 engines in 1892 (Nos.54-63); and the Belgian constructors SA Franco-Belge were subcontracted to complete 5 B1s, which they did in 1899-1900 (Nos.122-126). Before dispatch to Wales No.126 was displayed at the Paris Exhibition of 1900.

The class thus constituted 42 engines and remained much the largest of Barry's locomotive roster – their close cousins and progenitors the Bs were a class of 25,

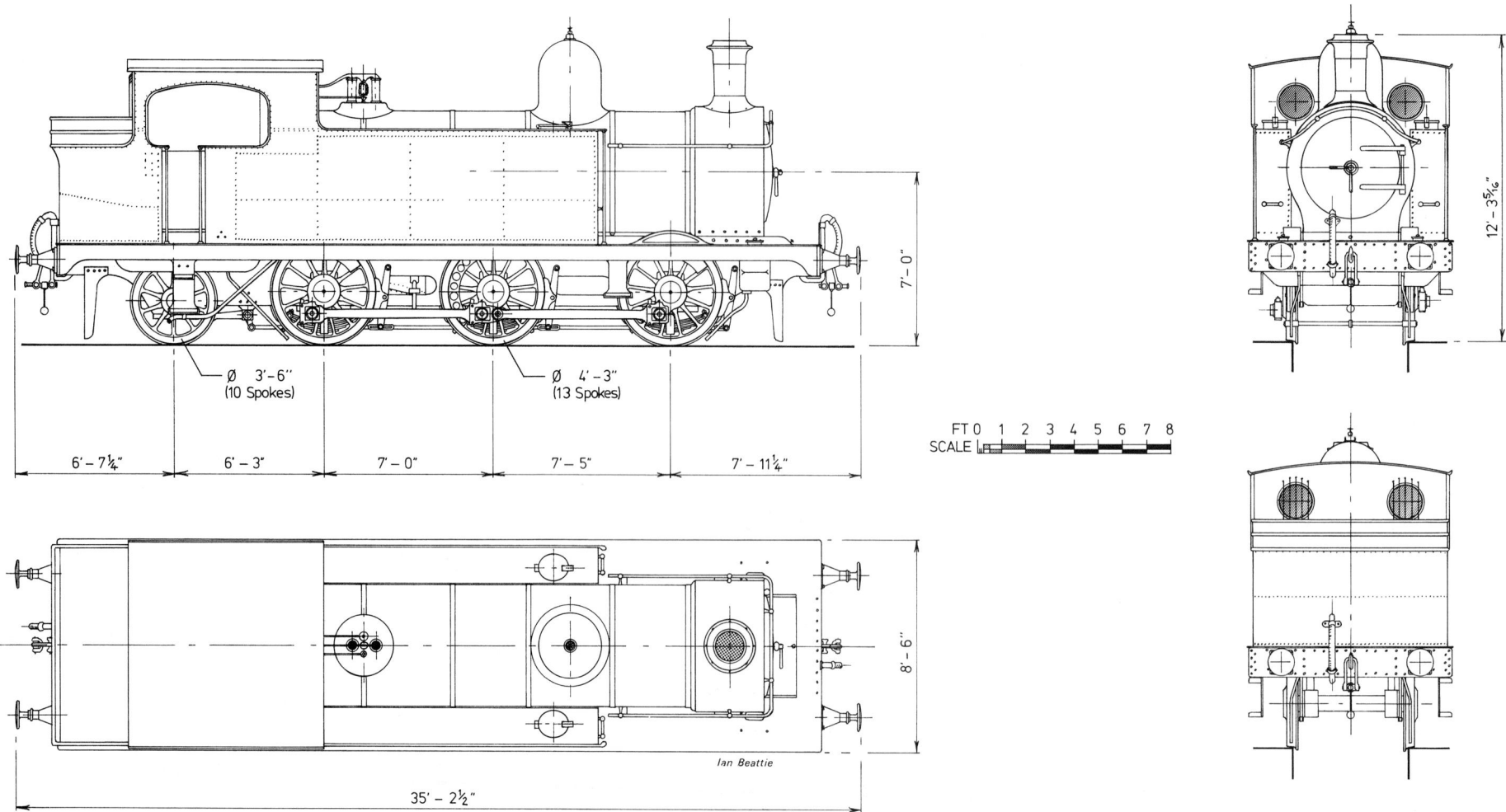

Ian Beattie

and both classes tended to be spatchcocked together after grouping as withdrawals eventually created considerable gaps in their numbers, especially beyond nationalisation in 1948.

Following grouping the B1s underwent erratic and seemingly random modification to their minor fittings, with consequent problems for the present-day historian and the modeller. In many instances Barry boilers were directly displaced by Swindon Standard No.9 counterparts: all B1s were equipped with GWR mountings and very many with replacement GW smokeboxes, others received GW-style bunker extensions. The distinctive GW safety valve bonnets were applied throughout which led to some interesting whistle sitings – on the roof, behind the bonnet or (mimicking the original position) placed laterally high up on the bonnet. As stated so many times when considering locomotives in these pages, to model a Barry B1 it really is necessary to find a picture of an example photographed during the desired period for modelling and faithfully replicate it, which should avoid solecisms.

Beware also that with three manufacturers involved three different overall lengths were found over the class, the variations being in the frame length forward of the leading axle: that shown in the drawings, 35'5½", and 35'10½". Additionally, most B1s sported vacuum braking apparatus for the rare passenger or fitted van duty, in which event screw couplings were *de rigueur*; unfitted engines were witnessed sporting either these or the simpler three-link couplings, interchangeably it appears from photographic evidence.

Withdrawals commenced in 1932 and 19 B1 0-6-2Ts survived into BR ownership, with the last examples removed from revenue-earning service in 1951. However a number escaped the cutting torch for a few more years as Swindon Works shunters but these too inexorably joined their classmates at the last.

Type:	Six-coupled Goods Tank
Cylinders:	2, 17½" x 26" bore/stroke
Mean Weight in Working Order:	53½ tons
Coal Capacity:	2¼ tons
Water Capacity:	1590 gallons
Number Built:	42, 1890-1900
Preserved:	None

ABOVE: an intriguing view taken at Barry shed on 26 May 1929 of Sharp Stewart engine of 1900 No.265 (ex-Barry No.110) under the gantry crane, its frame shored up for attention to the carrying axle – open-air overhaul was common on smaller British railways. The engine carries a Barry boiler with GW bonnet and smokebox.
PHOTOGRAPH: THE LATE W.G.BOYDEN, FRANK HORNBY COLLECTION.

RIGHT: built by Franco-Belge in 1899, No.276, ex-Barry No.125 stands on Barry shed not far from withdrawal, 11 June 1949; note GWR boiler and bunker extension.

Taff Vale Railway Class A 0-6-2T

THE BIGGEST, oldest and financially most remunerative of the many railways that thrived on coal haulage in South Wales, the Taff Vale Railway always maintained a close working relationship with the Great Western – historically both concerns were linked by their common engineer, Isambard Kingdom Brunel – opening their tracks at around the same period: the TVR route from Cardiff to Merthyr opened in 1840 and the Pontypridd-Treherbert line followed (in its entirety) 16 years thereafter, both routes possessing manifold spurs that constituted the bulk of the TVR system.

The TVR Class O4 0-6-2 tank class has already been dealt with in this series (see RM April 1986), but whereas that was specifically designed for mineral traffic the Class A engines of the same wheel arrangement were primarily intended for passenger traffic, of which there was a sizable degree on the network, though little enough compared with the immense coal workings.

The fairly large-diameter coupled wheels indicate the engines' usage, with the ability to switch onto mineral haulage when necessary, and to this end were equipped with vacuum braking from the outset (the steam heating apparatus came later). Designed by F.Cameron, fifty-eight examples were erected between 1914 and 1921 by three private builders, the Vulcan Foundry, North British and Hawthorn Leslie. As outshopped the class sported a squat parallel boiler with Belpaire firebox, much as the coal-hauling equivalents, and were numbered quite haphazardly by the owning company. Livery was black throughout during TVR days, whilst the GWR tended to repaint them green as befitted their passenger-hauling status.

Unusually in this series I have elected to show the Class as rebuilt by the GWR after 1923, when the TVR merged into the Group alongside other Welsh railways. Class A No.120 was the prototype 0-6-2T to undergo reboilering, in June 1924, being renumbered GWR No.441, and on the obvious success of the Standard No.10 boiler as applied thereon the remaining 57 members were similarly rejigged, between 1926 and 1932. There were very many variations in fixtures and fittings between the engines, a function in part no doubt of the time span involved in rebuilding them, so that although the boiler was common to all, some engines received 17½" diameter cylinders coupled with boilers pressurised to 200 lbs sq in (whereupon the tractive effort rose to 21480 lbs); tapered and straight-flanked chimneys were noted, as were tall or short safety valve bonnets; roof-style variations also obtained, amongst

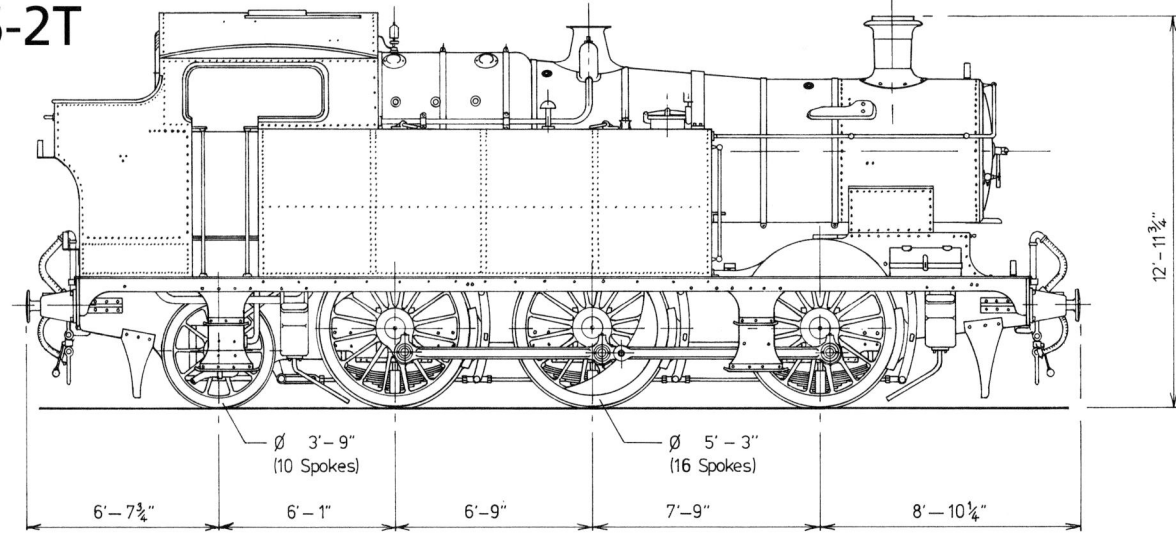

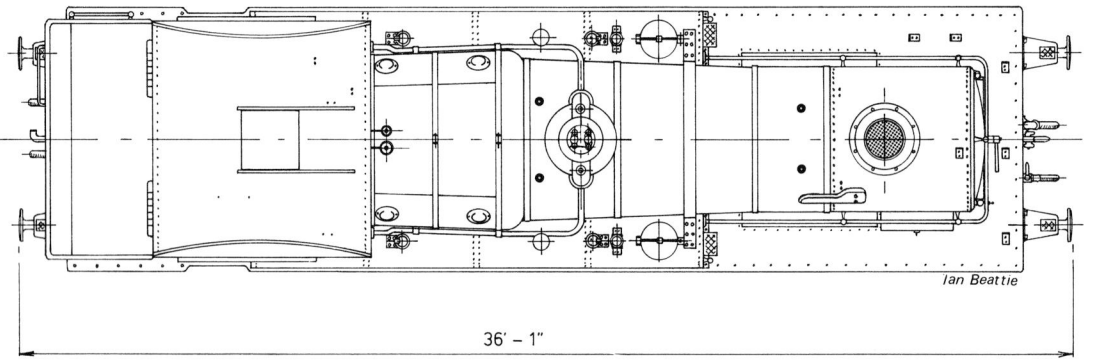

Ian Beattie

RIGHT: vintage Vulcan Foundry 1921, ex-Taff Vale A No.306 basks in the sunshine on Barry shed on 22 May 1955. The valleys workhorse had eleven months' service left to run.

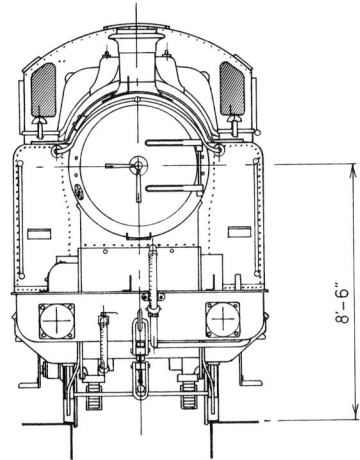

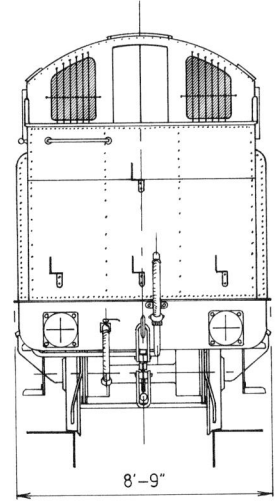

Gloriously immaculate bar a weathered smokebox, 1908-vintage No.4014 *Knight of the Bath* poses impressively outside Swindon Works on 8 September 1935. Note the recently-added outside steampipes. PHOTOGRAPH: THE LATE W.G.BOYDEN, FRANK HORNBY COLLECTION.

Churchward 'Star' Class 4-6-0 and 4-4-2 No.40

ARGUABLY the most influential British steam locomotive of the century and incontrovertibly George Jackson Churchward's masterpiece, the 4-cylinder 'Star' Class 4-6-0 premier passenger design was a huge technological step forward on its appearance in 1906/7; it also set the Great Western top link blueprint for the ensuing forty years – encapsulating the 'Castles' and 'Kings' – until the Company was subsumed by nationalisation into British Railways in 1948.

Chief Mechanical Engineer from 1902 until his retirement in December 1922, the Devonian Churchward (he was born in Stoke Gabriel, near Totnes in 1857) introduced a series of superbly designed and thoroughly engineered machines, from branch tanks through freight and mixed-traffic to express tender engines, which galvanised GWR haulage services and handed the Company such a technical supremacy that only on the advent of Grouping some twenty years hence did other railways begin to catch up.

Early in his incumbency Churchward had prevailed upon the GW Directors to purchase an eventual total of three French de Glehn/du Bousquet 4-cylinder compound Atlantics, which impressed hugely by their smooth application of power. Whilst his 2-cylinder 4-6-0s (the 'Saints') and associated 4-4-2s of 1902 onwards were superb engines in their own right they were not premium passenger hauliers in this vein and could not match the sheer vivacity of the French Atlantics. Many features of the latter appealed and were incorporated into the 'Stars', however compounding was deemed too extreme for GW use; to test the 4-cylinder divided-drive layout (that is, inside cylinders driving the leading coupled axle whilst outside cylinders were linked to the trailing axle) within a simple format a singleton 4-cylinder 4-4-2 was ordered from Swindon Works. Duly outshopped in 1906, No.40 underwent a comprehensive sequence of trials from which emerged such a triumphant success that Churchward rapidly processed an order of ten replicas for delivery in 1907.

No.40 remained nonetheless unique: the 4-6-0 wheel arrangement was decided upon in preference, chiefly in view of its advantageous adhesion over the 4-4-2 format together with twin inside-mounted Walschaert's valve gear with derived outside linkage in place of a complex 'scissors' motion fitted to No.40 which had been adapted from that installed on Deeley's Midland Railway compound 4-4-0s. Whereas No.40 had followed its 2-cylinder counterparts in sporting a severely 'squared' running plate mounted atop which the cab necessitated tall, 3-tread footsteps, the 'Stars' proper featured much more elegant curved stepdown fillets to the running plates fore and aft, requiring just 2-tread steps onto lowered cab panels.

Numbered from 4001, the ten 4-6-0s were provided with names first supplied to the original broad gauge express passenger engines, the eponymous 'Stars'. So overwhelming was the engines' performance that further batches were outshopped in quick succession: ten in 1908, numbered from 4011 and named for Knights;

---

other more minor variations in equipment. A few engines eventually received square-topped side tanks as opposed to the typical TVR 'round-shouldered' design, which further complicates the issue of their appearance.

Being comparatively new engines at the time of Grouping, the Class As lasted unbroken as a class throughout GW ownership and well into BR days. Withdrawal took place from 1955 with the final 0-6-2T being removed in 1958.

Cylinders:	2, 18½" x 26" bore/stroke
Boiler Pressure:	175 lbs sq in
Coal Capacity:	3¾ tons
Mean Weight in Working Order:	69 tons
Tractive Effort:	21000 lbs
Number Built:	58, 1914-21
Preserved:	None

9

ten each in 1908 and 1909 (Kings and Queens respectively); five in 1913 (Princes); fifteen Princesses in 1914 and finally after an interruption owing to World War 1, twelve Abbeys in 1922-23. The sole Atlantic, No.40 *North Star*, was rebuilt as a Ten-wheeler in 1909, renumbered 4000 in 1912 and eventually rebuilt as a 'Castle' in 1929.

As to be expected with such a radical design and not least to keep the class at the cutting edge of loco technology, manifold changes were effected both during the production period and for long afterwards. Superheating was standardised with No.4031 in 1910 after considerable experimentation on earlier 'Stars'; from 1908 the original swing link-type bogie was replaced by the de Glehn-style version with external bearings and side-control springs familiar on all subsequent GW 4-6-0s and fitted retroactively to older class members; topfeed was an early modification; 15" diameter cylinders became standardised from No.4041 in 1913; neater scalloped inside valve covers arose in 1909 with No.4021; and outside steam pipes made their appearance in BR days.

The cessation of 'Star' production in 1923 coincided with the launch of the 'Castle' Class 4-6-0, an intimate, updated derivative of the 'Stars' supervised by Churchward's successor as CME, Charles Benjamin Collett; the close kinship of the two classes is emphasised by the fact that 16 'Stars' were converted to 'Castle' guise between 1925 and 1940.

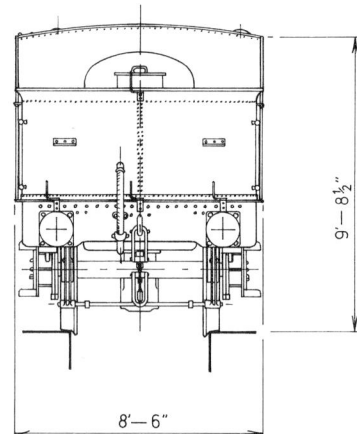

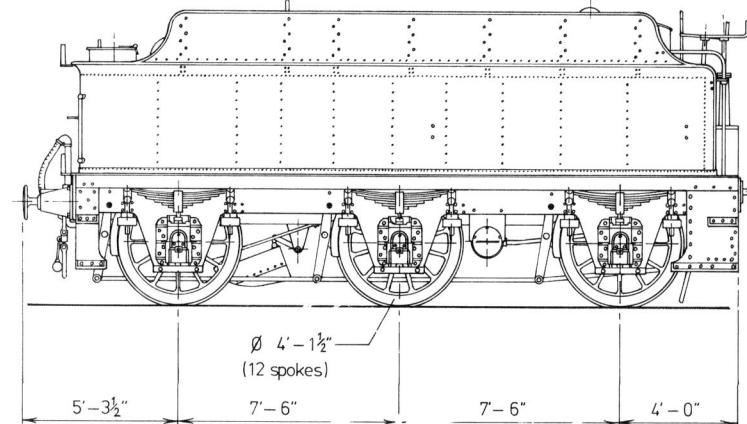

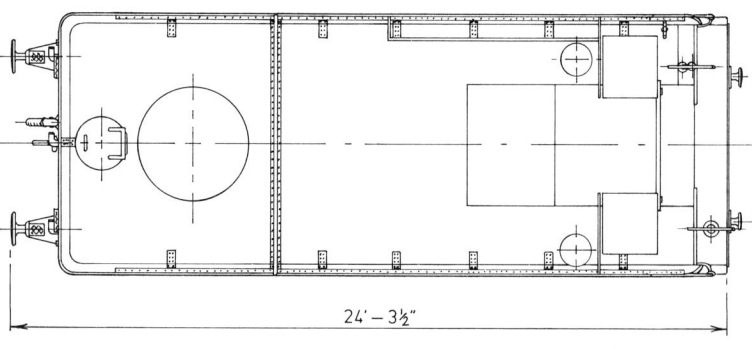

One of the originals, 4-6-0 No.4008 *Royal Star* wears its 23 years lightly in this atmospheric shot alongside the coal heap at Old Oak Common on 1 April 1933. Still carrying the early 'biscuit tin' inside valve cover but otherwise much modified, the engine lacks splasher brightwork, removed en masse during the First World War. PHOTOGRAPH: THE LATE W.G.BOYDEN, FRANK HORNBY COLLECTION.

These seminal express engines were withdrawn over a long period: the first in 1932 and the last, No.4056 *Princess Margaret*, in October 1957 – not counting those rebuilt as 'Castles', no fewer than forty-seven had entered BR service in 1948, performing with immense despatch on express trains to the last. Fortunately No.4003 Lode Star, one of the initial 1910-vintage batch, survives today *[at the NRM, York – Ed.]* in superb external but non-operational order.

Notes on the drawings
All the locomotive views here portray the 'Star' class in early format, incorporating unsuperheated boiler (identical in both side views bar the larger, capuchoned

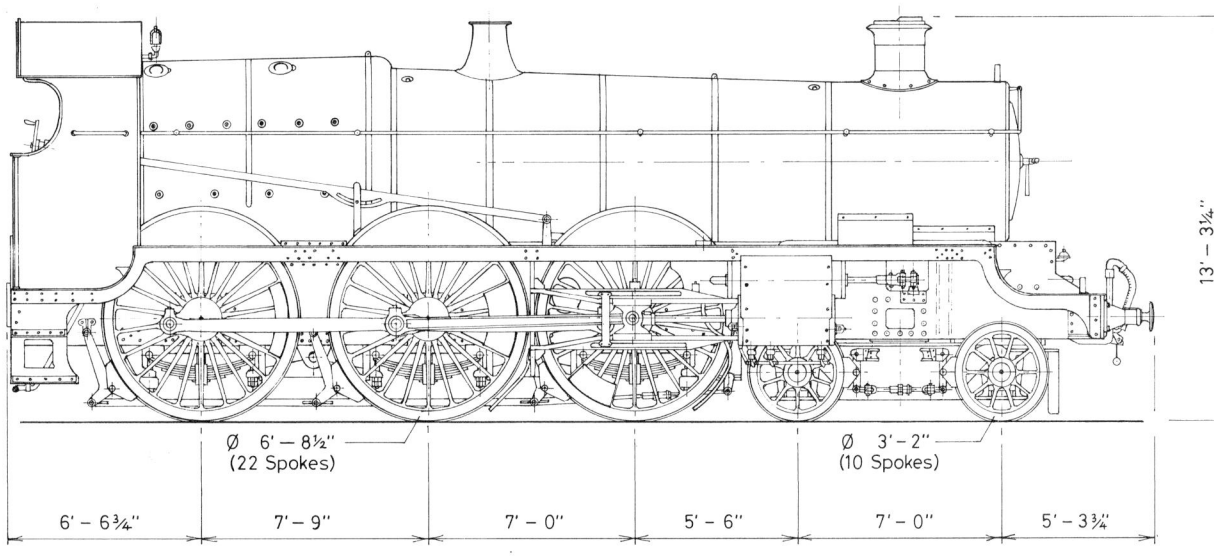
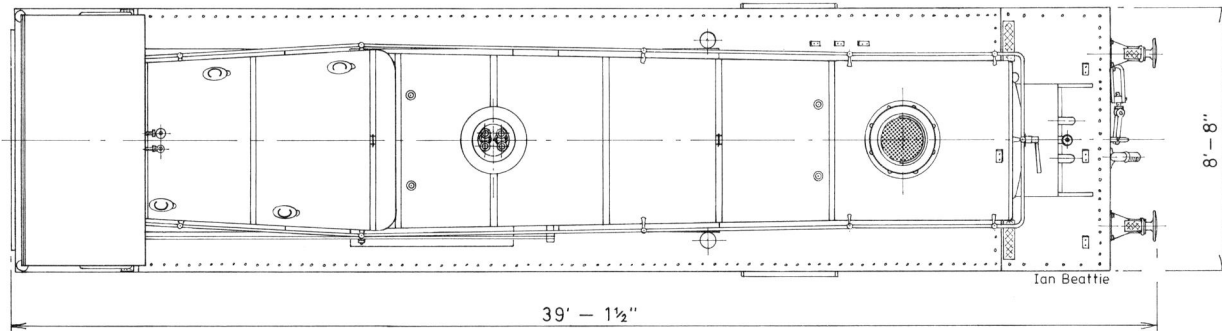
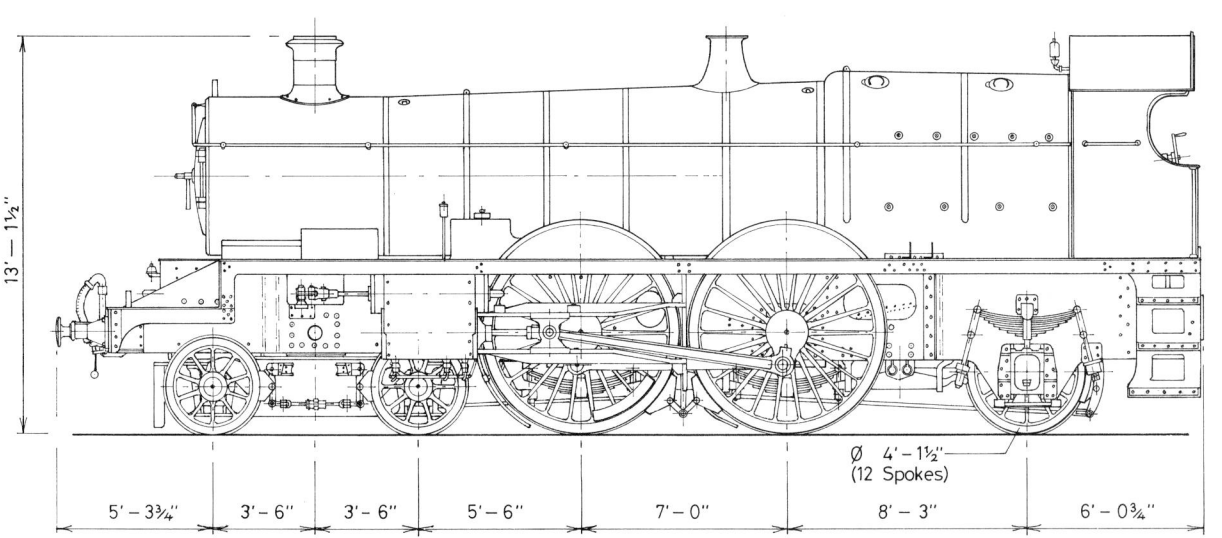
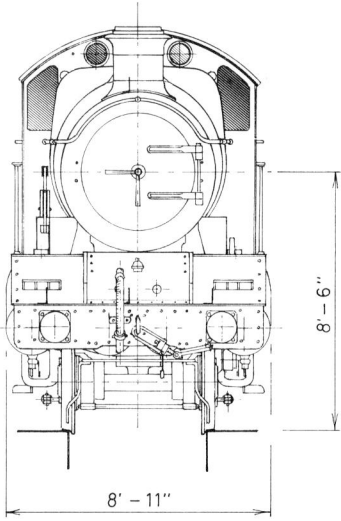

chimney of the 4-6-0), bogie brakes – removed 1923-25 – alongside swing-link bogies, equalising suspension beams between coupled wheels (made superfluous in time by more flexible springs) *inter alia*.

The Atlantic profile demonstrates the quite different and more archaic running plate arrangement, together with a partial outside frame surrounding the rear carrying axle. Once the 4-4-2 was adorned with a name – in 1907 – it, like the 4-6-0 and most evident in plan, was given a widened right-hand central splasher in order to accommodate the reverser rodding behind the nameplate. Note too that both engine types sported main frames that swung inboard to allow the front bogie wheel adequate clearance on curves.

The specifications apply to the earliest, unsuperheated Standard No.1 boiler as shown in the illustrations; the overall weight of No.40 was 114 tons 10 cwt.

Tenders used throughout the Class's collective life included 3000, 3500 and 4000 gallon types in several varieties; here the main tender drawings show a typical 3500-gallon version with 'long' coal rave(s), whilst the 'scrap' view of a 3500-gallon tank side displays the earlier, shorter coal rave plus flush-rivetted panelling.

Type:	Express Passenger
Overall Length:	64'1½"
Cylinders:	4, 14¼" x 26" bore/stroke
Boiler Pressure:	225 lbs/sq in
Heating Surface:	2142.9 sq ft
Grate Area:	27.07 sq ft
Tractive Effort:	25090 lbs
Mean Weight in Working Order:	115 tons 12 cwt
Coal Capacity:	6 tons
Water Capacity:	3500 gallons
Number Built:	73, 1906-23
Preserved:	1

Swindon-built diesel railcars Nos.19-38

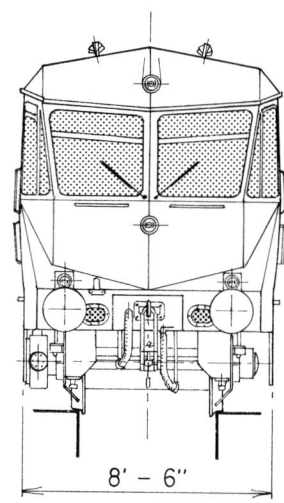

SELF-CONTAINED rail units or 'railcars' enjoyed a brief vogue in the early 1900s as a hopefully economic form of passenger transportation over branch and secondary lines. Many main line companies indulged in such railcars, 100% steam-powered in this era, which however quickly displayed numerous disadvantages in everyday use, not least of which was the fact that when either the 'engine' or 'coach' part of the equation required works maintenance the entire machine was laid up in non-revenue-earning mode. Hence the eventual preferment of separate units in push/pull guise or, in Great Western parlance, auto-trains.

Railcars were nonetheless reintroduced by the GWR during the early 1930s through the influence of burgeoning road traffic in direct competition with the railways; diesel power was by then a proven form of propulsion which in concert with lightweight bodywork resulted in railborne vehicles capable of competing with the ubiquitous road-going omnibus.

At this juncture I should state that it is not the intention to explore the pioneer GW railcars constructed in 1933-5 and known colloquially as 'Flying Bananas', however experience with these 17 machines in branch and local workings convinced the authorities that a further batch was not only desirable but that several fundamental modifications were necessary for enhanced utility, not least of which was an ability to haul one or more trailers when traffic required. To this end a singleton experimental version was outshopped within the 1935 batch of railcars in which *inter alia* a strengthened frame was united with straightforward buffers and couplings – the 'Bananas' had neither – and a square-rigged version of the shapely body style used hitherto.

Identified as No.18, the experimental machine effectively transformed the way in which the GWR employed railcars. Hitherto the streamlined cars, numbered 1 to 17, had successfully procured increased passenger usage by running over and beyond normal train services: by virtue of towing trailers No.18, plus the ensuing batch of 20 cars, was also capable of improving revenue on under-performing branch or secondary routes and even undertaking main line services on occasion.

Whereas the earlier cars were designed and built by the AEC bus and diesel engine facility at Southall, Middlesex, with bodies supplied by the Gloucester Railway Carriage & Wagon Co, the 20 strengthened machines emerged from the GW erecting shops at Swindon in 1940-42 sporting bodies, frames and bogies manufactured in-house but incorporating AEC powerplants and transmission assemblies.

Each railcar featured two 6-cylinder power units, each of which, when viewed from either side, was mounted left-of-centre and drove both axles of the right-hand bogie via a 5-speed Wilson epicyclic gearbox (plus fluid flywheel) and cardan shafts. Bodies consisted of steel panels cladding a teak frame with driving cabs present at both ends; seating for 48 – approached via a vestibule with doors either side of the body – plus handsome luggage area were provided in the 15 conventional versions, numbered 19-33. No.34 was constructed purely as a parcel-carrying vehicle, in which six double-door entries debouched into a 10-ton-capacity hold, joining an earlier parcels car (No.17 of 1936) at Southall shed for west London duties.

More radical departures to body specification were applied to the final 4 cars (they were however unchanged mechanically): designed to run in twin-car sets, each unit had a single driving cab and was coupled to another at the gangway end. Nos.35 and 37 contained seating for 60, plus a toilet and a small luggage compartment, whereas Nos.36 and 38 were completed as buffet cars accommodating 44 passengers; the sets comprised Nos.3516 and 3718 respectively.

Liveries originally included the smart chocolate-and-cream usual to GW coaching stock. First BR colours comprised 'blood and custard' which in fact suited the railcars (of both varieties) particularly well, the railcars ending their service in green paintwork with contrasting waistband applied from the late 1950s. Withdrawals were effected from 1957 into 1962 with the onset of BR's own DMUs, excepting No.37 which, damaged by fire in 1947, was scrapped in 1949 following a period in store. Fortunately two examples of the square-rigged GW railcar style survive in preservation for our delectation.

Notes on the drawings
The principal illustrations portray the conventional double-cabbed railcar, the second side of which although not shown is a mirror image, as can be

Outrigged in green plus 'whiskers' and typically towing a van, 1940-vintage No.W22W rests awhile at Tenbury Wells whilst on a gently timed service to Bewdley in August 1959. Note that drive to the outer axle has been disconnected. This railcar is now preserved, as GWR No.22, at the Didcot Railway Centre.

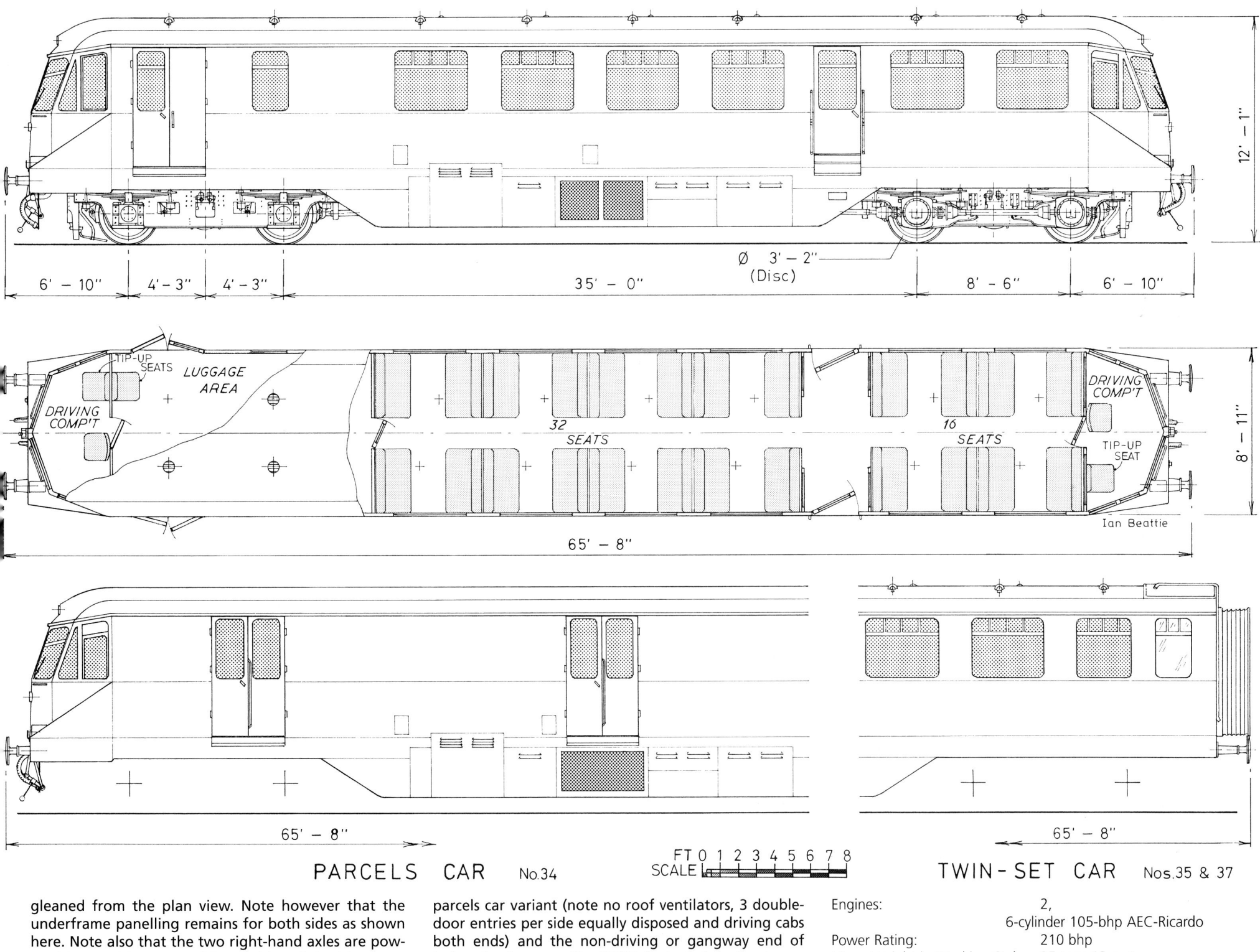

PARCELS CAR No.34

TWIN-SET CAR Nos.35 & 37

gleaned from the plan view. Note however that the underframe panelling remains for both sides as shown here. Note also that the two right-hand axles are powered by outside-mounted bevel drives linked by propshaft. The crosses in the plan view denote roof ventilator positions. The two part-side elevations display the parcels car variant (note no roof ventilators, 3 double-door entries per side equally disposed and driving cabs both ends) and the non-driving or gangway end of twin-set saloon car Nos.35/37 (note toilet at extreme end, indicated by the opaque window and roof-mounted water tank above).

Engines:	2, 6-cylinder 105-bhp AEC-Ricardo
Power Rating:	210 bhp
Mean Weight in Working Order:	35 tons 13 cwt
Number Built:	20, 1940-42
Preserved:	2

13

'Large Prairie' 2-6-2T

TO CELEBRATE the return to steam of preserved Great Western 2-6-2T No.4160 on the West Somerset Railway, the spotlight this month *[August 1993 – Ed.]* centres on the sizeable fleet of these big passenger locomotives assembled over 45 years – a protracted period which bears ample testimony to the engines' modernity from their very outset, way back in 1903.

At the time of pioneer No.99's introduction in that year, the GW Chief Mechanical Engineer was the inestimable George Jackson Churchward. In common with most of his motive power handiwork, Churchward insisted that the hefty, singleton 2-6-2T be tested thoroughly and exhaustively to prove its worth before a production line was contemplated. In the event No.99 met all requirements and construction of replicas began in 1905. Perennially and generically known (from genesis at Swindon Works to withdrawal in 1957-65) appositely as 'Large Prairies', to distinguish them from Churchward's somewhat earlier and equally successful 44/45xx Class branch line 2-6-2Ts (the 'Small Prairies'), 81 examples were initially outshopped within 3 years and numbered into the 31xx series. These machines were later lightly modified and thence renumbered into the 51xx sequence, the prototype amongst them.

Owing to a huge increase in short-haul passenger traffic, particularly in and around London, production of 'Large Prairies' restarted in 1929, in a minimally revised version of the original series. Churchward had retired at the end of 1921 and his exceptionally able assistant Charles Collett had become CME: Collett effected sundry localised alterations to the Edwardian 2-6-2T design in sanctioning continued assembly, and the results poured out of Swindon erecting shops in successive batches for the next 20 years, wartime excepted, into and beyond Nationalisation under the auspices of the newly created British Railways.

A total of 140 2-6-2Ts thence emerged and were numbered in the 51xx series, later examples including the BR builds utilising vacant 41xx numbers; no fewer than 10 have been preserved, including the aforementioned 1948-vintage No.4160.

Interspersed with these were three sets of variants on the theme, the first and most important of which comprised the installation of boilers pressed to 225 psi (otherwise unchanged) giving enhanced tractive effort specifically for London commuter haulage, where flashing acceleration, high speed potential and powerful brakes were desirable assets – as of course they still are. Numbered in the 61xx sequence, 70 'Large Prairies' of this nature hit the rails in 1931-35, only being displaced from work in the Capital by ubiquitous DMUs in the mid to late 1950s: No.6106 has survived the cutting torch.

During 1938-39 a number of elderly 51xx 'Large Prairies', mainly with origins as pre-World War I 31xx engines, were updated and converted with 61xx boilers together with 5'6" coupled wheels; which gave a higher figure for tractive effort than the 61xx tanks. Ten engines were completed, which were re-identified with 81xx numbers.

A contemporaneous rebuilding scheme, likewise involving former 31xx 2-6-2Ts, similarly used 225 psi boilers in concert with even smaller, 5'3" diameter wheels, further increasing the already fulsome tractive effort (but at the expense of speed potential) for banking purposes; just five tanks were thus converted, with reversion to 31xx numbering. Outbreak of war caused abandonment of both schemes, which were not recommenced thereafter – possibly because, beyond any fiscal or economic grounds, the 15 engines performed less dramatically than intended alongside their already formidably powerful progenitors.

During GW ownership the fleet was painted in standard green, however under BR aegis black was *de rigueur* (following the austere wartime livery, from which many 2-6-2Ts escaped repainting between war's end and nationalisation) until the dashing lined green livery was restored in 1957.

Designed for short-distance passenger workings that called for hearty acceleration and considerable velocity, the exceptionally handsome 'Large Prairies' met these desiderata and more. Fitted freight haulage was undertaken with panache, given the engines' superb steaming and free-running qualities, and even the mundane tasks allotted them in their final years (banking, pick-up goods *et al)* were likewise fulfilled with élan.

Notes on the drawings

If there be such a phenomenon in this class of complex history, a typical 'Large Prairie' is represented in the drawings. The curved plating beneath the smokebox linking the two levels of running plate bespeaks its Collett design origin – the Churchward 31xxs sported vertical drops between these plates (though rebuilds sported the newer variety) – and sliding cabside shutters first appeared in 1934, whilst earlier locomotives were so fitted retrospectively.

The customarily lavish GW brass and copper adornment was present too, included amongst which were

ABOVE: the subject of the opening sentence itself: No.4160, immaculate in BR mixed-traffic lined black livery, rolls into Williton, the principal crossing point on the West Somerset Railway, Minehead-bound on 31 August 1996. PHOTOGRAPH: ANDREW BURNHAM.

Right: fellow survivor of Barry yard, No.4141 was captured on film running round at 'wartime' Llangollen on 1 May 1994.

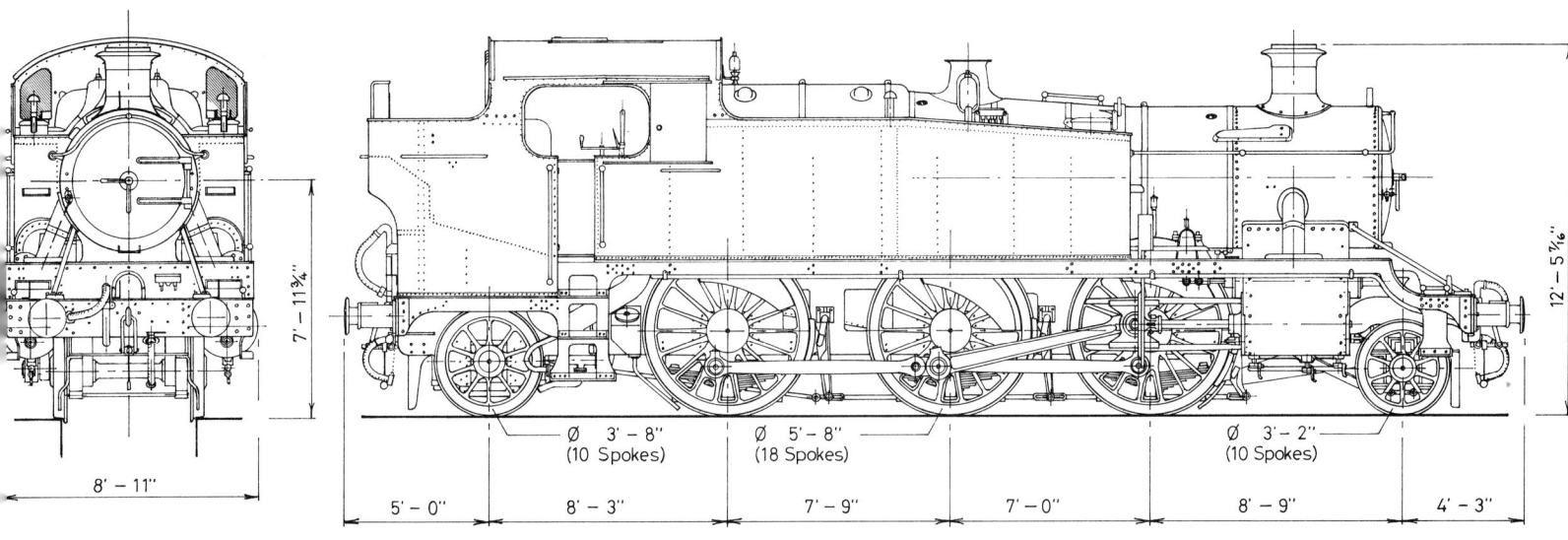
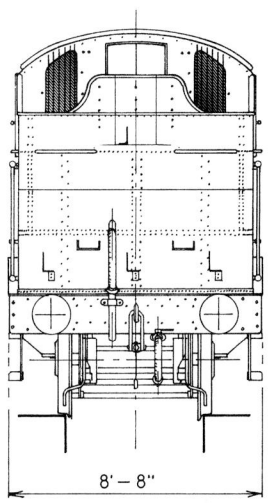
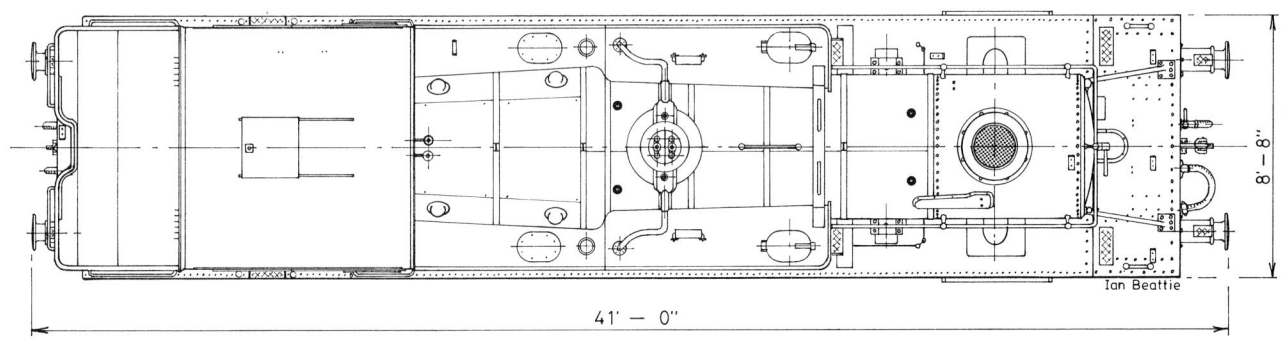

copper-capped chimneys and brass safety valve bonnets; the latter came in two sizes on these 2-6-2Ts, a tall version was the original fitment but a lower, squatter alternative was applied to later builds and thence to older machines – haphazardly it would seem, since many 2-6-2Ts went to the scrapyards with the older style still aboard. Compare the drawings and the photographs to ascertain the difference in bonnets.

Note that the upper bunker lamp iron is mounted in a recess and protected from damage when coaling by a tall vertical plate attached to the lip of the bunker.

Type:	Passenger Tank
Cylinders:	2, 18" x 30" bore/stroke
Boiler pressure:	200lbs/sq in
Heating Surface:	1348.95 sq in
Grate Area	20.35 sq ft
Tractive Effort:	24,300lbs
Mean Weight in Working Order:	78 tons 9cwt
Coal Capacity:	4 tons
Water Capacity:	2000 gallons
Number Built:	292, 1903-49 (see text)
Preserved:	10

15

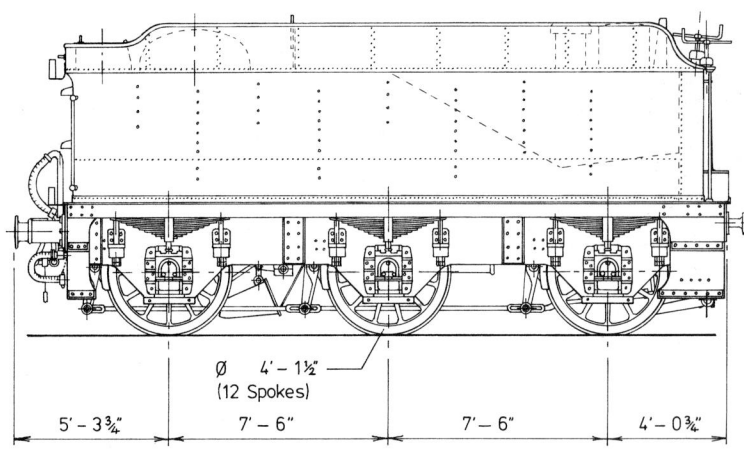
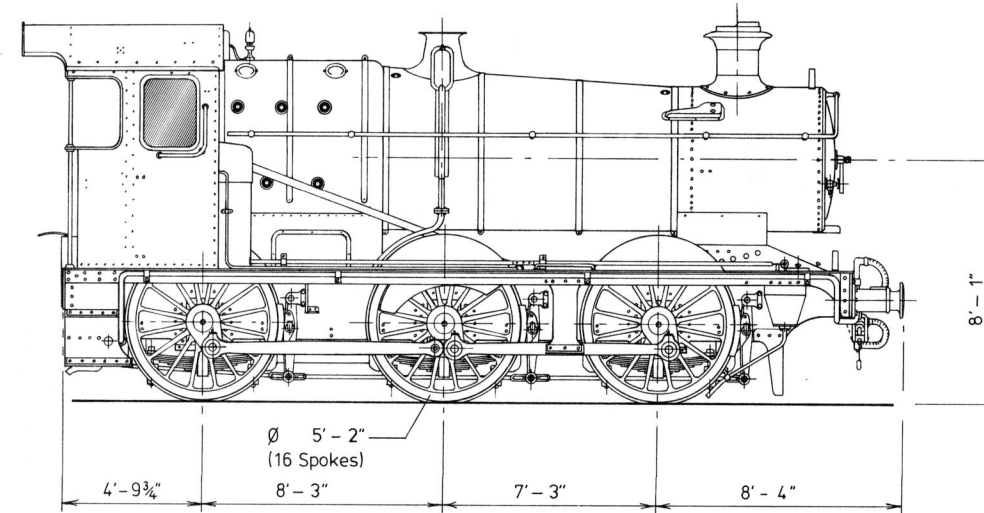
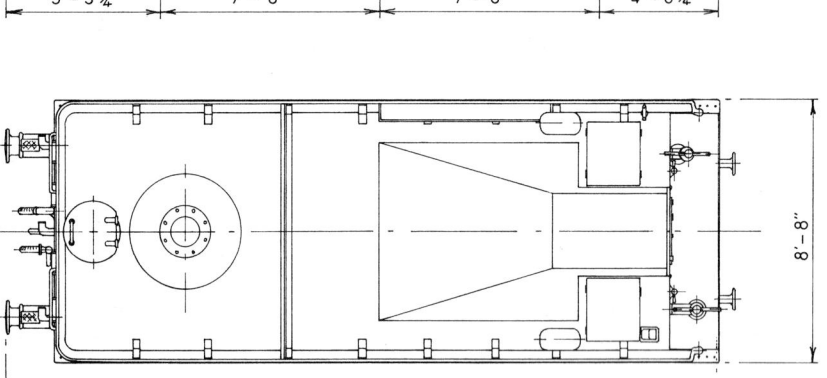
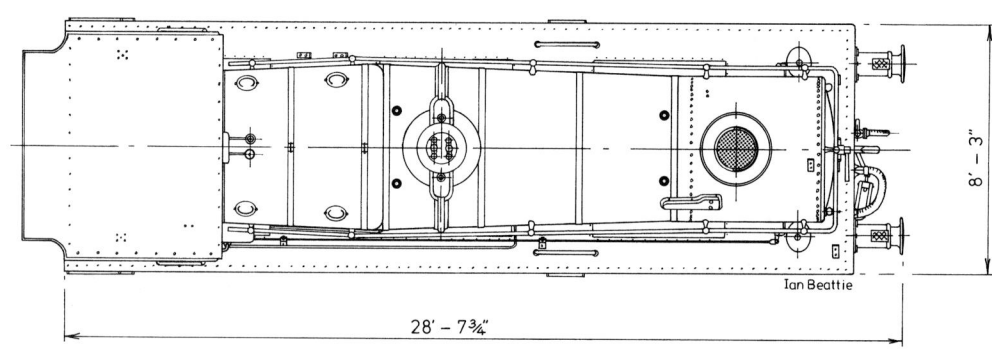

Ian Beattie

2251 Class 0-6-0

THE FREIGHT locomotive roster of the Great Western Railway was dominated by 2-6-0s and 2-8-0s, of the 43xx and 28xx Classes respectively together with their variants, such that the emergence of a new class of 0-6-0s in 1930 seemed somewhat of an unnecessary and retrograde step. In addition, humble pick-up and cross-country goods workings were competently handled by hordes of Victorian 'Dean Goods' 0-6-0s and remnants of their even more venerable antecedent the 'Armstrong Goods' Class of sandwich-framed six-coupled locomotives.

The answer to the conundrum lay in Central Wales, where the lightly-laid lines of companies absorbed by the GWR upon Grouping in 1923 were worked by indigenous engines. The increase in traffic density and weight in the area during the 1920s called for motive power augmentation and, because the larger GWR freight haulers were banned due to weight considerations, 'Dean' and 'Armstrong Goods' 0-6-0s were

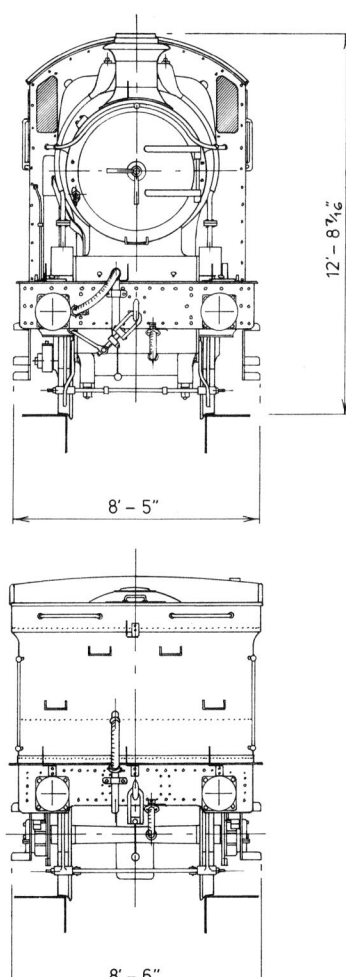

drafted in. However the numbers available remained insufficient, hence the need for a new breed of modern, lightweight 0-6-0s in the guise of Mr.Collett's 2251 Class.

The little 0-6-0s' utility spread far beyond the bounds of Central Wales however: no fewer than 120 engines were outshopped from Swindon, over a period of 18 years. The design comprised adapted frames and motion of 57xx pannier tanks surmounted by a GW Standard No.10 boiler, itself designed for modernising locomotives absorbed in the Grouping. Built in eight successive batches, locomotive No. 2251 was the first of the type, and thus the class title (although lower numbers were assigned to subsequent batches: eg No.2200, erected in 1938). Very few changes were made to the specification over the attenuated production span, the most evident being that in which 20 engines were constructed in wartime without cabside windows, in an effort to reduce the glare from open fireboxes during the blackout. Windows were eventually installed after the risk of enemy strafing had abated, although one or two engines entered BR service before alteration.

The little engines quickly proved immensely versatile over an extraordinary range of work and moreover were popular with crews, not least for their unusually stable ride at all but the highest speeds – and attainable speeds were high thanks to relatively tall wheels: 60 mph plus was readily approachable given the right set of circumstances. Whilst never entirely superseding the 'Dean Goods' 0-6-0s owing to the latter's very low axle weight, unmatchable by the 2251s and thus slightly restricted in route availability compared with their veteran forerunners, the Collett locos were shedded throughout the GWR and the Western Region of BR. They could be seen on main lines as well as their habitual stamping ground of branch lines and on diverse forms of duty, from main line stopping passenger to standby snowplough. Withdrawals commenced rather early in the locomotives' expected lifespan, due chiefly to mass closure of branches and dieselisation of the remainder; the first 2251 disappeared in December 1958 and the last during June 1965. One example, 1946-built No.3205 was rescued from oblivion and currently displays its demonstrable power on the preserved South Devon Railway.

Notes on the drawings
These depict a representative 2251 engine as built; beyond fitment of BR AWS equipment very little in the way of modification was made. Some 2251s sported typical GWR whistle shields when new but most were not carried for long. Note the 'modern' appearance of this otherwise traditionally British 0-6-0 delineated by the tapered boiler, its associated 'drumhead' smokebox and the commodious cab. The final 20 engines, including preserved No.3205, featured rear sandboxes, the fillers for which projected prominently forward of the cab steps (see photo). The capuchoned chimney was properly copper-capped!

An astounding variety of tenders was attached to the engines, including ancient but rebuilt Dean designs, sundry Churchward tenders and ex-Great Central Railway versions (from scrapped 'ROD' 2-8-0s) to brand-new Collett styles. Although a subjective opinion, the most appropriate tender for this stylish little engine – not for nothing was it nicknamed the 'Baby Castle' – was Collett's 3500-gallon version, which I have opted to show here complete with 'second-style' frames. The profile includes internal detailing (dashed lines) of the coal space, plus (l-to-r) water filler, scoop fountain, coal barrier, tank breather, toolbox and water level gauge respectively.

ABOVE: a fine view of a clean and well-coaled GWR 0-6-0 No.3217, actually 1948-vintage and therefore built by BR, resting between duties on Tyseley shed, 27 May 1956. Note the Collett 3500-gallon tender as per the drawings.

LEFT: a grimy 'Baby Castle', No.3208, tops up its 3500-gallon tender deep in the heart of the ex-Cambrian Railways system at Barmouth in June 1962. PHOTOGRAPH: NORMAN BROWNE.

Type:	Six-Coupled Mixed Traffic
Overall Length:	53'8¼"
Cylinders:	2, 17½" x 24" bore/stroke
Boiler Pressure:	200 lbs/sq in
Heating Surface:	1247.5 sq ft
Grate Area:	17.4 sq ft
Tractive Effort:	20155 lbs
Mean Weight in Working Order:	84 tons
Coal Capacity:	5 tons
Water Capacity:	3500 gallons
Number Built:	120, 1930-48
Preserved:	1

Churchward 47xx 2-8-0

THE HISTORY of these noble machines is a simple and in a sense a sad one, for their weight and coupled wheelbase restricted their area of use and their numbers; yet they were extremely powerful prime movers, free steaming and very much 'drivers' engines'.

During and just after the 1st World War the Great Western Railway experienced an upsurge in heavy fast fitted freight traffic, for which in locomotive terms the company was not too well equipped – the solitary Pacific, No.111 *The Great Bear* undertook such a task most successfully however, which led Churchward towards a similarly large eight-coupled machine in response to the Traffic Department's urgent request for a locomotive to match the traffic.

The ensuing 2-8-0 design emerged in 1919, looking much like a 28xx version albeit with much taller coupled wheels. No.4700 was given a standard No.1 boiler – as fitted to the 'Saint' and 'Star' 4-6-0s – added to which was a much extended smokebox in order to reach the saddle (the Pacific boiler was overlarge altogether), and it ran in this somewhat inadequate condition until re-equipped in May 1921 with the new standard No.7 boiler.

Churchward had intended to utilise this boiler on his 4-6-0s which would have resulted in some spectacular performances no doubt: but the Civil Engineer vetoed the project on grounds of axle weight. Thus the boilers were ultimately restricted to the 47xxs alone, another factor in their Cinderella-style role within the GWR, and much more suited to the engines than the No.1 boiler they were too. In customary Churchward fashion the prototype 2-8-0 was not followed by a production line for a considerable period, during which all manner of tests and running trials were conducted in order to prove the design; No.4701 was outshopped from Swindon in December 1921 and the final engine, ninth in the class, hit the rails in April 1923.

Though the 47s rapidly proved enormously successful in their sphere as fitted freight hauliers they evinced equal facility on express passenger and other heavy-duty work as well; in short they were capable of handling anything put their way with panache and great speed (those large driving wheels worked wonders). Their downfall, as already indicated, was their axle loading, restricting their athleticism to solely the best of GW main lines. The fact that much of their work was performed during the dark hours – they were masters of the night-time heavy fitted freight traffic – meant that their exploits were barely witnessed by the public at large.

Throughout Great Western days the 47s wore plain Brunswick green livery (No.4700 was fully lined-out for display in the Railway 100th Anniversary celebrations at

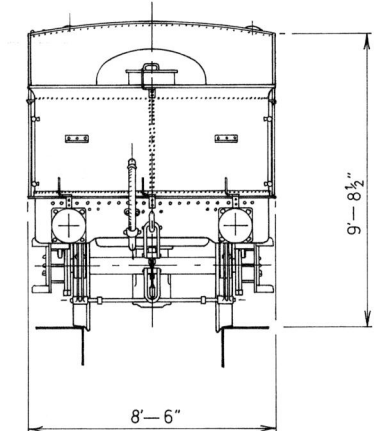

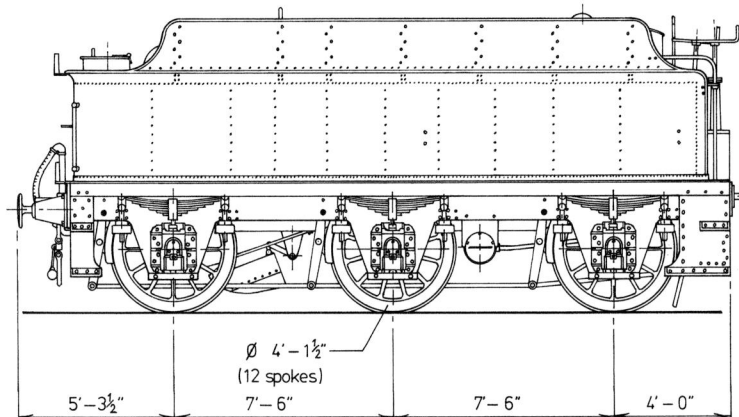
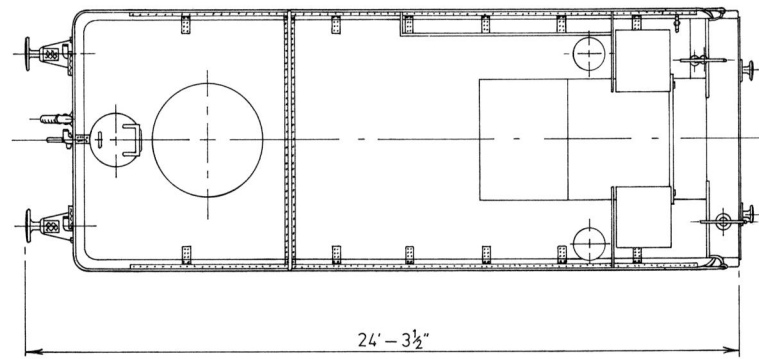

Darlington in 1925) and at first under the BR umbrella they sported black overall with one lined out, then in 1957 green once again was applied, this time complete with full 'express passenger' lining which smartened the huge engines no end. After a lifetime of comprehensive and always heavy work the nine constituents of the class were withdrawn, between 1962 and 1964.

Note on the drawings
This depicts a 47xx as it appeared in the early-to-mid 1920s complete with original-equipment 3500-gallon tender (replaced 1932-33 by 4000-gallon versions). Comparison with Frank Hornby's excellent photograph indicates many ways in which the 47s were modified over the years – though all were minor. The cab roof was given a 10½" rearward extension; 5 of the 9 engines had when new their valve chest snifting valves fitted on the smokebox saddle behind the steampipes rather than on the cylinder casting as shown here; the small circular cab windows were blanked in; and a cover of bell-like shape was provided for the exposed pony truck pivot.

Note also that the top lamp bracket was repositioned, the vacuum pipe was lowered on the buffer beam (it interrupted tube cleaning in its 'tall' guise), the steam connector on the smokebox face was relocated on the other side and new buffers were eventually installed. Each 47 had the rear three right-hand wheel splashers shaped to accommodate the lever-actuated reverse rod, and note the drive to the air pump from the right-hand crosshead. On the full-size locomotive the 2nd and 3rd coupled wheels sported thinner-than-standard flanges which, with spherical joints in the coupling rods, gave a measure of side-play to the very long wheelbase.

As Churchward's final design before retirement the 47xx was magnificent and the pity is that an example was not set aside for preservation. The fact is that their linear successors, the 'Halls' and other mixed-traffic 4-6-0s from Collett and Hawksworth with their wider

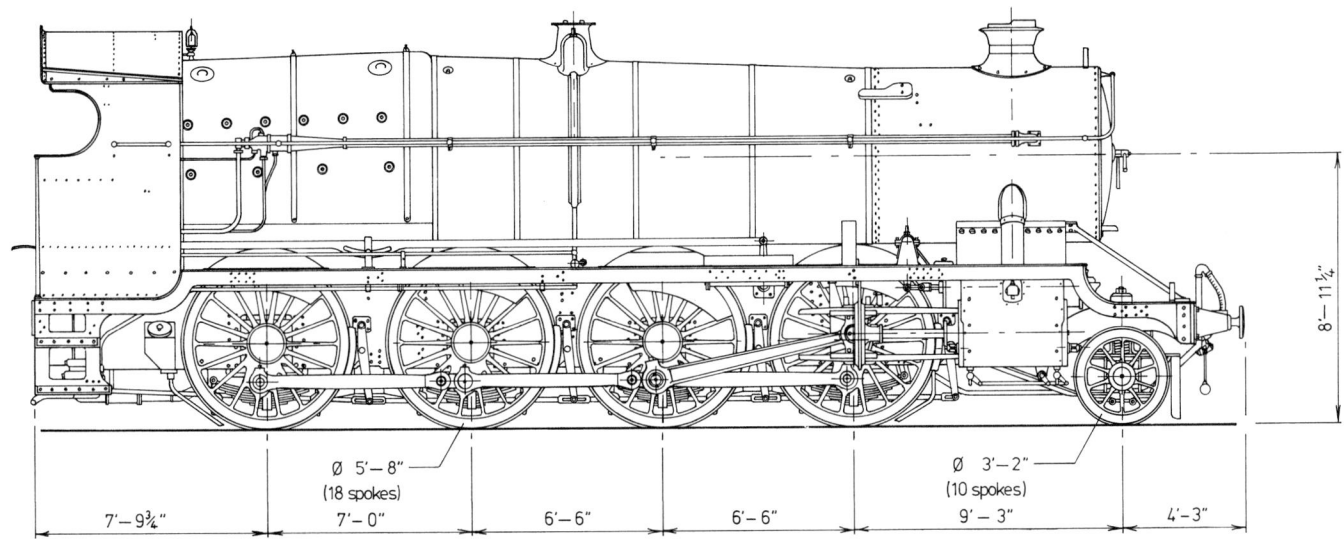
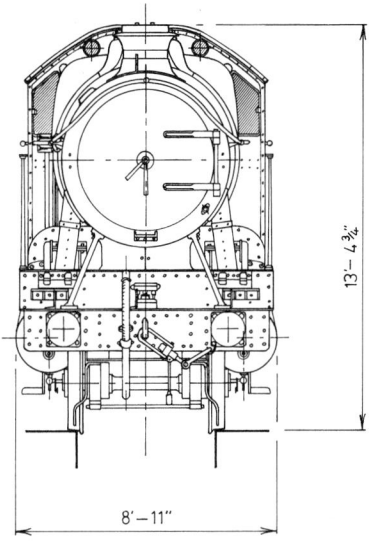
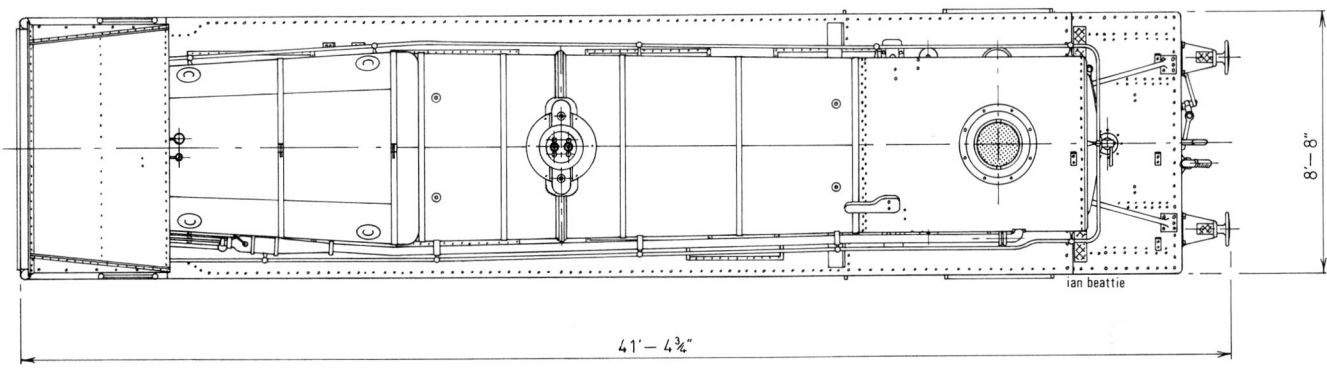

utility, were preferred by the GWR...and by modellers too it appears!

Type:	8-coupled
Overall Length:	66'4¼"
Cylinders:	2, 19" x 30" bore/stroke
Boiler Pressure:	225 lbs/sq in
Heating Surface:	2556 sq ft
Grate Area:	30.28 sq ft
Tractive Effort:	30460 lbs
*Mean Weight in Working Order:	122 tons
*Coal Capacity:	6 tons
*Water Capacity:	3500 gallons
Number Built:	9, 1919 & 1921-23
Preserved:	None

*Equipped with 3500-gallon tender

First of the 47xx class, 1919-built No.4700 rests on Tyseley shed on 21 May 1956. The engine is in final condition apart from its black livery, soon to be changed for fully lined GWR green.

56xx 0-6-2T

THE former independent railways of South Wales, the Rhymney, Taff Vale, Barry and other more minor systems that were merged into the Great Western Railway network, served the major coalfields of the region and in particular linked them to coastal ports, coal thence being either exported overseas or shipped to points in the United Kingdom. Much of the medium-weight mineral haulage was undertaken by fleets of 0-6-2 side tank locomotives, of a type arising in the 1890s especially designed for such a use in such a location.

About the time of Grouping in 1923 many of these tanks were superannuated so that, with the pits not yet affected by depression and in full production, the GW Chief Mechanical Engineer, Charles Collett, was required to institute a new class of locomotive to boost the flagging native motive power roster. Since the 0-6-2 wheel arrangement was well proven in this context Collett saw no reason to experiment with or substitute other variants; much of the engine hardware was standard GWR issue including the coupled wheels and the Swindon No.2 boiler (which was to be found on species of 2-6-2T and later on the 2251-class 0-6-0). The trailing axle was given a predetermined measure of sideplay and to accommodate this the engine main frames were jinked inwards – towards the centre line – from the rear sandbox position rearwards.

The prototype 0-6-2T, No.5600 (thereby determining the class identity 56xx) was outshopped from the GW works at Swindon in 1924, followed quite rapidly by a production line of facsimilies; no fewer than 150 emanated from Swindon altogether (Nos.5600-6649) and a further 50 were built by Messrs Armstrong Whitworth in 1928 (Nos.6650-6699) bringing the class total to 200 constituents.

ABOVE: Caught cold amongst the undergrowth of Swansea East Dock on 7 June 1953, No.6644 (vintage September 1928) poses for the camera. One of the last of the batch built at Swindon works, this trusty workhorse here sports grimy BR black livery.

BELOW: end of the road for No.5685, pictured in the scrap lines at Swindon Works on 22 March 1964.

Whilst certainly very successful on the duty for which they had been propagated the 56xx tanks were no less useful at hauling passenger trains in the South Wales terrain and therefore ought to be regarded as mixed traffic engines – shades of Mr. Webb's 'Coal Tank' of an earlier period. A few examples were directed away to other parts of the GW empire to act as shunters – for which their surefootedness and smooth running characteristics were eminently suited – and although equipped with small-diameter 'GW goods' wheels could be wound up to a considerable turn of speed, ultimately restricted by piston speed in the inside-mounted, Stephenson's-motion controlled cylinders. Withdrawal began under BR auspices in 1962 and was completed in 1966: to date no fewer than seven 0-6-2Ts have been selected for preservation, though not all are able of being steamed – yet. *[In fact eight machines departed Woodham's yard at Barry, between 1971 and 1988. Ed.]*

Notes on the drawings
As to be expected in a class of 200 locomotives surviving for 40-odd years apiece, there was a multitude of small differences in fixtures and fittings between batches and over their lifespans. For instance, the drawing here shows an 0-6-2T equipped with a rear bunker

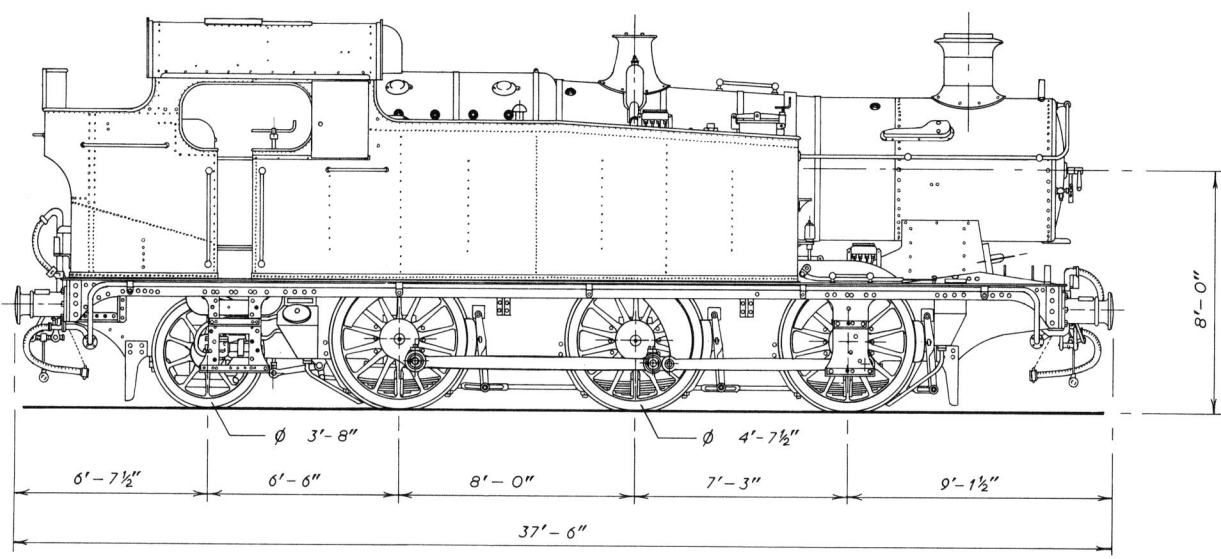
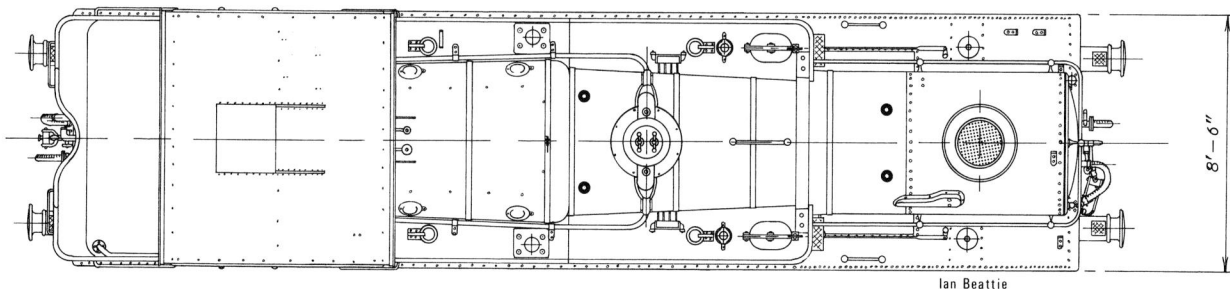
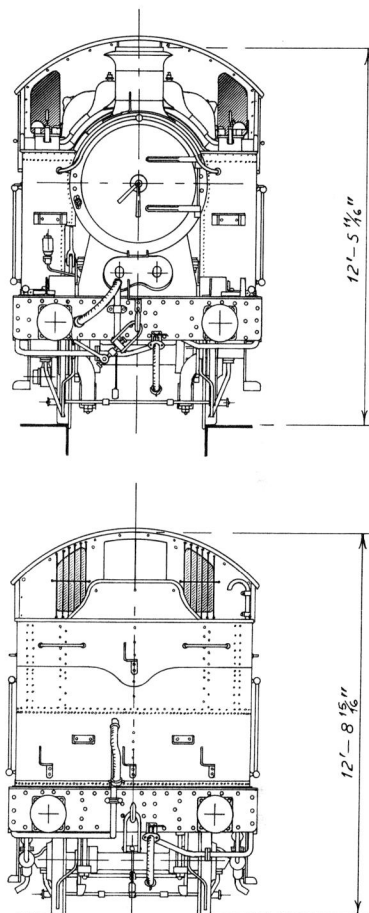

Ian Beattie

panel recessed to protect the rear lamp from damage in coaling; originally the locomotives sported plain bunker panels with one (left-hand) handrail only, the modification being made in 1934 to each engine as it entered the shops for repair... This course proved insufficient to prevent lamp breakage so that subsequently a shield was also fitted, as shown. Whereas vacuum and steam heating pipework is depicted the Automatic Train Control with which most 56/66xxs were equipped is omitted here. The initial batch of engines received front spectacle plates incorporating typical Churchward 'portholes' in addition to the openable windows, sited either side of the whistles; these extra items of glazing were eventually blanked off in conformity with the rest of the class. Again, earlier versions carried the Matthews taper-shanked buffers which were replaced during the 1930s into alignment with later 0-6-2Ts having the parallel-shanked Turton buffing installations.

At the beginning of the engines' relatively long careers some problems were experienced in the drive-

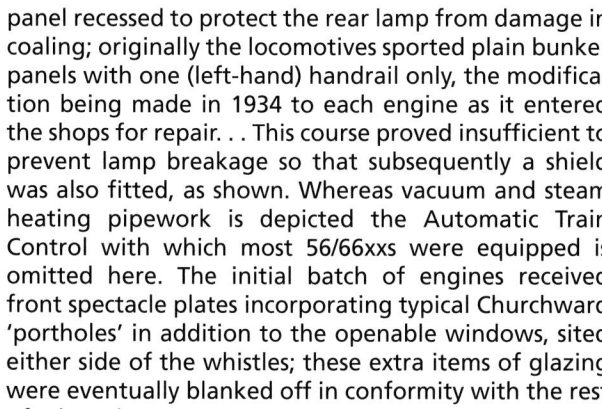

A powerful view of the 56xx preserved at Didcot by the Great Western Society, No.6697 of 1928. PHOTOGRAPH COURTESY GWS.

line necessitating reworked crank axles; later troubles occurred with wheel balancing anomalies, cured by giving driving wheels much larger and repositioned balance weights. Many other very minor variances in equipment were distinguishable between engines at one time or another. Incidentally the centre line of the front steps does not quite match that of the wheel; look at the hub in relation to the step backplate.

Type:	0-6-2T
Cylinders:	2, 18" x 26" bore/stroke
Boiler Pressure:	200 lbs/sq in
Heating Surface:	1349 sq ft
Grate Area:	20.35 sq ft
Tractive Effort:	25800 lbs
Water Capacity:	1900 gallons
Coal Capacity:	3¾ tons
Mean Weight in Working Order:	68½ tons
Number Built:	200, 1924-28
Preserved:	8

15xx 0-6-0PT

STRICTLY speaking, being built after nationalisation, these locomotives were products of British Railways, however in all other respects they bore instantly recognisable Great Western characteristics – technical novelties notwithstanding. Alongside their more traditionally shaped 0-6-0PT counterparts the 16xx series these squat, heavy and superficially Americanised pannier tanks were destined to become the final essence of GW steam technology; a technology refined over more than a century at Swindon through a lineage of supremely competent chief engineers from Daniel Gooch and the Broad Gauge in the 1840s to Frederick Hawksworth in the wartorn 1940s.

Compared with his predecessors' lengthy tenures in office Hawksworth's reign was brief indeed; before nationalisation overwhelmed the Company he had little opportunity to set his personal stamp on matters locomotive, yet he was imbued with Swindon methods and practices. Hawksworth spent his entire working life with the Company, reaching advanced posts as Chief Draughtsman and then assistant to his immediate predecessor Charles Collett; as CME he steered the GWR through much of World War Two and into the short austere interregnum before nationalisation in 1948. Hawksworth retired in December 1949, some six months after the 15xx class appeared, and died only quite recently *[July 1976 – Ed.]* in his mid-90s.

The archetypal Great Western pannier tank engine was an inside-cylindered machine with Stephenson's valve motion, plus a simple but free-steaming parallel boiler that punched out considerable power relative to the engine's small size. The 15xx class thus broke all these carefully laid, traditional ground rules. Not only had it a tapered boiler – the standard No.10 with which Hawksworth also equipped his otherwise typically adorned 94xx 0-6-0PT class without superheater but also outside cylinders: low-slung on the deep frames and controlled via outside-mounted Walschaert's valve gear. Compounding these novelties was an obvious lack of wheel splashers and running plates to lend a somewhat American appearance overall – Hawksworth may have inspected wartime United States Transportation Corps 0-6-0Ts common in Britain during the war and have been duly impressed (an apocryphal tale perhaps). There were sound reasons behind the design, as one would expect.

Intended for heavy shunting and freight haulage, the tanks were provided with a very short wheelbase of 12'10" in order to negotiate sharply-radiused curves found in most yards (the minimum requirement was negotiation of 3½ chains' radius; that's 231'). The resultant long overhangs front and rear gave rise to uncomfortable and (ultimately) dangerous yawing when haul-

The initial engine of the class, No.1500 hesitates on its habitual carriage-moving duty at Paddington terminus on 29 September 1962, within months of withdrawal. Note the comprehensive step and handrail arrangements easing the lot of the crew on this running plate-less locomotive.

ing trains at any reasonable speed, which obviated both passenger work and the freight haulage for which they were partly intended; the overhangs also proved a nuisance in tightly packed yards which further narrowed the engine's utility.

Outshopped in BR lined black livery, the initial five tanks were despatched direct to Old Oak Common, for empty carriage movement into and out of Paddington. The remainder were directed to various suitable yards throughout the Western Region – principally in South Wales, and Newport in particular and eventually some of these joined their brethren at Paddington. With lining removed on repainting, the class worked stolidly on until withdrawals began in 1962, the last of the line disappearing the next year, having served for just 12-13 years only, a pitifully short and economically wasteful existence. However three 15xxs (Nos.1501-2 and 1509) were sold out of service to the National Coal Board for colliery working in 1959-61; reliveried bright maroon though retaining their BR numbers, these tough little machines survived until 1970 when two were broken up. Fortunately one of the NCB 15xxs, No.1501, was rescued for preservation and is the property of the 15xx Fund on the Severn Valley Railway.

Notes on the drawings
Very little modification was applied to these engines, just small variations in lamp-iron fittings and application of toolboxes (under the bunker on the left hand side) for example. The valve rodding was quite massive and the hefty motion carrier casting is very evident (the reason behind the outside motion was to avoid the

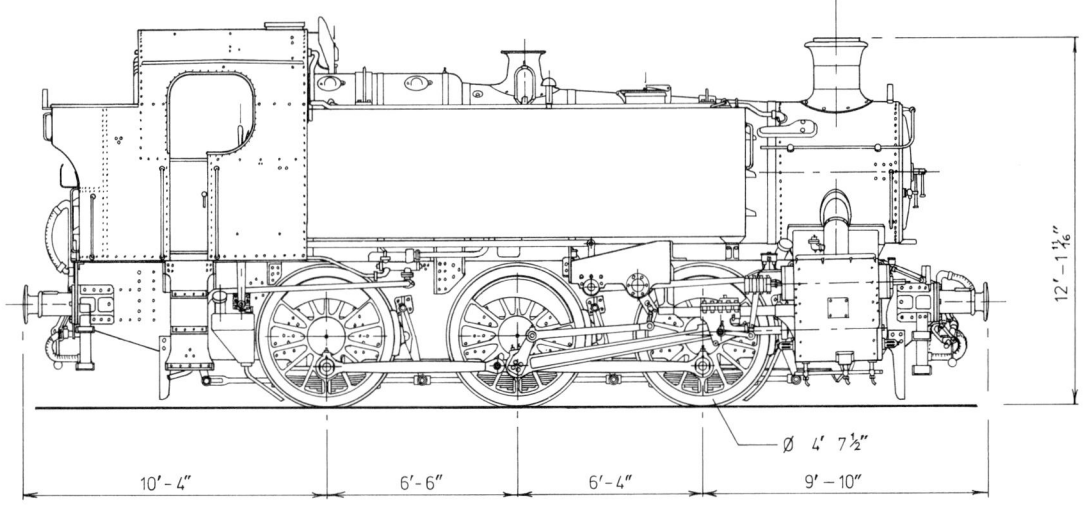
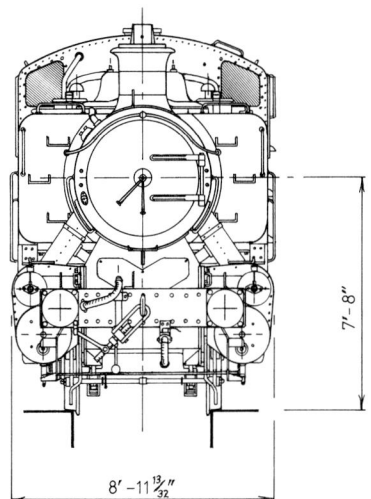
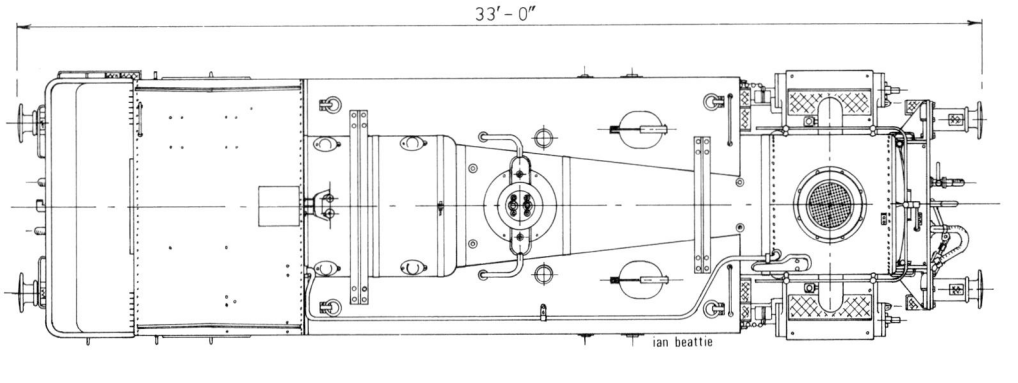
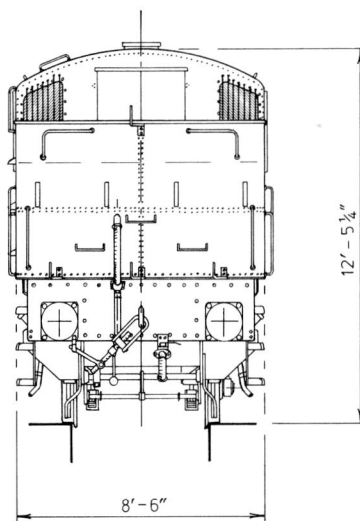
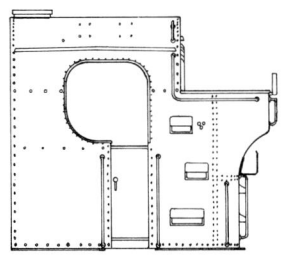
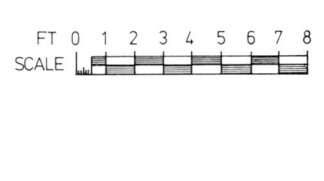

necessity for a pit when oiling the moving parts and thus maintain the engines in as constant state of readiness as possible: '24-hour shunting' was the original theme and hence also the large coal and water capacities) in drawings and the photo. Whistle hoods varied in shape; some tall as shown, others were severely truncated or (as in the photo) removed altogether.

Type:	0-6-0 Pannier tank	Tractive Effort:	22515 lbs
Wheels:	4'7½" dia. 14 spokes	Water Capacity:	1350 gallons
Cylinders:	2, 17½" x 24" bore/stroke	Coal Capacity:	3.3 tons
Boiler Pressure:	200 lbs/sq in	Mean Weight in Working Order:	58.2 tons
Heating Surface:	1347.4 sq ft	Number Built:	10, in 1949
Grate Area:	17.4 sq ft	Preserved:	1

Section 2
London, Midland & Scottish Railway (and constituents)

Locomotive	Page	Locomotive	Page
LMS-built 'Tilbury Tanks'	24-25	Ivatt Class 2 2-6-2T	36-37
Stanier 'Black 5' 4-6-0	26-28	Lancashire & Yorkshire Railway 'Dreadnought' 4-6-0	38-39
Fowler freight engines: LMS 4F 0-6-0 and 7F 0-8-0	29-31	Stanier 2-6-0	40-41
Highland Railway 'Jones Goods' 4-6-0	32-33	Stanier 'Princess Royal' 4-6-2	42-43
LNWR G1 'Super D' 0-8-0	34-35		

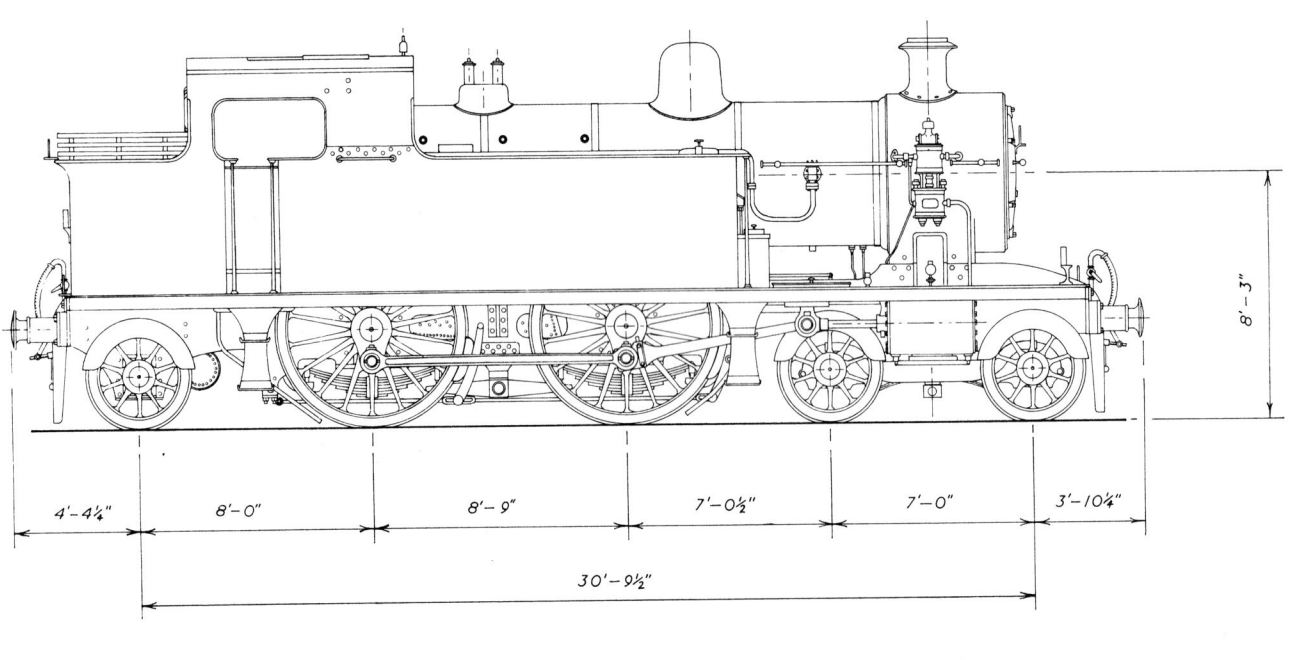
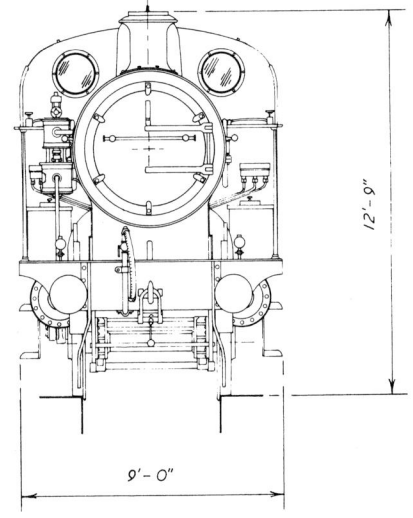
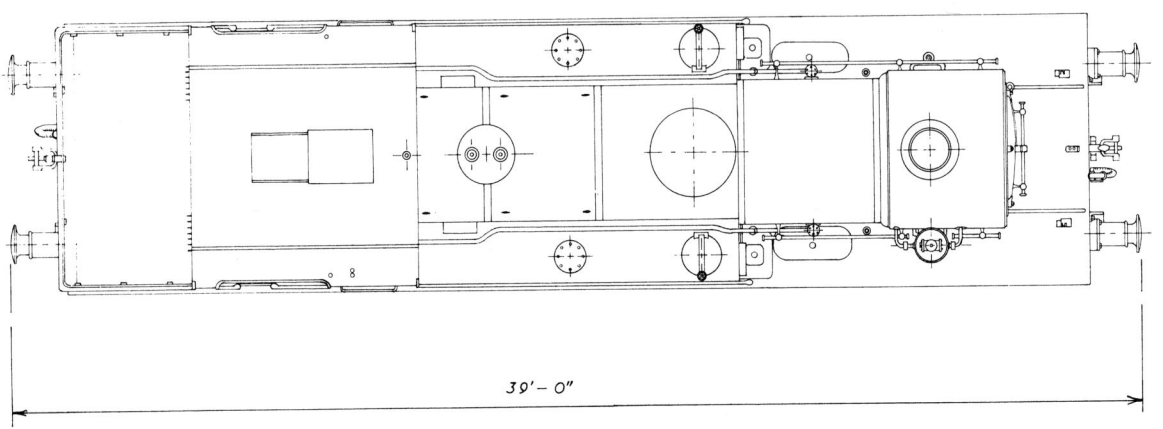
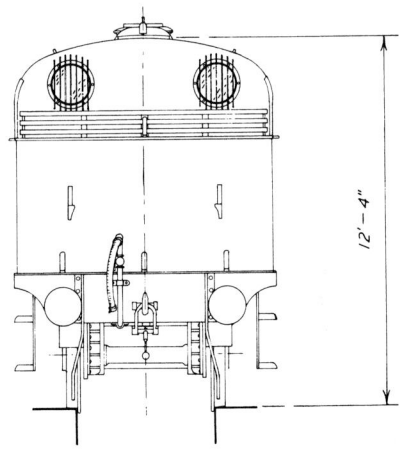

LMS-built 'Tilbury Tanks'

INAUGURATED in 1854 and acquired by the Midland Railway in 1912, the London, Tilbury & Southend Railway was an undertaking primarily concerned with daily high-density passenger movement to and from London and Essex dormitory towns and, as a result, large, powerful locomotives figured prominently thereon; generally tank engines since the limited track mileage and requirement to run either chimney- or bunker-first mitigated against tender equivalents. In the main suitable locomotives were at first purchased from the adjacent Great Eastern system, but when in the late 1870s an especially potent class of tank became necessary for hauling the ever-increasing commuter traffic an indigenous Atlantic design was proposed.

Three varieties of 4-4-2T eventually fulfilled this role, in progressively increased power ratings. The smallest and least powerful, designed by GER superintendent William Adams was outshopped from 1880. Hereafter came the so-called 'Intermediate' class 37 versions under the aegis of LTSR chief Thomas Whitelegg; 12 were built in 1897-8 and were rebuilt with larger boilers and bored-out cylinders in 1907 to align with the 'Large' class 51 engines. In turn these rebuilds inspired a batch of four new locomotives in 1909 classified 79.

These engines, collectively celebrated as the 'Tilbury Tanks', were immensely successful, being extremely economical and free-steaming, their large driving wheels enabling high speeds to be attained between stations.

Although the Midland and its successor the LMS attempted to replace the Atlantics with standardised locomotives none could match the needs of the line so well as the indigenous engines, thus the LMS not only rebuilt many of them but also perpetuated the species by building a further 35 in four lots between 1923 and 1930; all but five were erected at Derby, those remaining contracted out to Nasmyth Wilson in 1925, and the initial batch of ten had in fact been ordered by the Midland Railway shortly before Grouping.

Basically the LMS 4-4-2Ts were still Whitelegg's design, with LMS fittings from the running-plate upwards, and therefore vaunted all the usual LTSR features including right-hand driving, air brakes (via Westinghouse pump mounted on the smokebox flank) and destination board hangers at either end. Unlike the originals however they were dressed overall in LMS rather than the elaborate LTSR livery. The drawings show just such a 'Tilbury Tank', whereas the photo, taken in BR days, illustrates the changes necessary when these 4-4-2Ts were dispersed to other territories: vacuum braking being the principal revision. Whilst as capable and powerful as their forebears the updated engines were joined within four years of the last being placed in service by Stanier's big, fleet 2-6-4Ts of both two- and three-cylinder configuration; the levels of performance shown by these modern locomotives rather overshadowed the still worthy efforts of the 4-4-2Ts, resulting in eventual dispersal away from their native tracks for a sizeable number.

Whereas new numbers were allocated to the Atlantics under the 1947 LMS renumbering scheme none in fact bore those numbers (a belated scheme in any event given the imminence of Nationalisation), all being reassigned numbers by BR in 1948.

All 35 LMS-built 4-4-2Ts were withdrawn between 1951 and 1960, with a representative singleton preserved – not however an LMS origin engine but an older 'Large' tank rebuilt with LMS fitments. Recalling LTSR days when all 'Tilbury Tanks' were named, after localities served by the network, this example runs in LTSR green livery as No.80 *Thundersley*.

Built 1930 as No.2157, Class 3P 4-4-2T No.41975 pauses between duties at Seaton, on the Uppingham branch on 28th March 1959.

Type:	4-4-2T, LMS Power Class 3
Cylinders:	2, 19"x 26" bore/stroke
Boiler Pressure:	170 lbs/sq in
Heating Surface:	1086 sq ft
Grate Area:	19¾ sq ft
Water Capacity:	1800 gallons
Coal Capacity:	2¾ tons
Mean Weight in Working Order:	71 tons 10 cwt
Number Built:	35 (by LMS), 1923-1930
Preserved:	1

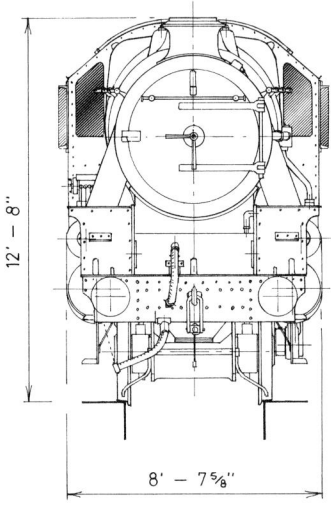

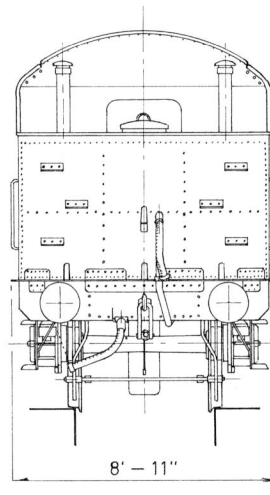

ABOVE: No.44823, with domed boiler, accelerates an express out of York and back towards home metals. PHOTO: DOUGLAS DOHERTY.

RIGHT: terminally grubby domeless No.45134 waits on Crewe South shed on 30 August 1967, a year before the end of steam.

Stanier 'Black 5' 4-6-0

THIS IS the archetypal general-purpose locomotive, the yardstick by which any rival is measured; and, beyond the top link passenger performers, much the best-known of all British steamers. William Stanier's genius evolved a design able to travel almost the entire LMS network (widening throughout Britain after nationalisation) on as broad a selection of workings imaginable.

The vast number of 842 Black 5s were assembled over a lengthy period of 17 years, a class total exceeded only by their LMS 2-8-0 freight equivalents at 852 examples many of which however eked out their lives overseas, thus making the Black 5s numerically the largest class of steam engines to be used on British trackage.

Such a sizeable class spawned a great many modifications and alterations, additions and developments, basic and trivial alike, over both the production span and collective service life; of necessity this present potted history can include only the most important changes wrought, lest this entire issue be filled with Black 5 lore! The old saw of choosing a particular loco at a particular period for modelling purposes is more pertinent than ever in this case.

So widespread from the mid-1930s onwards were the hugely successful Black 5s (named for their habitual black livery and class 5 power category) that most railfans took their all-pervading, even comforting presence utterly for granted; only after 4th August 1968, the final day of normal steam working on BR, was the absence of those workhorse 4-6-0s keenly felt. Not surprisingly given the class size, no fewer than 18 survived the call of the scrapyards into well-earned preservation: the most numerous of all preserved types and justifiably so.

As is well-known, the 55-year-old William Stanier was appointed Chief Mechanical Engineer of the London Midland & Scottish Railway in 1932, ending a hiatus following the MR-oriented Sir Henry Fowler's resignation in 1930. Stanier was more than simply a breath of fresh air in what had become a stultified system; he transformed LMS engineering practice not just through his own Great Western-bred instincts but by recognising and moreover using to the full the talents of staff already in place.

The Group's requirement for a 'maid of all work' mixed-traffic class had been admirably met by Hughes' 'Horwich Crab' Mogul (see RM December 1992), however the traffic authorities came to prefer the notion of extra security from 2 leading carrying axles as opposed to the single-axle truck endemic to the 2-6-0 wheel arrangement. Stanier's Class 5 4-6-0 filled the ticket ideally from the outset, from this and most other angles.

Continued on page 28.

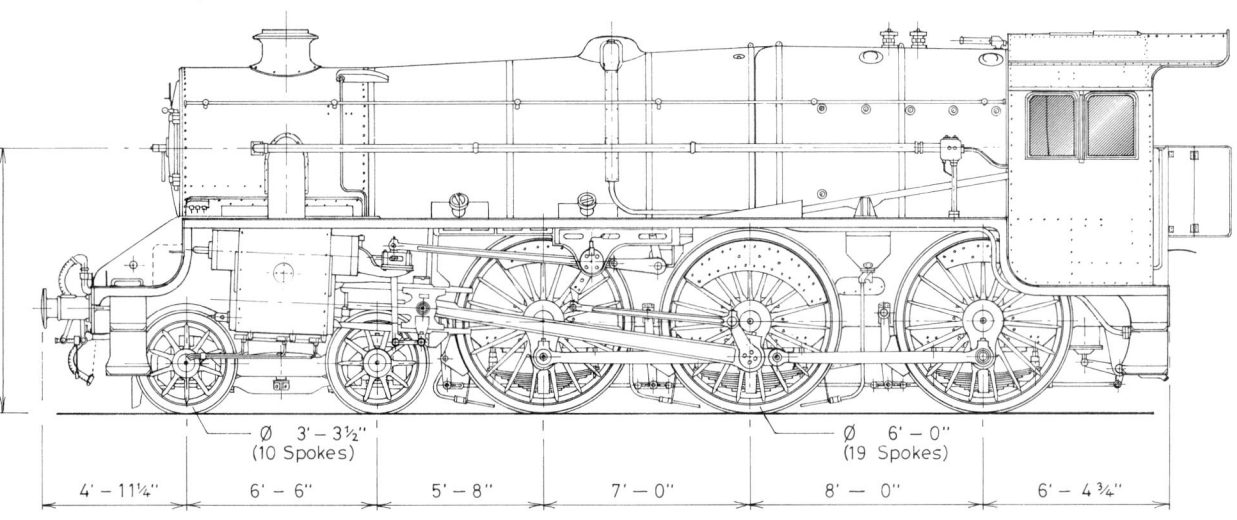
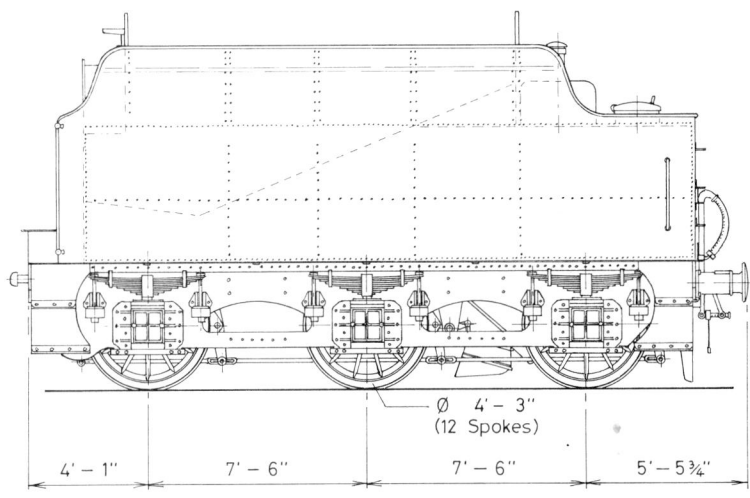
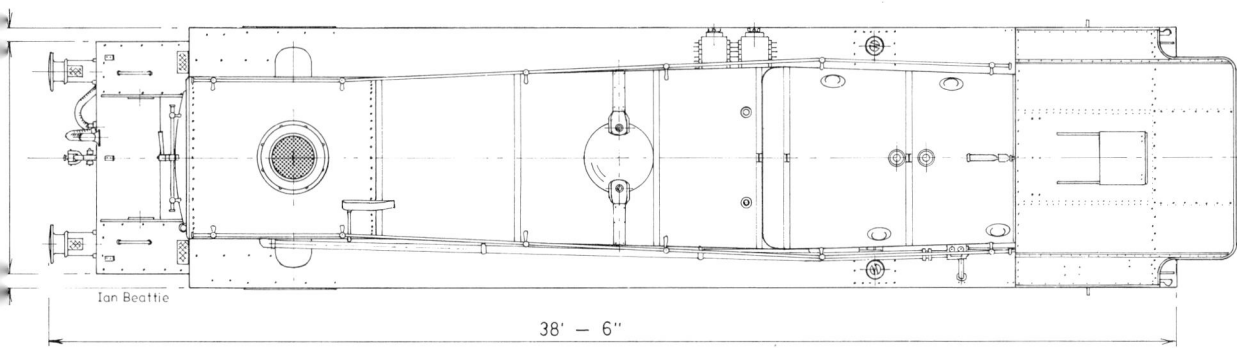
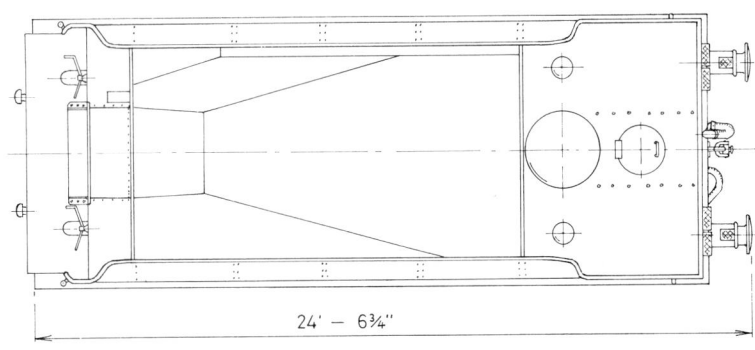
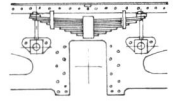

Alternative Spring Hangers

Type:	Mixed-traffic
Overall Length:	63'7¾"
Cylinders:	2, 18½" x 28" bore/stroke
Boiler Pressure:	225 lbs/sq in
Heating Surface:	1998 sq ft
Grate Area:	28.65 sq ft
Tractive Effort:	25455 lbs
Mean Weight in Working Order:	125 tons 5 cwt
Coal Capacity:	9 tons
Water Capacity:	4000 gallons
Number Built:	842, 1934-51
Preserved:	18

ABOVE: No.45161 has a rake of empty suburban stock behind it as it nears Carlisle Canal yard. PHOTOGRAPH: PHIL CALEY.

BELOW: No.5025, restored to LMS condition, is seen here at Aviemore on the Strathspey Railway in 1990. PHOTOGRAPH: ALAN PIKE.

Quite naturally teething troubles afflict any type of new machine and the Black 5s were not immune; compared however with Stanier's preceding 'Princess Royal' (see RM May 1990) and 'Jubilee' designs the 5s were models of perfection. Of the initial 472 examples constructed during 1934-38 100 were supplied by the Vulcan Foundry and the remainder by Armstrong Whitworth of Newcastle; otherwise production was concentrated 'in house' at Crewe and Horwich until cessation in 1951, under BR auspices and in favour of the BR Standard Class 5 4-6-0 (see RM September 1990), itself largely based on the precursive LMS specifications.

The first 225 Black 5s featured domeless boilers – the apparent dome cover acted merely as a mount for the topfeed clack valves – together with (on the first 57 engines) low-degree superheating, general over the GWR network and which the new CME deemed adequate. Whilst the operating authorities were generally delighted with the new 4-6-0s uprated superheating proved efficacious and was fitted retroactively to the earliest engines; at first domeless boilers were retained as standard – indeed many Black 5s featured such boilers till the end of steam – but domed versions were installed from the 226th engine onwards (No.5225, outshopped from Newcastle in 1936). To confuse the issue, many domeless boilers were also converted with domes...

Production ceased during 1938 but was restarted in 1943, following Stanier's secondment onto wartime work, under the guidance of Charles Fairburn (who became CME in 1944 on Stanier's eventual resignation from the LMS), continuing under Fairburn's successor George Ivatt who instituted several American-inspired labour-saving fitments onto new Black 5s plus a series of fundamental modernising changes to the 4-6-0 format, which will be covered by a future article in these pages [see RM March 1999, in fact – Ed.].

Attached to Black 5s were Stanier's LMS standard 9-ton coal, 4000-gallon water capacity tenders, with bodies of either rivetted (exposed or flush) or welded construction. Later tenders – chiefly the welded variants – sported a simpler, neater form of spring hanging illustrated here by a 'scrap' elevation.

Withdrawal of these ultimately most useful of locomotives took place from 1961 onwards, a remarkable number staying in service to the very end of everyday steam.

Notes on the drawings

Such a wide variety of modifications, made during production and in service, over such a numerically enormous class brings its own special problems when it comes to illustrating a 'standard' example, however the drawings herewith are reasonably typical of such a Black 5.

The boiler is of the domeless style with feedwater pipes sunk within the cladding. Flush (ie invisible) rivetting was general on pre-war Black 5s, exposed rivets being normal for postwar assembly and overhauls, the latter especially in BR times; the rivet patterns shown are representative but not necessarily true for each and every 'standard' Black 5. The tender is depicted with full rivetting; the welded counterpart is otherwise identical. Note that the table quoted contains general specifications reasonably representative of the 'standard' 4-6-0.

Fowler freight engines: LMS Classes 4F and 7F

THE two principal freight engine classes that Sir Henry Fowler introduced for the London Midland & Scottish Railway have a number of factors in common, including of course a distinct family resemblance, so that it is convenient to consider both these designs together – a further reason being that generally they shared the same tender type, Fowler's 3500-gallon version that became an LMS standard used throughout his incumbency as Chief Mechanical Engineer and well into that of his successor, Sir William Stanier.

4F 0-6-0

The Class 4F 0-6-0 was far from brand-new to the LMS: the first example rolled out of the Midland Railway works at Derby in October 1911, itself being the latest of a long line of increasingly more powerful goods 0-6-0s that had begun with Matthew Kirtley in the very early days of the MR. In fact the 4F was at base an update of its precursor and could hardly be deemed a totally original concept. The Midland concern built 197 4Fs until Grouping swallowed up the railway in 1923, including five for use as mixed-traffic locomotives on the Somerset & Dorset Joint Railway.

The fledgling LMS was dominated by Midland thinking and practice, so that continuation of the building programme of Class 4 engines as a standard goods design for the new group was entirely natural. The Midland 4Fs were built to be driven from the right-hand side of the cab and the first few LMS-built 0-6-0s followed suit, however successive batches conformed to the decreed left-hand drive for LMS engines (the MR and early LMS 0-6-0s were never altered in this respect). No fewer than 575 examples were outshopped by the LMS, principally between 1924 and 1928, and during Stanier's regime from 1937 to 1941. Private builders, and other erecting shops beyond Derby in the LMS empire, swelled the totals of six-coupled engines' ranks to an eventual class strength of 772, a measure of their general utility.

The 4Fs were powerful, sturdy locomotives with plenty of the stamina needed in the coal traffic that constituted so much of the MR and LMS revenue. Unfortunately the MR 'small-engine' policy, whereby small but efficient engines in multiple, leading to doubleheading as a common and entirely accepted routine, were favoured over bigger and more potent machines, led to lack of experience in detail fittings when eventually big engines were desperately needed. This also showed itself in some shortcomings in the MR 4Fs that were never corrected in the LMS variants: chiefly involved were axlebox bearings that were far too parsimonious in their bearing area for the increasingly heavy demands made upon the engines. Valve chest characteristics were none too modern either, leading to constricted breathing, and again no real development took place.

All LMS 4Fs were vacuum-brake fitted, many with steam heating too, for fitted freight duties and the occasional passenger working, which their quite large wheels allowed. General throughout the LMS system and subsequent BR regions, the big 0-6-0s contributed heavily if mundanely to the overall operating picture of the railway. The 4Fs were withdrawn between 1954 and 1966, with four being retained for preservation.

7F 0-8-0

Pertinently nicknamed 'Austin Seven' on their appearance in 1929, as a play on their power classification and obvious antithesis to the minute, hugely popular motor car of the time, the hefty Class 7F 0-8-0s were intended as intermediaries in the power stakes between the 4F 0-6-0s and the huge newly-launched Beyer-Garratt articulated engines, the latter specialising in main line coal-running from the Nottingham coalfields to the immense marshalling yards at Cricklewood in north London.

The boiler used for the 0-8-0s was based on that fitted to the very successful ex-LNWR Class G1 and G2 0-8-0s and emerged as a simply superb steam-raising plant, but once again the extraordinary Achilles Heel endemic in Fowler's goods engines was allied to an otherwise very sound mechanism: the same axlebox bearings as installed on the 4Fs, far too small either for reliability or the sustained working stresses imposed by the much heavier and more powerful 7Fs. Thus, sadly (albeit with the advantage of hindsight), the effectiveness of the big 'Austin Sevens' was undermined from the start: maintenance costs were unduly high and an additional batch of five already sanctioned shortly before his appointment was cancelled by Stanier (who was responsible thereafter for a far better freight machine, the Class 8F 2-8-0).

Altogether 175 7Fs were erected, at the ex-LNWR workshops at Crewe, in four batches from 1929 to 1932; three of the 1932 output were equipped from new with ACFI feedwater heaters, a popular experimental installation on British railways at the time, especially with the LNER, but the gains to be found on the 7Fs were more than nullified by their expense and the heaters were removed in the early 1940s. None of the 7F fleet was vacuum-brake fitted and to underline their purely goods role most were supplied with simple 3-link couplings.

One of the quartet of preserved 4Fs is No.4422, seen here away from home turf in fine fettle at Llangollen. PHOTOGRAPH: LEN WEAL.

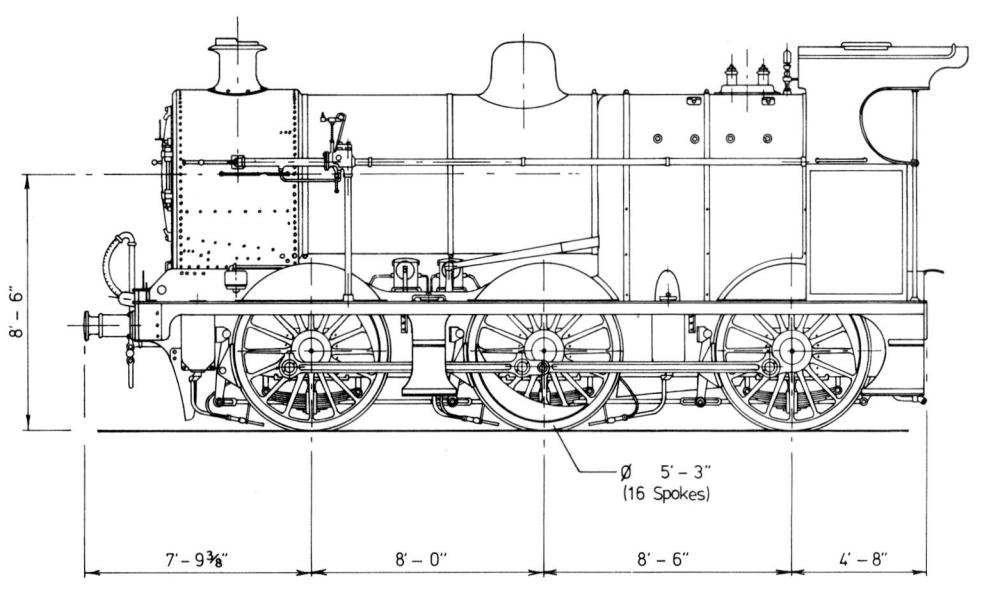
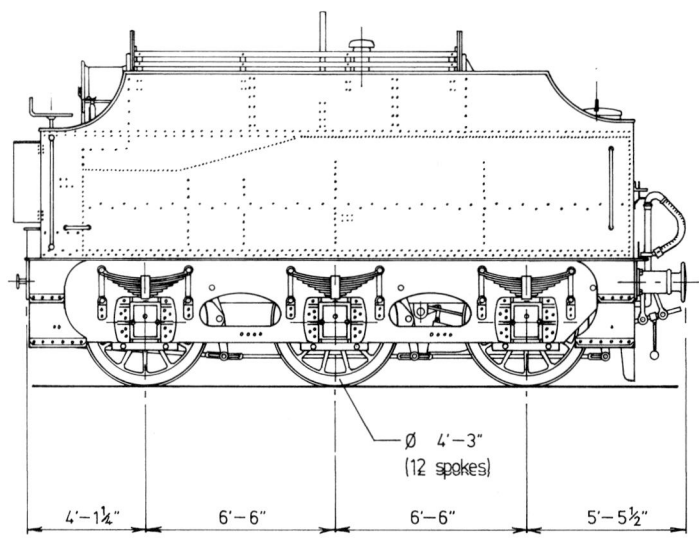
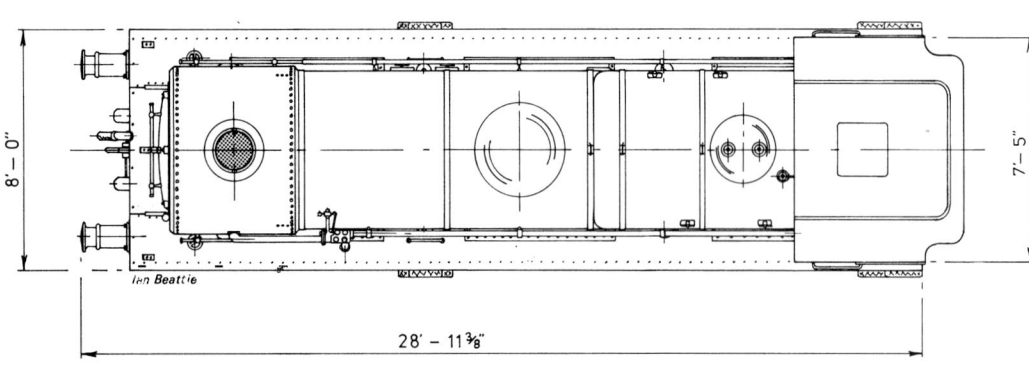
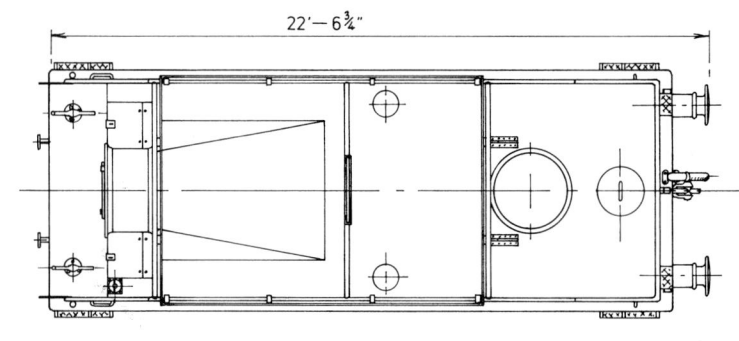
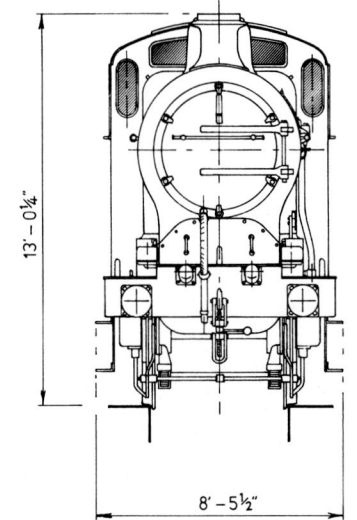
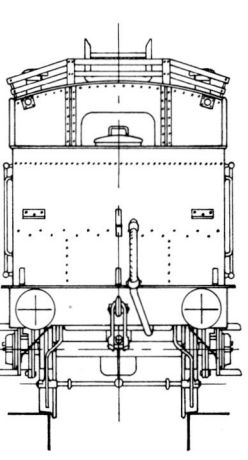

	4F	7F
Overall Length:	52'0 1/8"	56'1"
Cylinders:	2, 20" x 26" bore/stroke	2, 19 1/2" x 26" bore/stroke
Boiler Pressure:	175 lbs/sq in	200 lbs/sq in
Heating Surface:	1157 sq in	1786 sq in
Grate Area:	21 sq ft	23.5 sq ft
Tractive Effort:	24560 lbs	29747 lbs
Mean Weight in Working Order:	90 tons	102 tons
Coal Capacity:	4 tons	4 tons
Water Capacity:	3500 gallons	3500 gallons
Number Built:	772, 1911-41	175, 1929-32
Preserved:	4	None

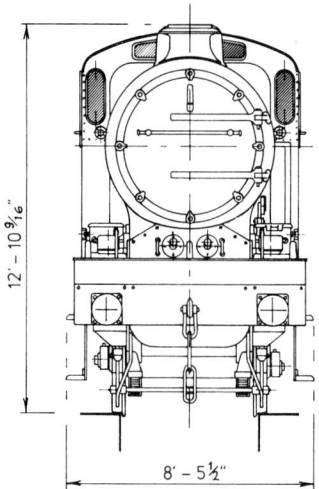

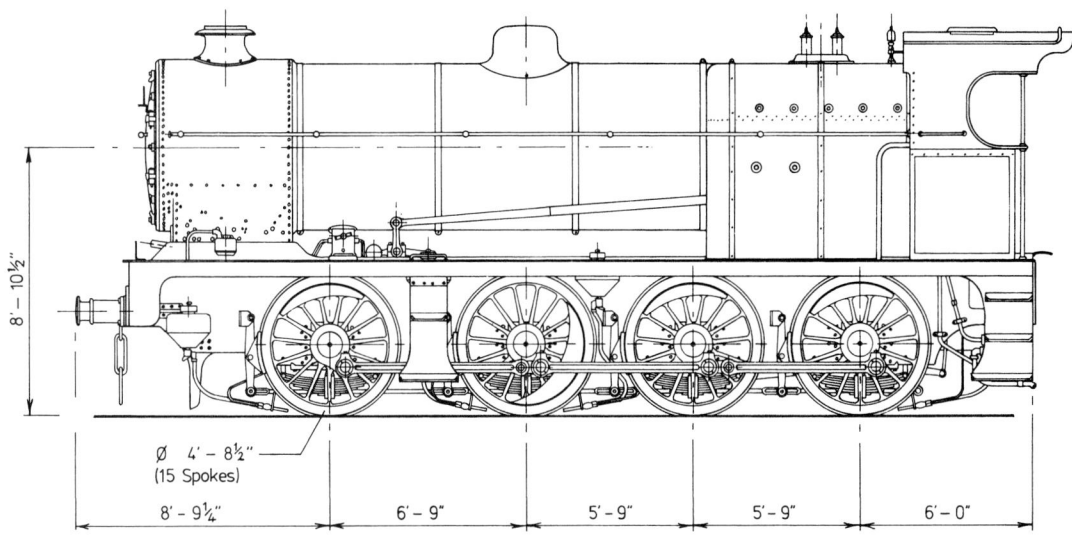

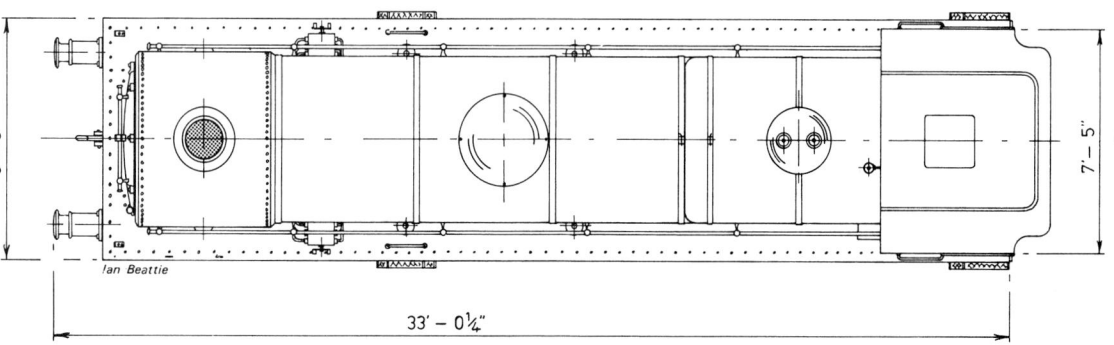

Given some thoughtful development the burly 0-8-0s could have proved magnificent locomotives for their purposes instead of merely adequate, but the somewhat motley fleet of new and rebuilt LNWR eight-coupled freight machines was uniformly reliable and in abundant supply with a renowned longevity; in the 1930s the emergence of Stanier's rightly celebrated freight 2-8-0 further demonstrated the Fowler engines' weaknesses, so that flawed 'Austin Sevens' eked out their humble existence on main line coal trains before a protracted withdrawal period, taking place between 1949 and 1962.

Notes on the drawings
The drawings of the Class 4F 0-6-0 show a typical example as built in the late 1920s, complete with piston tail-rod covers (removed by BR) protruding from the specially raised central portion of the buffer beam. As indicated by the siting of the reverse rod and brake ejector equipment, the locomotive is driven from the left-hand side of the cab. The Fowler chimney has a capuchon which was later removed, after which the height from rail level was 12'10 3/8" – the 4Fs built from 1937 onwards sported some small detail differences over the pure Fowler versions, notably the use of a Stanier chimney (which maintained the same height as the non-capuchoned Fowler ditto).

And as-built condition is illustrated by the Class 7F drawings; note the slightly flattened underside of the smokebox front plate (to accommodate and for access to the valve chests), and the small difference in the shape of the cabside opening *vis-a-vis* the pure MR ditto of the 4F. Both classes utilised the Fowler Standard tender style shown.

RIGHT: in its 30th year, 7F No.49618 rests on Agecroft shed, Manchester. Withdrawal was but two months away when it was photographed on 13 August 1961.

Gleaming in anachronistic Stroudley ochre, No.103 poses for the official photographer in August 1959. PHOTOGRAPH: BR(ScR).

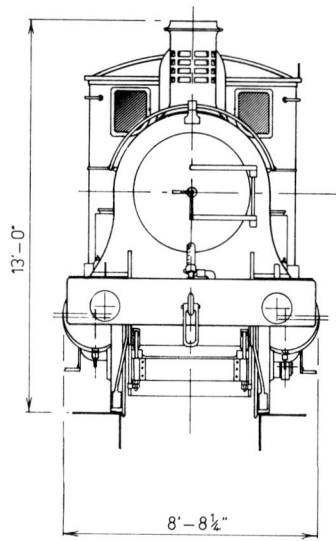

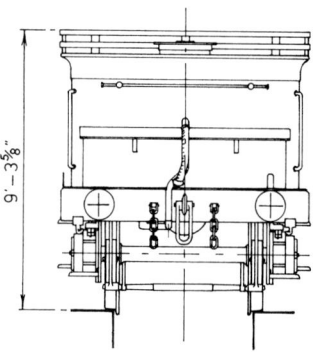

Highland Railway 'Jones Goods' 4-6-0

A SPECTACULAR undertaking set in some of the most magnificent – and rugged – scenery Britain has to offer, the Highland Railway worked, as its title implies, the area of Scotland north of Inverness, in which population was small and communities isolated by distance and topography: in short a railway engineer's nightmare. Incorporated in 1865 and worked as a fiercely independent company until absorption into the LMS Group in 1923, the HR required tough, powerful engines to work its services, and those supplied by David Jones by and large admirably coincided with that premium necessity.

Appointed in 1870 as locomotive superintendent in succession to William Stroudley (who went on to greater fame on the LBSCR, almost as far south of the HR as it is possible to get), Jones initiated several classes of 4-4-0 passenger locomotives that achieved lasting fame for their exploits down the years. Well aware of advances in locomotive technology in other countries, though rather belied by the old-fashioned 'Crewe' style of double frames and cylinders built in unit with smokeboxes that characterised his 4-4-0s, Jones elected to design a class on the 4-6-0 principle that had been long employed in the United States and was becoming well-favoured in Europe. That it was intended for goods traffic alone slightly offset the glamour of its multiple 'firsts' – first of that wheel arrangement and most powerful as well as heaviest locomotive in Britain at the time of unveiling in September 1894.

Being a small network the HR had neither resources nor, given the multiplicity of private Scottish engine builders, had it need to erect its own prime movers: all fifteen 'Jones' or 'Big Goods' (to differentiate them from Jones' 0-6-0 goods design) were outshopped by Messrs Sharp Stewart of Glasgow between September and November 1894. Unusually for Highland engines none received names; numbering was 103-117 inclusive.

The work the class performed completely vindicated the confidence shown in their pioneering mechanical specification, hauling premium freight trains throughout the Highland system and, being equipped from the outset with vacuum braking, passenger train duties were frequently undertaken with considerable élan. Many features in the engines' constitution comprised archetypal Jones fittings, such as the cab shape (derived it must be said from Stroudley in the first instance) and his famed louvred chimney; being double skinned, the louvres were supposed to admit air between the liners to lift the exhaust clear, and the principle seemed to work on HR engines if no others. The Crewe-inspired Allan straight-link motion was perpetuated on the 'Jones Goods', and livery was composed of apple green with olive green bands, fully lined, with deep maroon beneath the running plates downwards.

Transference to the LMSR in 1923 saw no change in the duties carried out by the 4-6-0s, and very few wandered beyond the confines of the Highland section. Renumbered 17916-30 respectively, the fifteen engines were painted black overall. Modifications were applied at various times to all the engines though none seemed identically equipped so modellers should consult plenteous photos of their chosen example! All 'Jones Goods' sported flangeless central coupled (ie driving) wheels but a number were refitted with flanged versions eventually. Most engines carried Peter Drummond chimneys after a period – Drummond succeeded Jones, who resigned in 1896 following injuries sustained during trials with a 'Jones Goods' – also Ross 'pop' safety valves were installed and smokeboxes rebuilt, when the wingplates were excised.

Withdrawals of the hard-worked 4-6-0s took place quite protractedly for what was by then a small,

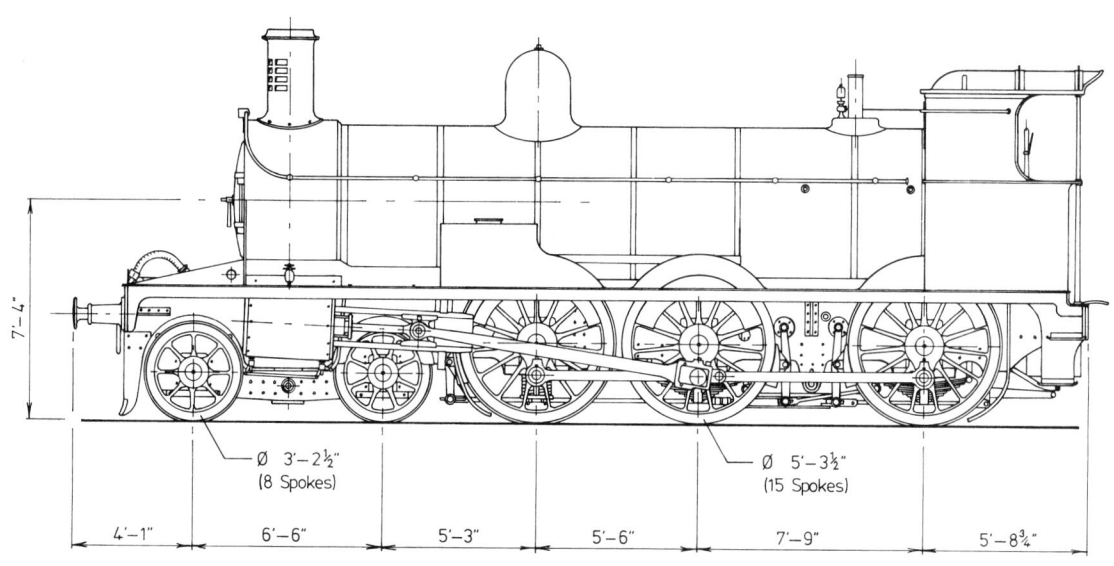
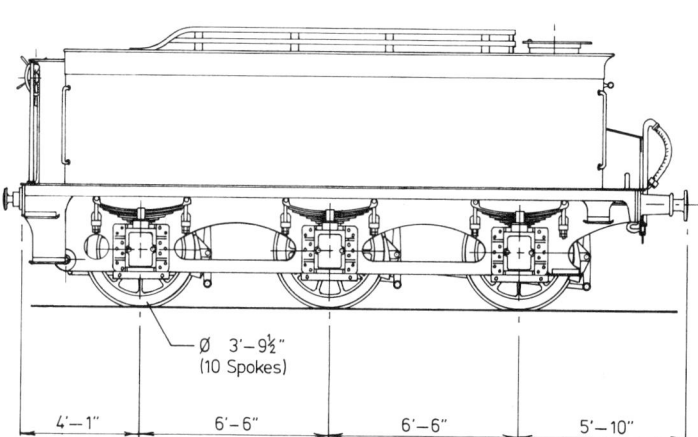
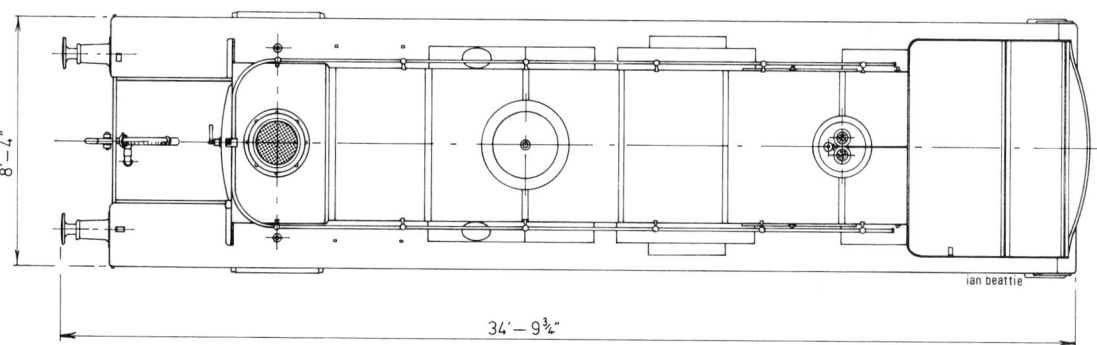
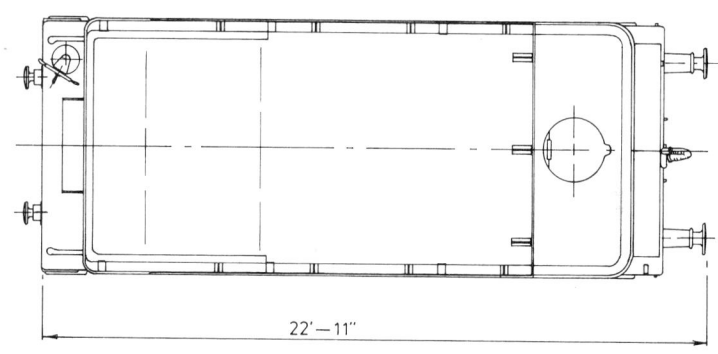

Taken at Inverness shed on 16 June 1934, this historic photograph illustrates No.103 in its incarnation as LMS No.17916, within days of withdrawal for preservation in July that year. Note Ross valves, rejigged smokebox and Drummond chimney as the hardy old 4-6-0 awaits its next turn of duty.

PHOTOGRAPH: THE LATE W.G.BOYDEN, FRANK HORNBY COLLECTION.

non-standard class, between 1929 and 1940. The original 'Jones Goods', No.17916 was renumbered 103 and preserved by the LMS; it was restored to full working order in 1959, including the choice of Stroudley's HR (and LBSCR) ochre-yellow livery, a curiosity since although Jones continued this style for some fifteen years into his superintendency, by the time his 4-6-0s were designed the green livery outlined above had long been in force. Following several years of enthusiast train working No.103 was finally retired and now resides in state at the Glasgow Museum of Transport, still wearing early HR paintwork.

Notes on the drawings
These show a typical 'Jones Goods' in original condition as erected in 1894. A tablet exchange mechanism was fitted against the right-hand tender tank but is not depicted here for clarity. Note that the cylinders were inclined at 1 in 24, and the HR lamp-irons in which the bufferbeam-mounted versions were turned through 90° from left to right, with a lamp socket used atop the smokebox and a spare iron on the cab roof. Present too is the typical HR folding front vacuum hose; the running plate between bufferbeam and smokebox was at first inset between the frames, below the level of the side plates this was later raised in line as seen in the photographs.

Overall Length:	58'4½"
Cylinders:	2, 20" x 26" bore/stroke
Boiler Pressure:	175 lbs/sq in
Heating Surface:	1672.5 sq ft
Grate Area:	22.6 sq ft
Tractive Effort:	23666 lbs
Mean Weight in Working Order:	94.35 tons
Coal Capacity:	5 tons
Water Capacity:	3000 gallons
Number Built:	15, in 1894
Preserved:	1

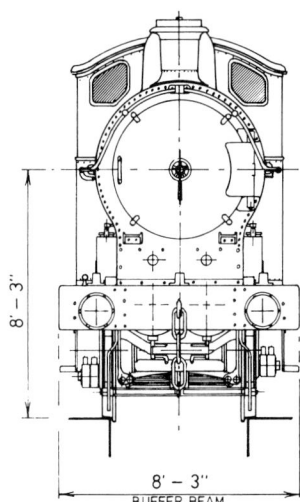

Complete with cab – a fairly common feature – on its Bowen Cooke standard tender, 1922-vintage G2a 0-8-0 No.49454 was the last of 60 G2 Class engines to be assembled: caught by Frank Hornby's well-travelled camera at Crewe South shed on 8 April 1962.

London & North Western Railway G1 0-8-0

THE STORY behind the huge fleet of legendary 0-8-0 freight engines amassed by the London & North Western Railway, the erstwhile 'Premier Line', is as convoluted as any yet described in these pages and any attempt to portray such complexity within the customary half-dozen drawings is foredoomed to failure. The sole recourse therefore is to review a single class as representative of the fleet; but first a bit of background history.

Instigated in 1892 on the LNWR (as was much else innovatory) by Francis Webb, famed Chief Mechanical Engineer for almost 30 years, the initial 0-8-0 was essentially a stretched 0-6-0 – of which format the railway had huge experience – sharing such features as two cylinders mounted between the frames combined with simple expansion of steam. Given Webb's proclivities for experimentation however, compound steam expansion in the form of 3- and 4-cylinder 0-8-0s quickly followed (Classes A and B respectively, comprising 111 and 170 members) after the singleton simple model.

Following Webb's resignation in 1903, his successor George Whale lost little time in modifying the relatively complex yet reasonably successful compound 0-8-0s, firstly by adding pony trucks to the hefty front ends of the B Class engines – thereafter reclassified E as 2-8-0s – and then, late in 1904, rebuilding the A Class machines as 2-cylinder simple units which then became Class C 0-8-0s. During 1906 a secondary Class D was formed from former A Class engines converted as Class Cs but with larger boilers; a further subclass involved refitting the remaining Bs as per the E Class but involving this bigger boiler, thence relabelled Class F.

The story continues to thicken. Also in 1906 the 32 remaining 4-cylinder Class B compound 0-8-0s underwent rebuilding into 2-cylinder simple guise complete with the large D Class boilers, retaining several original features such as their 'piano fronts', covers beneath the smokebox doors shaped like piano keyboard lids that were hinged for access to the steam chests. These rebuilds were joined in 1910 by 60 new locomotives to the same overall specification, but without the idiosyncratic fitments left over from compounding, to complete Class G.

Whale relinquished his position as CME in 1908 and was replaced by Charles Bowen Cooke, who was responsible for launching the principle of superheating on the LNWR. It was therefore natural that the company's hardworked heavy freight engines – on which for a goodly proportion of its income the railway depended – should be subjected to such improvement. The upshot was the Class G1 0-8-0.

Basically a developed Class G design plus superheater, conversion of all existing 0-8-0s (and derivative 2-8-0s) of whatever class, subclass or format began in January 1912. Taking into account units withdrawn without being subjected to this rebuilding programme, no fewer than 279 8-coupled engines converted to G1 status emerged from Crewe Works over more than 20

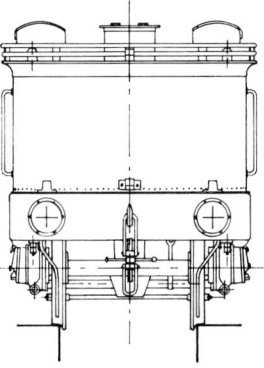

years, ie well into LMS days. A series of 170 new G1 engines was erected contemporaneously, the last outshopped in 1918, bringing the eventual class total to 449; this class formed the basis of the characteristic LNWR 0-8-0 which was so useful and well regarded that it endured right up to the final days of steam working on BR in 1968.

A G2 development followed in 1921-2, at the very end of the LNWR's autonomous existence, comprising 60 units almost identical to the foregoing G1s bar increased boiler pressure, set at 175 lbs/sq in. The final flowering emerged in 1935 as the G2a which sported strengthened motion parts and enhanced braking power.

Curiously not all 449 G1 engines could have been witnessed in service together, since before the last of the conversions to G1 format were instituted earlier members of the class had in turn been rebuilt to G2a specification!

The advent of Grouping had a considerable influence on the sturdy 0-8-0s. A new boiler containing a Belpaire firebox was developed by H.P.M.Beames, who had become CME of the LNWR after Bowen Cooke's death in office in 1920 but had been superseded by the more senior George Hughes of the LYR upon the merger of the two companies in 1922 (Hughes of course went on to stewardship of the LMS loco fortunes until his retirement in 1925). This design was standardised for the 0-8-0 in 1924 and it is with these boilers that the engines became so familiar in later LMS and especially BR days – at first these boilers were used turn and turn about with the orthodox LNWR round-topped-firebox versions until the latter wore out beyond redemption. Externally less drastic (and virtually the only other) LMS adjuncts were reprofiled roofs to suit the tighter ex-Midland loading gauge and substitution of Ross 'pop' safety valves. Under LMS and BR managements the engines were placed in power category 7F.

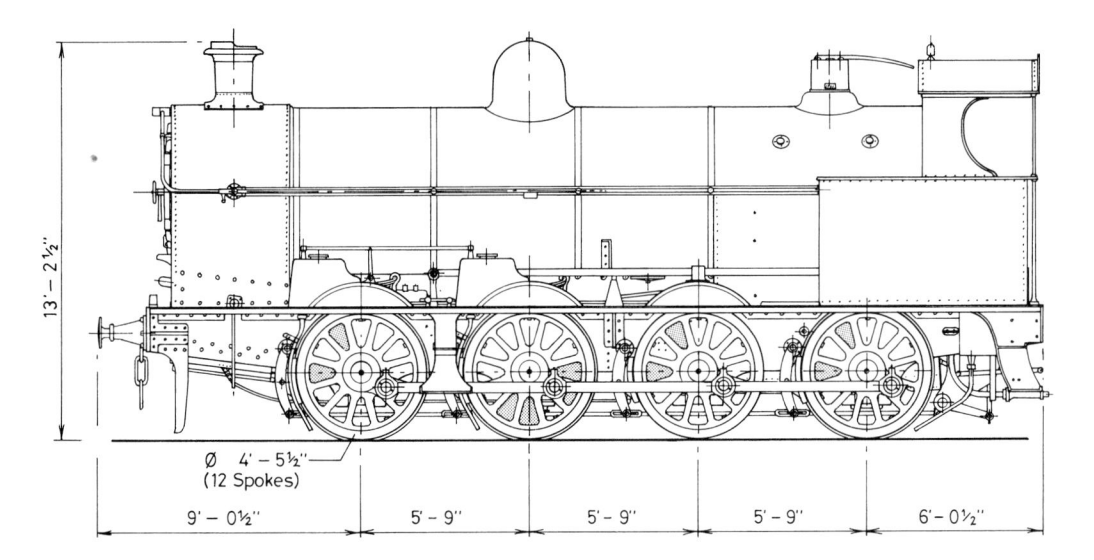

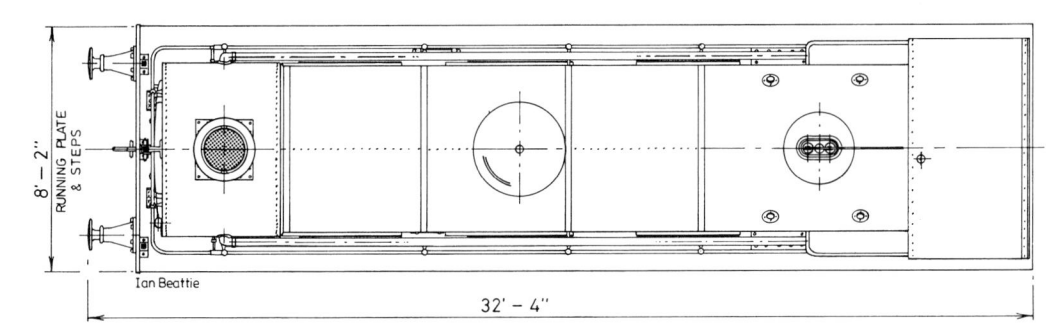

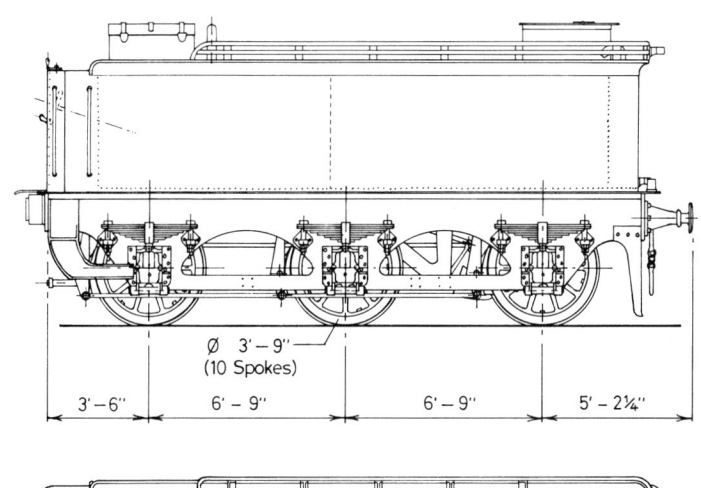

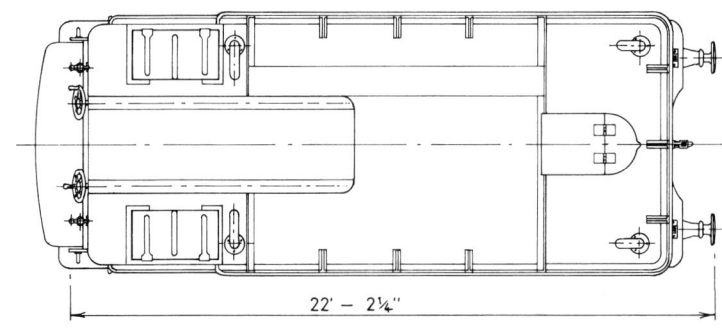

Because the LNW Running Department rather obscurely termed the G1/G2 0-8-0s 'D Superheated' the class in time collected the nickname 'Super D' (inevitably debased to 'Stupid D'), amongst other sobriquets such as 'Mourners', 'Choo Choos' and 'Fat Nancies'! One G2 survived the cutting torch and remains in fine working order as part of the National Collection, residing at the time of writing at the Midland Railway Centre. *[As this book goes to press, the locomotive is now back at the National Railway Museum in York – Ed.]*

Notes on the drawings
These are based on a G1 Class 0-8-0 as outshopped new from Crewe between 1912 and 1914 (from then onwards screw couplings and vacuum braking apparatus were standardised: previously 3-link couplings and steam brakes as shown were employed). Several items are worthy of note, namely flangeless wheels on the 3rd axle, the central coupling rods mounted outboard of the outer pair (later replaced as in the photos by conventional rods with articulated joints); though not discernible here the wheel spokes are H-section – a typical Webb feature – and balance weights fill gaps between spokes (their distribution is indicated by dot shading).

Unusually the rearmost two axles utilise transverse leaf springs, that on the 3rd axle mounted above the axleboxes and on the 4th axle beneath (the later visible in the front view here); the foremost axles are conventionally suspended.

Throughout their existence the LNWR 0-8-0s trailed a variety of tenders which from the days of the G1s onwards graduated towards those standard types designed by Whale and Bowen Cooke. That shown here is a typical Whale 3000-gallon tender, in this instance with screw coupling and twin toolboxes (those tenders sporting 3-link couplings with one or no boxes present were nonetheless just as common). Note the brake and waterscoop operating wheels set at quite a steep angle, shown dashed in the side view: the vertical line thereon indicates the limit of the coal space.

Type:	Heavy Freight
Overall Length:	55'4"
Cylinders:	2, 20½" x 24" bore/stroke
Boiler Pressure:	160 lbs/sq in
Heating Surface:	c.2500 sq ft
Grate Area:	23.6 sq ft
Tractive Effort:	25640 lbs
Mean Weight in Working Order:	97 tons 5 cwt
Coal Capacity:	5 tons
Water Capacity:	3000 gallons
Number Built:	449, 1912-18 (see text)
Preserved:	1 (Class G2)

ABOVE: demonstrating the ecumenical nature of this favoured LMS design, Class 2 2-6-2T No.41294 was not only one of those constructed in 1951 for allocation to the Southern Region of BR but was captured in well-scrubbed, recently-serviced condition outside the ex-GWR Swindon Works on 13 August 1956.

OPPOSITE: its home shed in the background, No.41224 shunts at Bournemouth Central, 30 May 1966. PHOTOGRAPH: DOUGLAS DOHERTY.

Ivatt Class 2 2-6-2T

BORN IN Ireland in 1886 and son of H.A.Ivatt, celebrated locomotive chief of the Great Northern Railway at the beginning of this century who introduced the 4-4-2 tender format to Britain's rails, Henry George Ivatt was thoroughly imbued in steam lore yet displayed an admirably modern approach to engine design during his years as firstly locomotive chief of the North Staffordshire Railway until Grouping, thence as a senior LMS engineer and, from October 1945, Group Chief Mechanical Engineer.

The immense impact of austere exigencies during wartime between 1939 and 1945, when staff numbers, maintenance and repair of infrastructure plus care of engines and rolling stock were drastically straitened weighed heavy on the LMS authorities: it was obvious too that the peacetime world to come would be vastly different to the old pre-war order. In his deliberations for the future and in common with other railway engineers, Ivatt inspected and was impressed by the many labour-saving devices sported by American engines, these becoming common on southern English metals in the early 1940s, especially in the intense military supply build-up to the Normandy Landings in 1944.

In 1943 Sir William Stanier had handed over the office of CME to C.E.Fairburn, whose duties, with a highly competent staff including Ivatt as Chief Assistant, included *inter alia* drawing up proposals for locomotives suitable for postwar usage. Whilst Fairburn was responsible for initiating the twin Class 2 2-6-0/2-6-2T format (a fact not often acknowledged) it was on George Ivatt's capable shoulders that the practicality of the design lay. Fairburn was not a fit man and, as his health deteriorated, much of the CME's work devolved on his Chief Assistant; on Fairburn's death in 1945 Ivatt was declared *de facto* CME by the LMS Board.

The operating division of the Group had originally requested a new 0-6-0 for general duties – a format after all perfectly familiar to engine crews and shed staff throughout the network over many decades – and it was principally due to Ivatt's persuasive character that the 2-6-0/2-6-2Ts were produced in lieu. Their versatility, wide route availability (thanks to low weight) and extraordinary power for such small machinery won enduring popularity with crews and shed personnel alike, likewise those who now drive and maintain examples in preservation. Note that the Class 2 twins are all but identical: the 'Mickey Mouse' Mogul (ie the 2-6-0 version) was featured in RM April 1982.

Ease of maintenance and use were key factors in the specification given the paucity of staff and expertise after the attritions and deprivations of war: smokebox self-cleaning apparatus and quick-emptying ashpans were examples of the benign American influence, together with an up-to-date boiler and highly accessible, outside mounted Walschaert's valve motion two cylinders only were employed to avoid unnecessary complication (the bore was increased to 16½" from outshopping of No.41290 onwards) and vacuum-operated push-pull control gear, which was mounted either side of the smokebox was installed on several engines.

Only 10 engines were completed by the LMS before Nationalisation (Nos.1200-8 in 1946 and, curiously a singleton No.1209 in 1947). but being a pre-eminent success the newly-created British Railways were happy to continue assembly of the design until a total of 130 filled the class.

Thus Nos.41210-41329 emerged between 1949 and 1952 – the final 10 tanks were built at Derby whereas all the remainder emanated from Crewe – and production of this useful machine only ceased as a political decision in favour of the BR Standard version which in actuality was virtually identical.

Operated habitually in lined black livery, the potent little tanks popped up in localities way beyond the ex-LMS network – indeed a batch of ten was constructed in 1951 especially for the Southern Region. Worked interchangeably on branch line, suburban and light cross-country mixed traffic duties with their twins the Class 2 Moguls (and of course their close cousins the BR variants), the tender engines being chosen where coal and water supplies were none too lavish, the 2-6-2Ts suffered the same fate as most modern BR hauliers – they were withdrawn years, even decades, before their useful life was run. We are fortunate in that four such tanks still work with customary verve in preservation.

Notes on the drawings
This is a typical Ivatt Class 2 tank of the LMS/early BR period: 3 types of chimney were fitted during production, of which that shown is the earliest style. From No.41290 (following tests at Swindon) a slimmer, tapered chimney was used – see the photo – and finally a broader, taller version became standard. Perhaps strangely, chimney interchangeability seemed rarely if ever practised within the class.

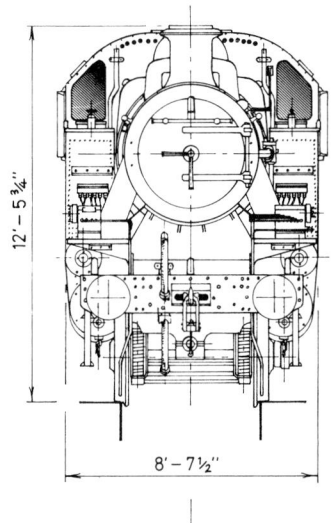

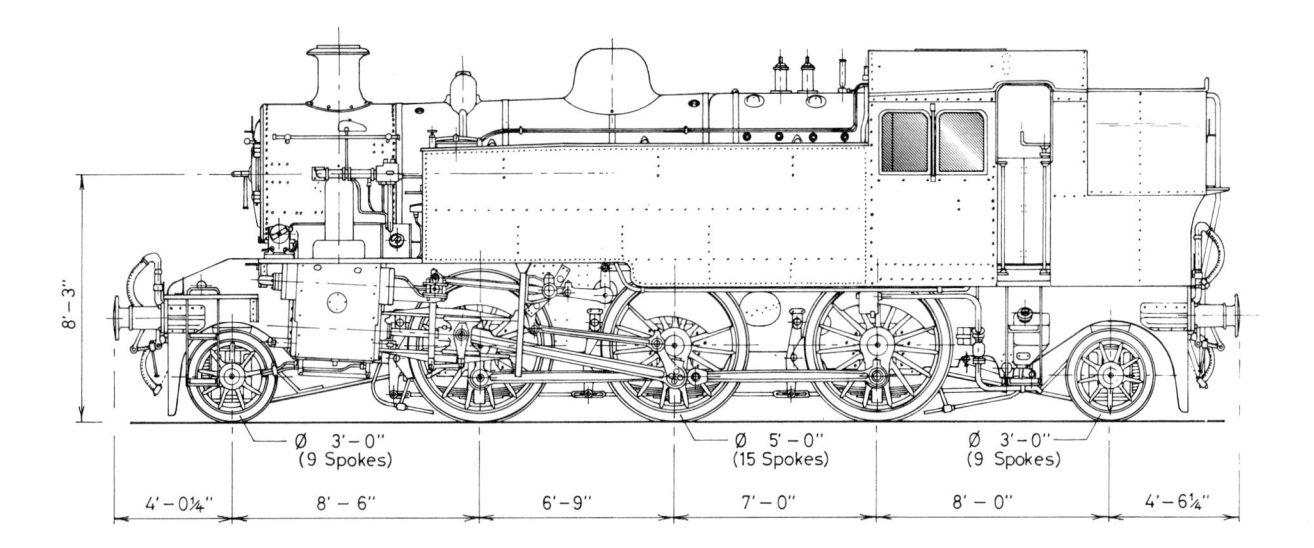

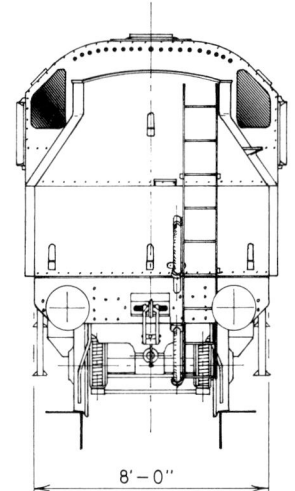

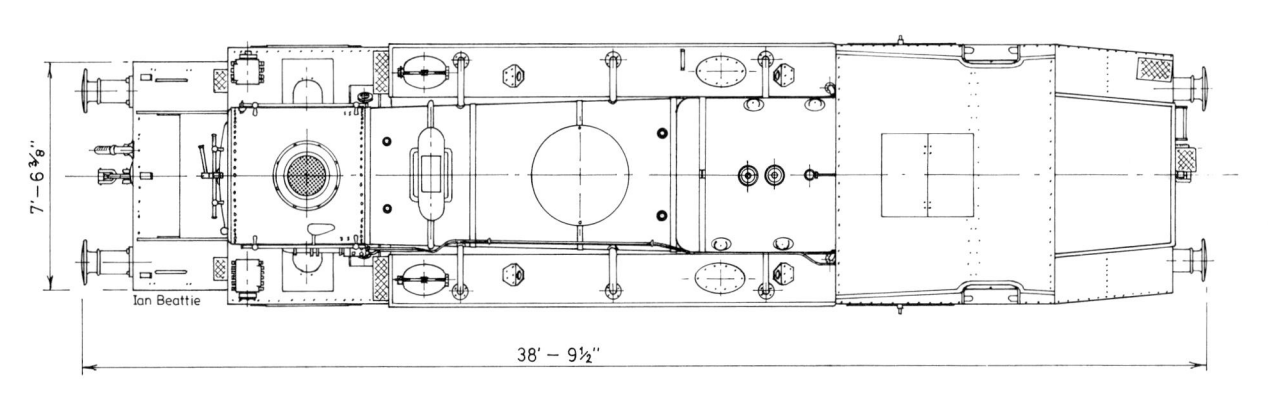

The design of front and rear trucks was amended somewhat during the assembly period, most apparently via heavily-flanged pivot struts (compare with illustrations of the 'Mickey Mouse' Mogul), also the roof ventilator underwent several changes of style, with that drawn here being the original LMS design.

Please note that pipe runs from the smokebox-flanking lubricators have been omitted from the plan view, for clarity's sake.

Type:	Mixed-traffic
Cylinders:	16" x 24" bore/stroke
Boiler Pressure:	200 lbs/sq in
Heating Surface:	1159.5 sq ft
Tractive Effort:	17400 lbs
Mean Weight in Working Order:	63 tons 5 cwt
Coal Capacity:	3 tons
Water Capacity:	1350 gallons
Number Built:	130, 1946-52
Preserved:	4

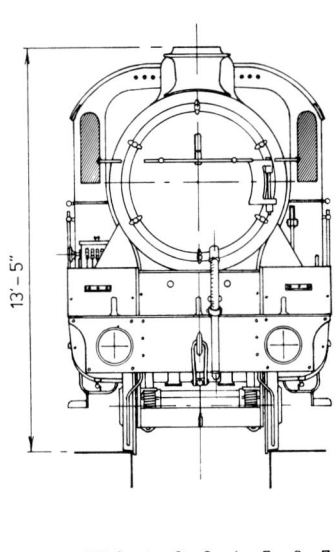

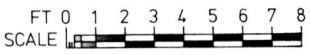

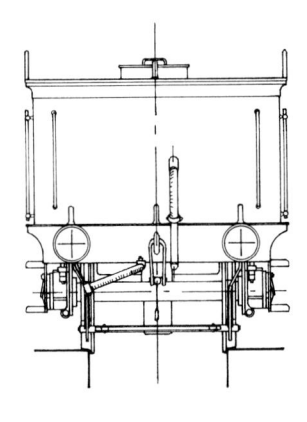

The unique Compound 'Dreadnought' caught historically by Walter Boyden's camera on 21 July 1929 at Carlisle Upperby, together with the justifiably proud shed foreman. No.10456 was withdrawn in 1936. PHOTO: THE LATE W.G.BOYDEN, FRANK HORNBY COLLECTION.

Lancashire & Yorkshire 'Dreadnought' 4-6-0

THE Lancashire & Yorkshire Railway did not contain the route mileage for sustained high-speed passenger operation, so that when a class of colossal 4-6-0 express engines emerged from the LYR works at Horwich beginning in 1908 there were many surprised reactions, and indeed the LYR's lack of experience in designing modern mainline hauliers (the Aspinall Atlantics notwithstanding) quickly became evident: the locomotives were asthmatic, sluggish, had a horrendous coal consumption and suffered from too many inherent faults such as inadequate bearing surfaces. On top of all this the 4-6-0s were very heavy on maintenance, to the point where at any one time up to 50% of the class were undergoing repairs simultaneously. Clearly something drastic had to be done to restitute the situation, and to the LYR locomotive chief George Hughes' great credit, he thoroughly revamped what should have been his masterpiece, though the advent of World War 1 delayed the planned rebuilding programme.

Having been launched at much the same time as the huge Royal Naval capital ships, Hughes' very big 4-6-0s were given the same name – 'Dreadnought' – which remained with the class throughout all its subsequent duplications and vicissitudes. Rebuilding entailed so complete a transfiguration that in essence the results were entirely new engines: the original 20 'Dreadnoughts' comprised saturated boilers (in an era when superheating was a very recent but recognisably desirable breakthrough) and four cylinders directed by inside-mounted Joy's valve gear beloved of the LYR – the outer cylinders were controlled by rocking arms. The rebuilds were equipped with the latest technology, ie. superheated boilers, four piston-valved cylinders controlled by outside Walschaert's valve motion (in the reverse of the original, the inside cylinders were linked by rocking arms to the gear), stretched wheelbase via new frames, windowed cabs and much more besides.

The rebuilt engines were still not perfect – five of the original batch were not revamped, and were scrapped in 1925-6 – but at least they could handle with confidence the greatly increased size of trains for which they had been hurriedly mooted in the first place. Ten further 'Dreadnoughts' were outshopped by the LYR in 1921, followed by 25 more in 1922-23 under the aegis first of the LNWR (the LYR and LNWR merged in January 1922) and then, upon the Grouping in January 1923, the newly formed London Midland & Scottish Railway. A series of 30 4-6-4 tank locomotives intimately based upon the 'Dreadnoughts' was propounded to release the 4-6-0s from mundane duties on to exclusively main line use, however after only ten hit the rails the remaining 20, for which components had been gathered, were turned out as tender locomotive and form the final, somewhat mechanically revised batch of 'Dreadnoughts' of 1924-5. These last engines sported longer (7' wheelbase) bogies, slightly redesigned boilers and – externally obvious – much more sharply angular cab rooflines; the longer frames are evident in their sweeping curve to the buffer beam, as shown in the photo, which provide the best visual balance of all the three 'Dreadnought' variations.

As performers the entire class was in actuality on a par with their close contemporaries the LNWR 'Claughton' 4-6-0s. The fact that George Hughes became CME of the LMS in 1923 was fortuitous for his largest designs, and they were put to use handling West Coast Main Line expresses alongside their LNW counterparts. Hughes retired in 1925, leading the way to different engine philosophies against which his 4-6-0s

38

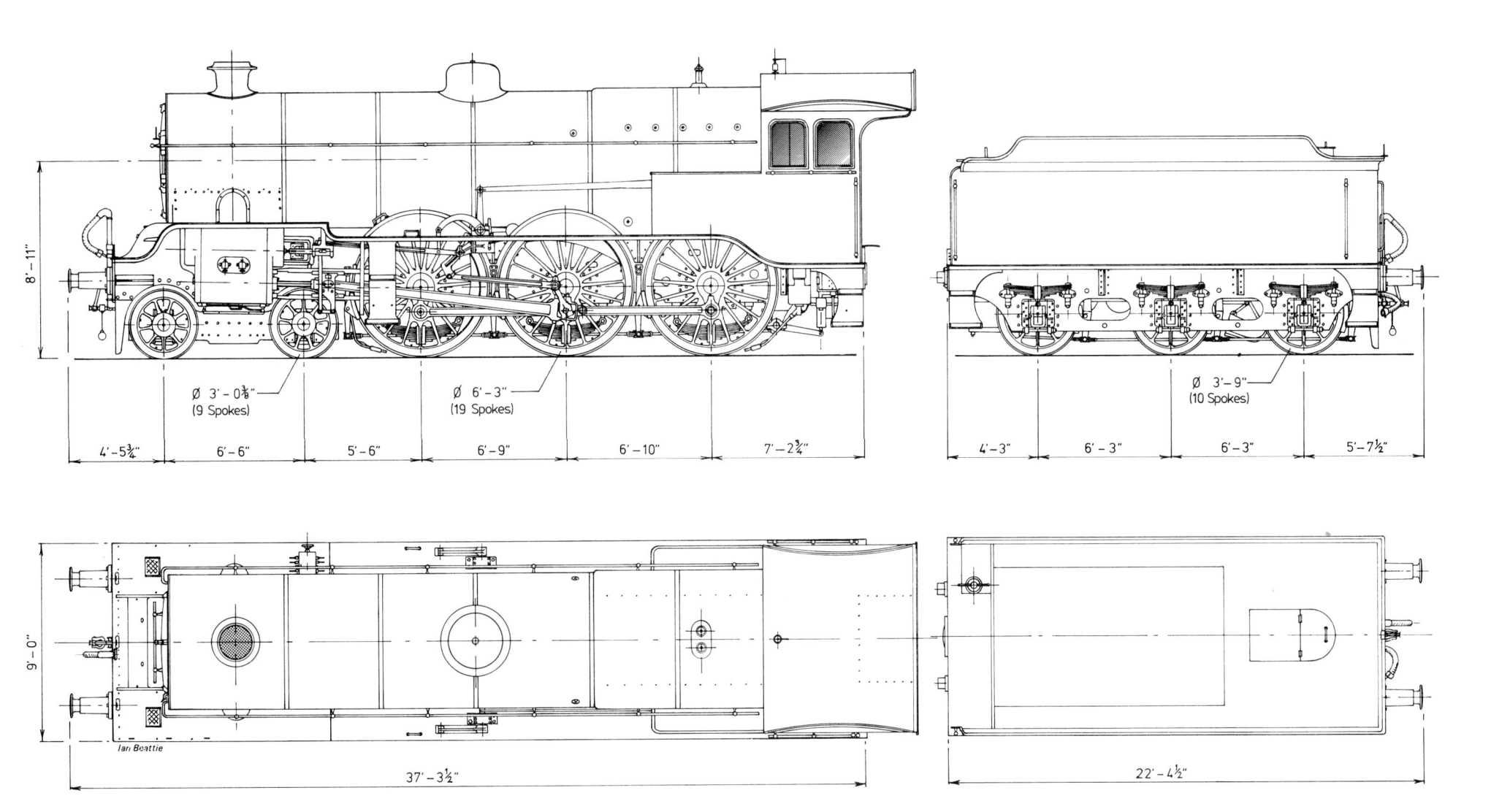

suffered by comparison: relative to the pure LMS 'Scots' and 'Patriots', and thereafter the excellent Stanier 4-6-0s, the 'Dreadnoughts' were far from competitive and, on boiler replacements falling due – no spares had been manufactured – the class was progressively withdrawn, from 1933 onwards. No fewer than 55 left revenue-earning service in 1934-7 and had World War 2 not intervened the class would have been extinct earlier than 1951, when the final example (No.50455, the only one to receive its BR number) was withdrawn and most unfortunately not preserved.

As an experiment 1924-built 'Dreadnought' No.10456 was converted in 1926 to compound working, incorporating 22" x 26" low pressure and 16" x 26" high pressure cylinders, to evaluate such a scheme for a proposed Hughes Pacific, which came to nought. Although very successful and certainly popular with footplate crews, the Compound eked out its existence working between Crewe and Carlisle and was shedded together with its 19 last-batch stablemates at Carlisle Upperby.

Notes on the drawings
The drawings and the specification table refers to the 'second' style of 'Dreadnought', ie. the rebuilds of the original engines plus the 1921-23 versions, comprising 50 engines in total or much the majority of the class. The tender is the large LYR-type fitted to most post-1923 engines (and earlier ones eventually) of LMS provenance. As a sop to clarity the fallplate is shown with the engine – in fact it was hinged to the tender footplate.

Type:	Express Passenger
Overall Length:	60'1¾"
Cylinders:	4, 16½" x 26" bore/stroke
Boiler Pressure:	180 lbs/sq in
Heating Surface:	2238 sq ft
Grate Area:	27 sq ft
Tractive Effort:	28800 lbs
Mean Weight in Working Order:	119 tons
Coal Capacity:	6 tons
Water Capacity:	3000 gallons
Number Built:	75, 1908-25
Preserved:	None

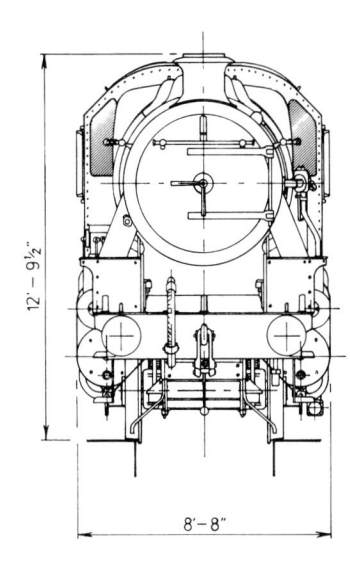

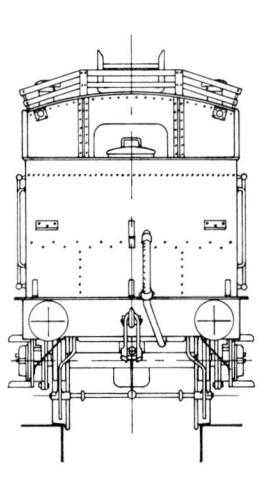

Since restoration and main line certification the singleton preserved Stanier 2-6-0, reunited with its LMS identity of 2968, has travelled far and wide. Witness the fine locomotive, toting its designer's breed of 4000-gallon tender for increased sphere of operation, in unfamiliar territory at Exeter St.David's with GWR cousin No.7325 on a special in late 1997. PHOTOGRAPH: ANDREW BURNHAM.

Stanier 2-6-0

WELL and truly overshadowed by its close cousin the ubiquitous 'Black Five' 4-6-0, William Stanier's version on the 2-6-0 theme is a relatively neglected class historically and certainly seldom seen on railway layouts, yet it was a competent and well-regarded design in its heyday that deserves a bit of an airing amongst the more elevated locomotive types.

Somewhat surprisingly the requirement for further Moguls that fell on the capable shoulders of William Arthur Stanier soon after his appointment as Chief Mechanical Engineer to the LMS in 1932 was fulfilled not by additional Fowler/Hughes 'Crab' 2-6-0s *[see RM December 1992 – Ed.]*, of which there were 245 on the engine roster, which perhaps may have been the simplest course of action, but by a design based on the earlier Mogul incorporating much equipment of Swindon origin. For prior to his posting Stanier (who was knighted in 1943) was a Great Western man through and through, having been trained and worked all his life on that railway and would have become CME of the GWR had fate not intervened by his being of similar age to Charles Collett, thus his stewardship would have endured only a matter of months had he continued to serve the GWR until retirement. The opportunity of heading the LMS mechanical engineering team was understandably grasped firmly by Stanier, who brought to the office great charm and diplomacy as well as formidable engineering talents; his tactfulness was a considerable factor in bringing together the warring factions within the Group that had festered since 1923 into a reasonably homogeneous entity. His distinctive style of locomotive design which was accepted throughout the LMS empire was another factor.

Alongside the 'Princess Royal' Pacifics *[see overleaf – Ed.]* the humble 2-6-0s were Stanier's first efforts for the Group; tapered boilers in the GW idiom were installed as the principal advance over previous LMS designs though retained were the then standard tenders, of Midland pattern, and LYR-style cabs of the 'Crabs'. All 40 2-6-0s were outshopped from Crewe works over the course of a year: the first off, No.13245, was equipped with a GWR-shaped safety valve bonnet as a well-meant gesture, however Stanier was furious when he saw it and ordered its instant removal – he rightly regarded it as too blatant a plagiarism on the Great Western.

The initial ten Moguls sported safety valves inset into the dome-style cover (not a steam dome), however the remaining 30 engines were given modified boilers having, amongst other alterations, Ross 'pop' valves mounted atop the Belpaire fireboxes. Interestingly the Moguls featured throughout their lives conventional whistles rather than the characteristic Caledonian hooters of all other Stanier locomotives. As they passed through the workshops on overhaul the first batch of

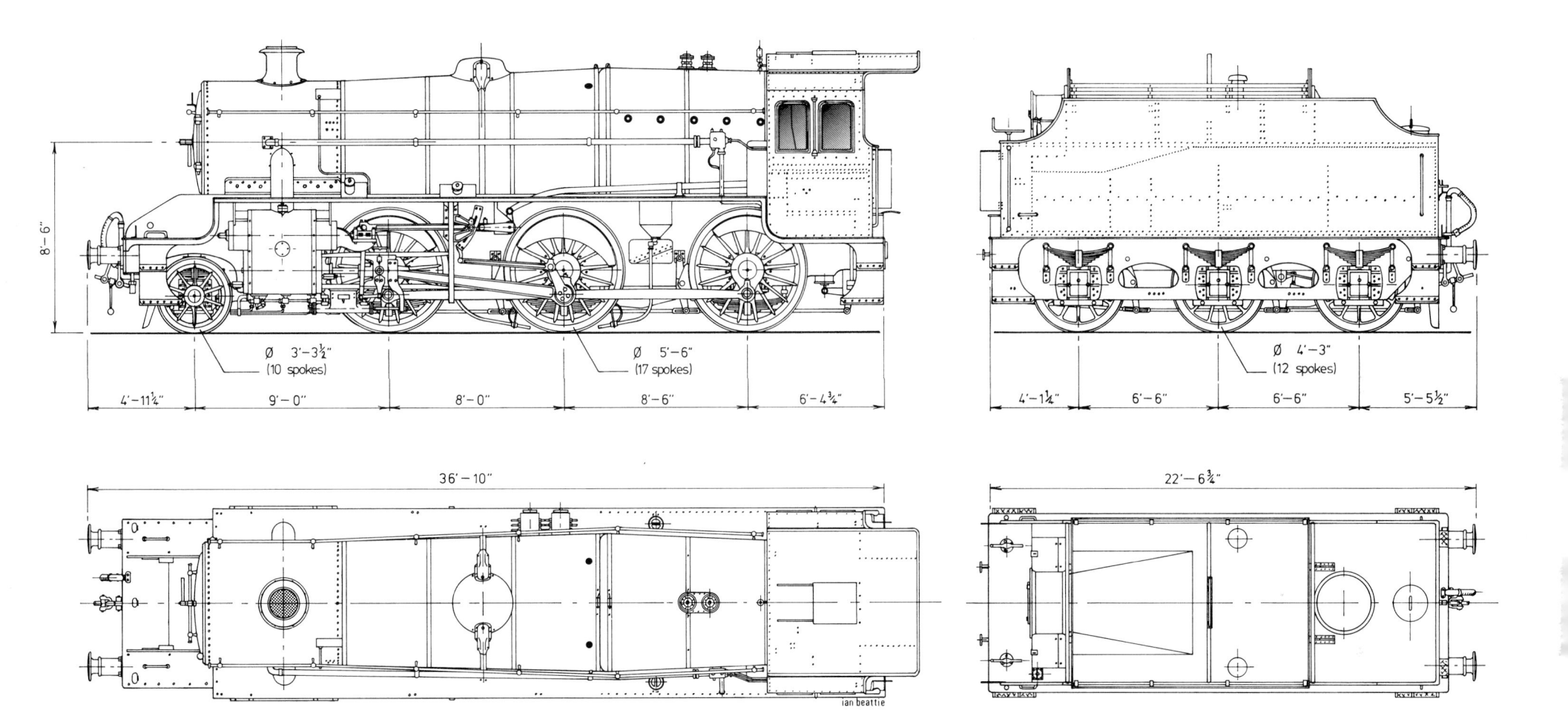

2-6-0s were provided with the second style of boiler, though this was undertaken over a period of many years and some 2-6-0s still had the original boiler design well into BR days.

Painted overall black, with lining details applied in early LMS and to some in LNWR-style BR mixed traffic livery, the 40 Moguls were at first widely distributed over the LMS network and only later tended to group together into more centralised areas where their usefulness was best exploited; as mixed traffic engines they were very capable performers and could certainly handle medium expresses with aplomb, notwithstanding their comparatively small coupled wheels. Nevertheless the quick success of their immediate successors in production terms, the remarkable 'Black Fives' which could accommodate any traffic the Moguls were capable of and much more besides, not only restricted the class's growth to just 40 members but tended to diminish their utility as the 4-6-0 numbers grew apace.

The entire class was withdrawn from traffic between 1963 and 1966, with the final engine being removed from revenue-earning service early in 1967. One example, No.42968, has fortunately been saved for posterity and is presently to be viewed on the Severn Valley Railway.

Notes on the drawings

This illustrates a typical example rather than the prototype in original condition, and the specifications also refer to the second-style and much better known boiler used by the Moguls and shown here. The buffer beam tended on later engines to sport prominent riveting (contersunk here), and the vacuum pump shown given by the (left hand) crosshead was removed in 1939 as a superfluity. The several batches of MR-derived tenders differed in detail and all were to be found attached to Stanier 2-6-0s at one period or another: that depicted is representative. All those used were fitted with coal rails.

Type:	Mogul
Overall Length:	59'10¾"
Cylinders:	2, 18" x 26" bore/stroke
Boiler Pressure:	225 lbs/sq in
Heating Surface:	1595 sq ft
Grate Area:	27.8 sq ft
Tractive Effort:	26288 lbs
Mean Weight in Working Order:	111.3 tons
Coal Capacity:	5 tons
Water Capacity:	3500 gallons
Number Built:	40, 1933-34
Preserved:	1

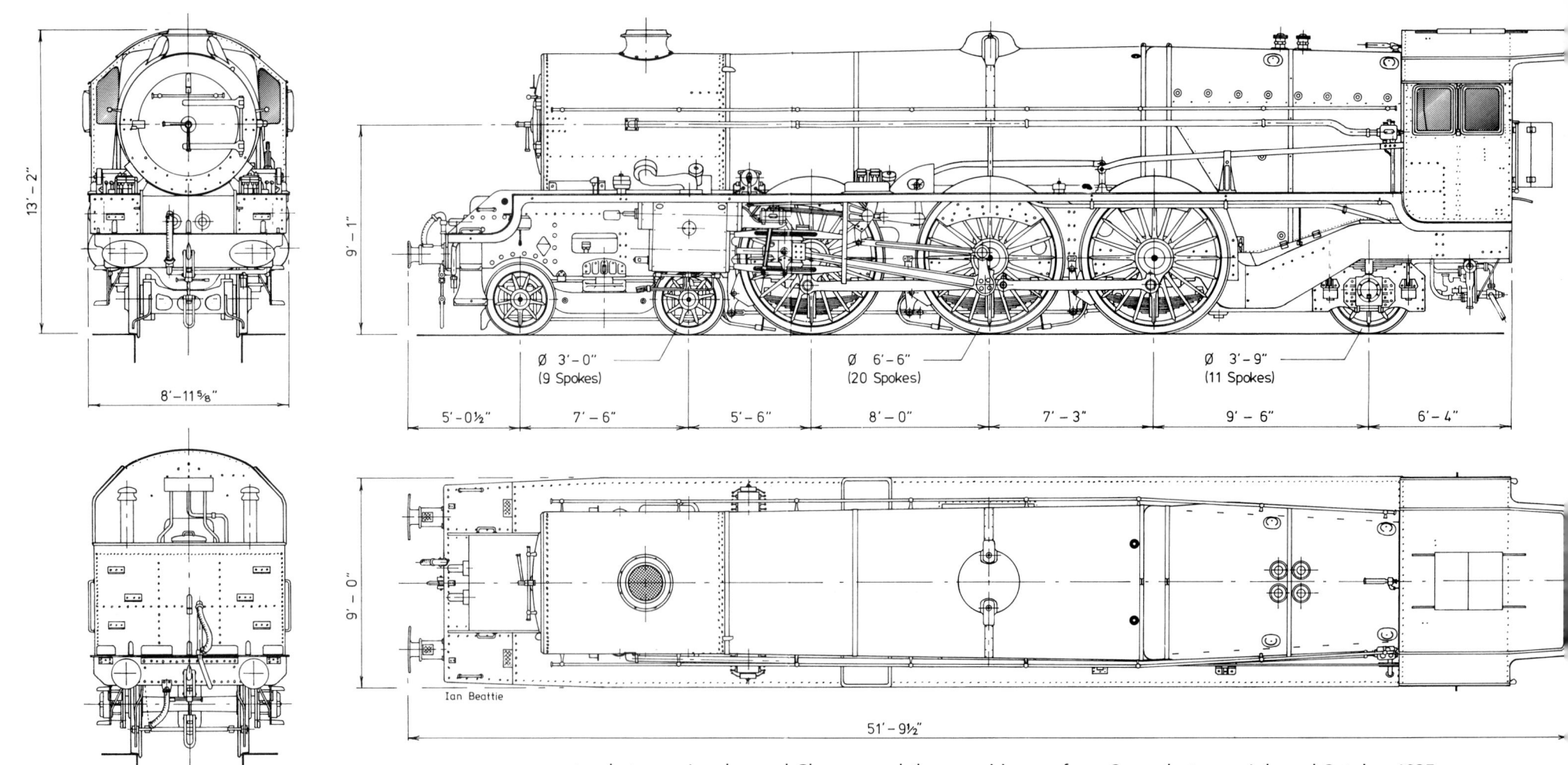

'Princess Royal' 4-6-2

FIRST entirely new fruit of William Stanier's period as CME of the London, Midland & Scottish Railway and making their debut only some 18 months after his move from Swindon, the handsome 'Princess Royal' Pacifics made (in the eyes of the LMS authorities at least) a gratifyingly deep impression on the first public showing in June 1933; top link express engines befitting the LMS's position as largest and wealthiest of the four Groups.

As an ex-GWR engineer Stanier could reasonably have been expected to produce an expanded 4-6-0 on the 'King' theme as a modernised version of the 'Royal Scots', in satisfying demands for an improved top link design to work principal expresses on the arterial West Coast Main Line. Whilst excellent engines and to all intents and purposes saviours of the LMS's shaky initial reputation for passenger haulage, the 'Royal Scots' displayed an increasingly awkward defect as passenger train weights rose in the 1930s – an inability to run non-stop between London and Glasgow and thus requiring engine changes at Carlisle. This was brought about by clinker in the fireboxes developing over a distance to the stage where the 4-6-0s were all but throttled to a stand, and hence the vital engine swap. To obviate this wasteful and expensive practice of change-over was a prime remit for Stanier's attention, best met by provision of much enlarged firebox grates, which in turn indicated a Pacific wheel arrangement that invited installation of suitably wide fireboxes over the rear carrying wheels as well proven by Gresley on the rival LNER.

Three 4-6-2s only were authorised at first, fortunately as it transpired since the design needed much modification and development before the engines' performance matched their outward promise. One of the three was outshopped as an experimental turbine locomotive, No.6202, the 'Turbomotive', which in due course will from a subject of its own for these pages and therefore disregarded at this juncture. Resulting from extensive and ultimately satisfactory mechanical rejigging of the two prototypes. Nos. 6200/1, a series of 10 production engines was instituted and all emerged from Crewe between July and October 1935.

Numbered 6203-12 and named for female members of the Royal Family, as were the two prototypes, the massive Pacifics sported huge domeless boilers incorporating high superheat and vast fireboxes with combustion chambers extended into the boiler space. Four cylinders were controlled by four sets of Walschaert's valve motion and reversing was effected by a split lever, although one engine (No.6205) was equipped with inside cylinders controlled via linkages from the outside-mounted valve gear, acting as the prototype in this respect for the forthcoming 'Princess Coronation' Pacifics, which were at bottom nothing less than ongoing developments of the 'Princess Royal' design.

The two 1933 engines were outshopped complete with Stanier's first essay in Standard tenders, based very largely (and obviously) on Fowler's standard design and certainly far too small both physically and visually for the lengthy Pacifics. These were rapidly exchanged for Stanier's own 9-ton standard versions as soon as these became available, and all 12 'production' 4-6-2s were likewise outfitted. While the engines displayed com-

42

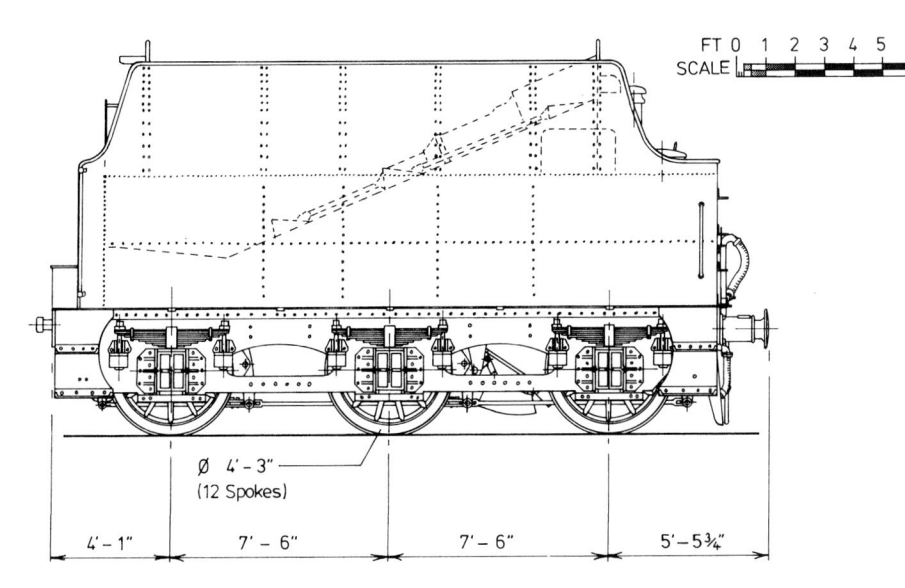

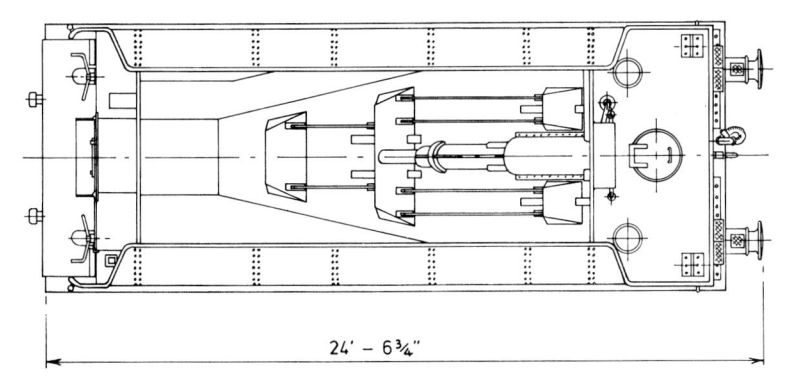

Fully coaled and with safety valves lifting, No.46208 *Princess Helena Victoria* looks every inch the mistress of her task, the Down 'Manxman', as she drifts down Camden bank to join the train on 25 August 1959. Note the domed boiler, as mentioned in the text. PHOTOGRAPH: DOUGLAS DOHERTY.

mendable coal consumption over the longest express routes the LMS system offered (which were run non-stop of course, as per the original remit), a slightly larger tender was evolved for handling a welcome extra ton of coal; the 12 Pacifics were duly re-equipped with these during 1936.

In their role as premier machines for the most prestigious expresses the 'Princess Royals' were extremely successful, although overshadowed later in the 1930s by their even more powerful developments the 'Princess Coronations', in both streamlined and orthodox format. Incidentally and fortunately, the elegant lines of the 'Princess Royals' were never disfigured by any sort of smokebox deflector.

Livery was in the first instance fully lined Crimson Lake of course, followed in wartime and for the remainder of the Group's existence thereafter in black, thence to BR's standard lined passenger green; four locomotives – Nos.46200/4/7/8 – were returned to the supremely attractive Crimson Lake paintwork in the late 1950s but by then steam was on the way out, and especially top link steam. The class was finally withdrawn in 1962, after a curious 'Indian summer' when many were exhumed from 'mothballing' in 1961 and returned to their old stamping ground for a few months. Two engines were saved from the cutting torch, of which No.6201 *Princess Elizabeth* is much the better known – and incidentally one of the 1933-vintage 'prototype' locomotives – the other survivor being No.6203 *Princess Margaret Rose*.

Notes on the drawings

These show a typical Pacific basically as the class appeared, post-1936, including a domeless boiler (the apparent 'dome' acted simply as a mount for the feedwater clack valves and did not house the regulator); latterly boilers were converted to a domed condition.

The tender is to the 10-ton Stanier standard design with which the 4-6-2s ran throughout their careers (all but a few months in most cases) and displayed the proud rivet heads common to earlier versions of this tender – flush-riveting became the norm during assembly for 'Coronation' engines in the late 1930s and thereafter. Also depicted is the steam-powered coal pusher installed in many of these tenders as a (welcome) aid for the hard-pressed fireman; strictly speaking this is an anachronism here since only one tender so fitted was supplied to the 'Princess Royal' class – for No.6206 *Princess Marie Louise* – but pushers became mandatory with the later LMS 4-6-2s, which will themselves feature here in the future. *[Sadly both 'Turbomotive' and 'Princess Coronations' eluded the Drawn & Described treatment – Ed.]*

Type:	Express Passenger
Overall Length:	74'4¼"
Cylinders:	4, 16¼" x 28" bore/stroke
Boiler Pressure:	250 lbs/sq in
Heating Surface:	2516 sq ft
Grate Area:	45 sq ft
Tractive Effort:	40300 lbs
Mean Weight in Working Order:	159 tons 3 cwt
Coal Capacity:	10 tons
Water Capacity:	4000 gallons
Number Built:	12, 1933 & 1935
Preserved:	2

Section 3
London & North Eastern Railway (and constituents)

Locomotive	Page	Locomotive	Page
Great Northern Railway N2 0-6-2T	44-45	Gresley J39 0-6-0	54-55
Great Central Railway 'Director' 4-4-0	46-47	Gresley V2 2-6-2	56-57
Great Eastern Railway 'Claud Hamilton' 4-4-0	48-49	Gresley K3 2-6-0	58-59
North Eastern Railway Raven 4-6-2	50-51	Thompson B1 4-6-0	60-61
North British Railway Reid 4-4-2	52-53	Peppercorn A1 4-6-2	62-63

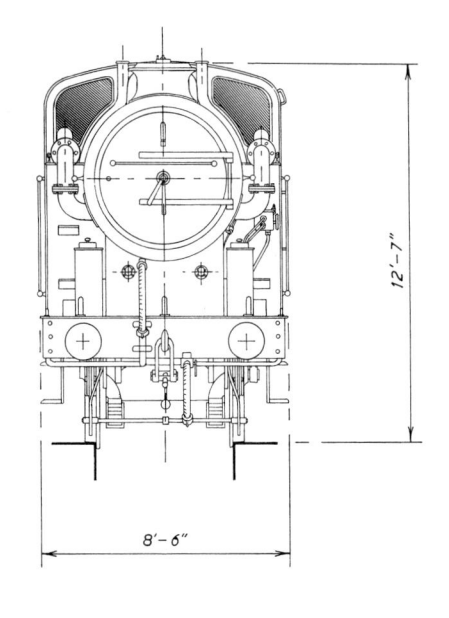

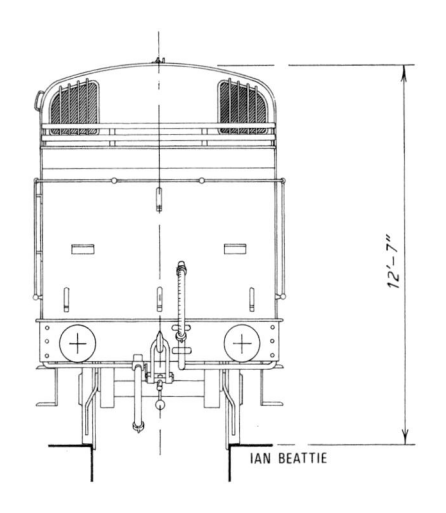

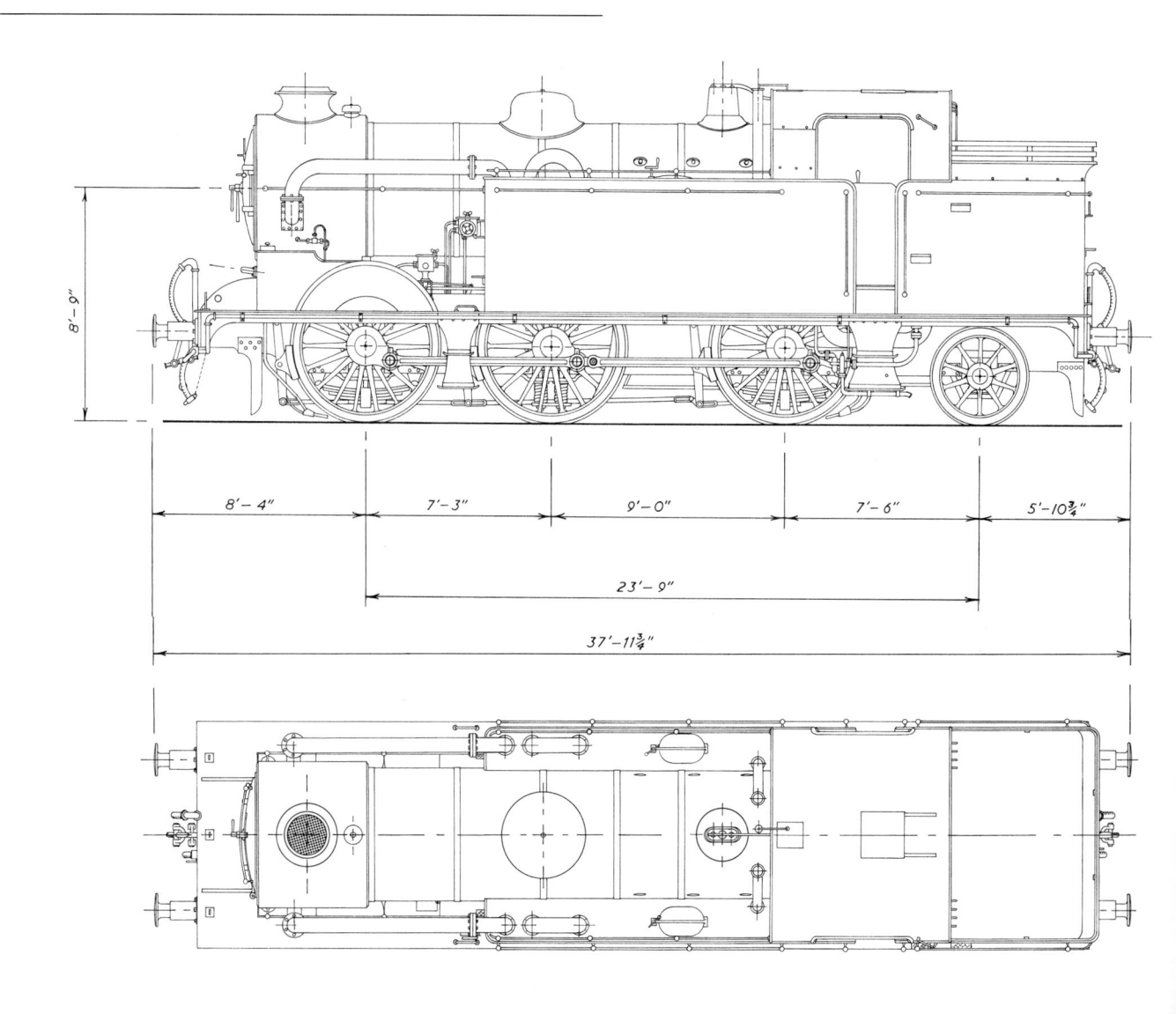

IAN BEATTIE

Gresley N2 0-6-2T

WITHIN the last remaining years of its independent existence and particularly following World War 1, the Great Northern Railway experienced a burgeoning of commuter services in and around London, the growing intensity of which required rather more speed and accelerative powers than those possessed by the staple GNR suburban passenger hauliers, the Ivatt N1 Class 0-6-2Ts of 1907 vintage.

Whilst formulating a variety of tank designs in replacement the young Nigel Gresley, who had succeeded Ivatt as Locomotive Carriage & Wagon Superintendent in 1911, was forced to recognise that a development of the 0-6-2 theme was the optimum answer to the problem: hence the N2 Class, closely based on the N1 and fitted with piston valves, Gresley's own brand of superheater (tested in 1919 on suburban work via a modified N1 with positive results), and a boiler of similar dimensions that however looked larger owing to its high pitch.

The initial N2 rolled out of Doncaster works in November 1920, to be followed in 1921 by 9 more from that source plus a further 50 outshopped by the North British Company for the GNR.

An immediate success on the London routes for which they were mooted, the N2s impressed for their considerable acceleration and high speed potentials, yet a few routes were barred to them owing to axle weight limitations. In common with other GNR locomotives the N2s built until Grouping were equipped with right-hand driving positions.

On formation of the London & North Eastern Railway in 1923 Gresley became the Group's first Chief Mechanical Engineer and, beyond designing new locomotives when required, embarked on a policy of continuing the building of proven pre-grouping engines. Among these were his own N2s, of which a further 47 were outshopped between 1925 and 1929. The much enlarged network of the LNER over the former GNR enhanced the scope of Gresley's potent suburban passenger tanks and several were sent to Scotland, to work such duties in the Edinburgh and Glasgow areas. Unlike their forebears the LNER-derived versions accommodated left-hand drive, amongst more minor differences in specification.

Fixtures and fittings applied to the class tended to vary widely according to use (for instance in GNR days the power of the N2s was put to unusual use in piloting expresses out of Kings Cross, and in later BR days handled much of the empty coaching stock movements to and from that terminus). Condensing gear was applied to all N2s bar those allocated to Scotland – the latter sported taller chimneys (by 3") – and Westinghouse air braking systems were installed where required. At first the GNR N2s ran with feedwater pumps before adequately reliable injectors became available, and all versions were given bonneted safety valves as shown in the drawings; the 1925-29 builds had pop valves as standard, to which the earlier locomotives eventually complied. The bars atop the coal bunkers were latterly sheeted in, to increase capacity but more importantly to aid mechanical loading.

Very little modification was necessary mechanically throughout the N2s' collective life, the most basic being replacement of Gresley's superheater with Robinson's more efficient equivalent during the 1940s.

Whilst completely at home in London's suburban heartlands the N2s were never totally acceptable in Scottish circles, because the lack of guiding pony wheels conflicted with the tightly radiused curves thereabouts, with the consequent design by Gresley of his V1 (and later V3) 2-6-2Ts *[see RM August 1992 – Ed.]* to alleviate this shortcoming.

During the late 1950s the London commuter lines were taken over by diesel power, ending a very long reign by the familiar N2s and hastening their withdrawal: by the end of 1962 all had been transferred to the scrapyards with a single preservation.

The single survivor of the 107-strong N2 fleet is No.69523, GNR No.1744 and built by North British in February 1921. When withdrawn, in September 1962 it was one of the final septet still on the BR books: it is seen here in lively condition at Weybourne, on the North Norfolk Railway, superbly presented in lined black with late BR crest.
PHOTOGRAPH: IAN FUTERS.

Type:	0-6-2T
Coupled Wheels:	5'8" dia. 18 spokes
Trailing Wheels:	3'8" dia. 10 spokes
Cylinders:	2, 19"x 26" bore/stroke
Boiler Pressure:	170 lbs/sq in
Heating Surface:	125 sq ft
Grate Area:	19 sq ft
Water Capacity:	2000 gallons
Coal Capacity:	4 tons
Tractive Effort:	19945 lbs
Mean Weight in Working Order:	70 tons 5 cwt
Number Built:	107, 1920-29
Preserved:	1

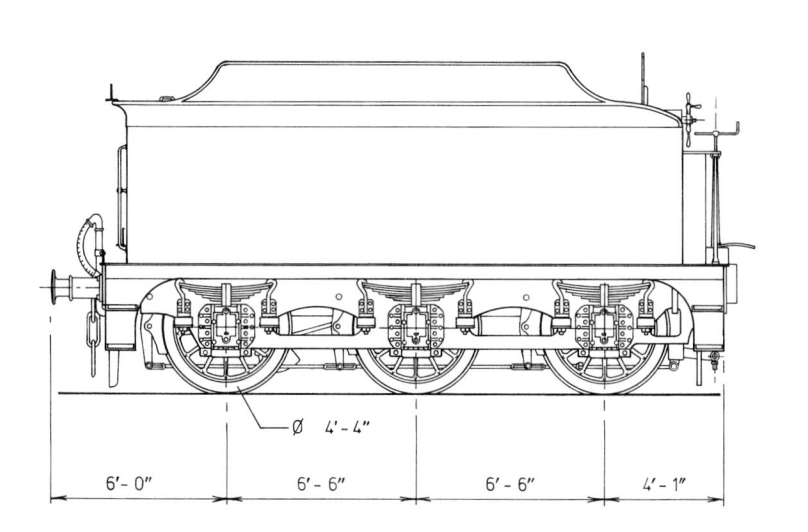

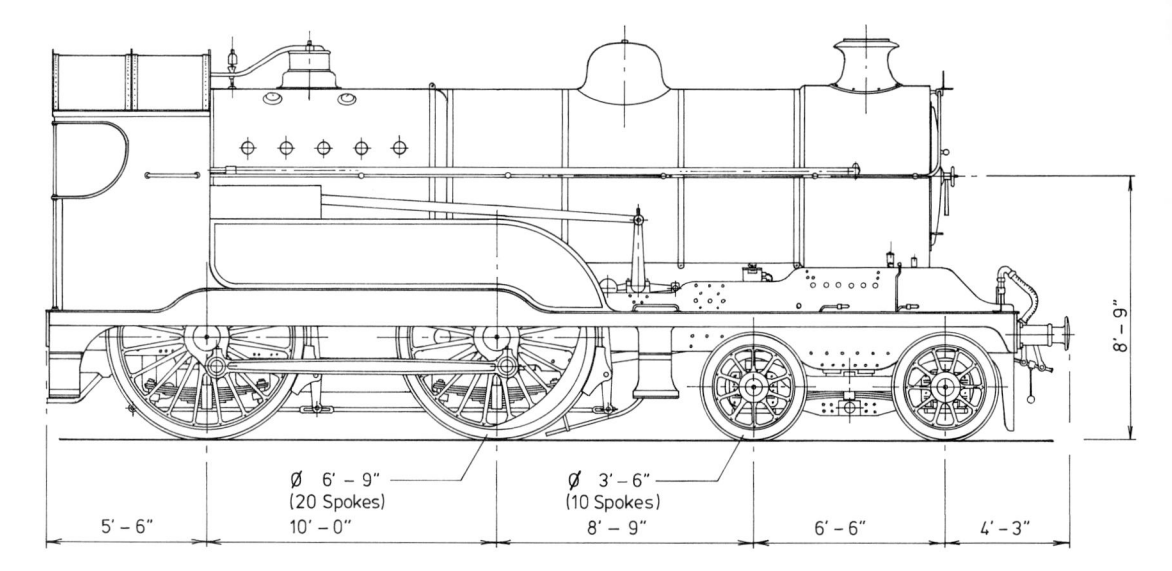

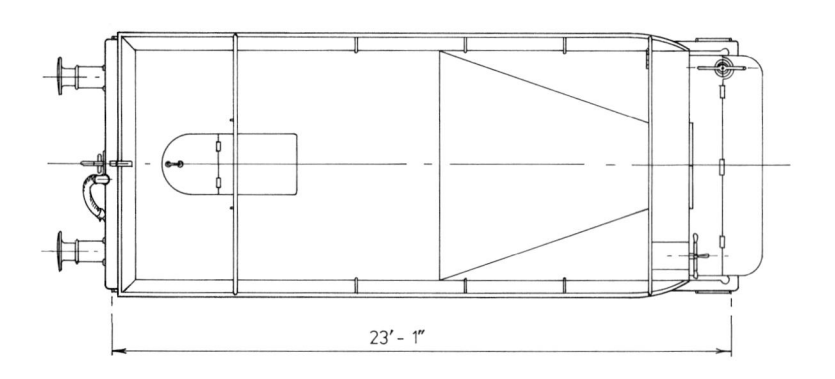

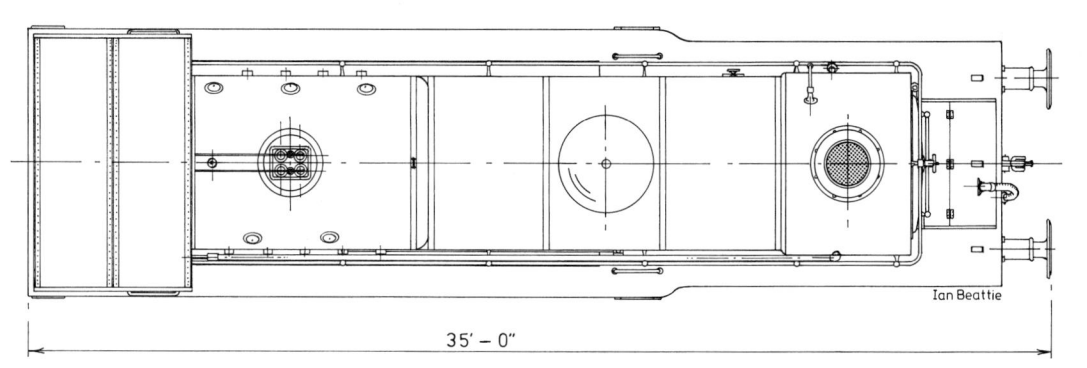

Great Central Class 11E/11F 'Director' 4-4-0

GENERALLY considered the masterpiece of John G. Robinson CBE, Chief Mechanical Engineer to the Great Central Railway 1900-23, the 'Director' Class locomotive constituted alongside its contemporaries the LNWR 'George the Fifth' and GER 'Claud Hamilton' designs *inter alia* the very cream of inspired railway engineering for its day and long afterwards. The fact that these were all 4-4-0s was no accident, for the advent of superheating together with rapid strides in cylinder technology in the years immediately preceding the First World War permitted the superficially curious use of an ancient, albeit well respected, wheel arrangement – the 4-4-0 – in place of more up-to-date and ostensibly more efficient multi-wheeled configurations.

In the GCR's case reversion to the 4-4-0 pattern for premier express passenger use arose in part due to flaws in Robinson's 'Sam Fay' 4-6-0s: so successful were the 'Director' 4-4-0s in fact that not only were the 'Sam Fays' displaced by them but so too in large measure were the famed and effective Atlantics (see RM June 1989) on premium traffic over the GCR 'London Extension' route between London and Nottingham.

The wide admiration for the running performance and haulage ability coupled with working economy evoked by the 'Directors' reached the ears of American technical journalists, at that time inured to European events through the pyrotechnic level of railway progress displayed in their own country, who nonetheless heaped praise on Robinson's creation as a paragon of contemporary technological artistry.

The initial batch of ten engines was outshopped from the GCR's Gorton erecting shops in 1913 and classified 11E. The first engine of this series, No.429, was built without coupling rod splasher skirts, however the result was deemed 'half-dressed' and full skirting was demanded, which was applied to this engine and indeed to all 21 'Directors' built by the GCR. A subjective opinion perhaps, but when in place these skirts lent the thoroughly modern machines a strangely old-fashioned demeanour; the skirts were subsequently removed under LNER ownership.

Although best known to railfans by their all-encompassing 'Director' name tag, only the initial ten engines commemorated members of the GCR Board without exception; thereafter name themes diversified into the fields of Royalty and First World War battles as well.

Two more batches were erected under GCR auspices, five locomotives in 1919-20 and a further six in 1922. Again all originated from Gorton but differed in several albeit minor respects from the initial 1913 batch, being classified 11F and known as 'Improved' or (inaccurately) 'Large Directors'. Chief adaptations were cabs equipped with twin side windows, Ross 'pop' safety valves in place of the Ramsbottom variety, redesigned front frame contours, and the boiler pitch from rail level raised by ½" (to 8'10½") with concomitant alterations to boiler mountings.

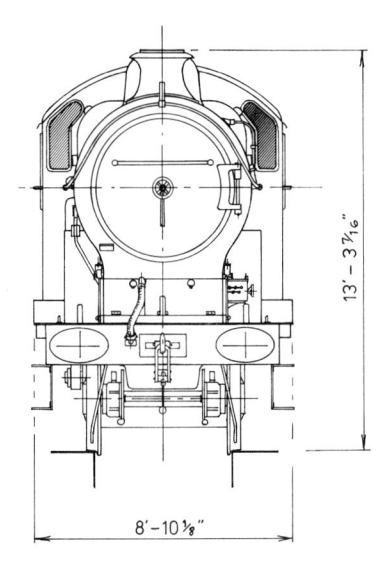

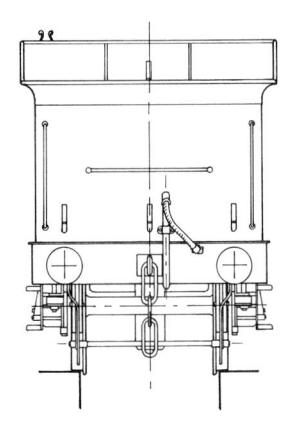

In grimy BR lined black livery and with cut-down boiler mountings, D11/2 No.62694 *James Fitzjames* departs Markinch on 9 September 1955 with an Edinburgh Waverley-Dundee stopping train. PHOTOGRAPH: W.HARDIN OSBORNE.

On the Great Central's transference into the LNER Group the 4-4-0s were usefully dispersed beyond their traditional London Extension stamping ground. In common with all inherited fleets, the engines were subjected to reclassification. The 1913-vintage class 11E was changed to D10 and the 'Improved Directors' became Class D11. The famed utility of the excellent 'Directors' was underscored by the LNER ordering no fewer than 24 further examples of the type, constructed during 1924 by private builders Armstrong Whitworth of Manchester and Kitson of Leeds (each company supplying 12 machines). They incorporated numerous modifications such as Gresley superheater anti-vacuum or 'snifting' valves, unskirted coupling rod splashers, plain wheel splashers and painted-on names (the GC engines' splashers were resplendently bordered in brass strip, and proper nameplates were *de rigueur*); cut-down boiler mountings were installed to suit the restricted loading gauge of the ex-North British Railway region of Scotland for which this batch of 'Directors' was commissioned: classified D11/2, their names were taken from characters in Sir Walter Scott's novels.

As befitted their top-link status the 4-4-0s were always maintained in magnificent condition by the GCR. Originally outfitted in the superb, rather complex GC passenger livery, by the time withdrawals began under BR auspices the fleet of once pre-eminent engines sported black paintwork, lined or unlined. Many 'Directors' ended their days on passenger duty over the erstwhile Cheshire Lines, still well able to give a rousing account of themselves; the earliest D10 machines disappeared in 1953-55, the ex-GCR D11s during 1959-60 and the youngest, Scots-based LNER versions lasted until 1958-62.

By great good fortune Class 11F No.506 *Butler Henderson* of 1920 vintage survives as representative of this much-admired design, in full working order complete with GC livery – and full 'modesty skirting' – on the present Great Central Railway. *[Since the article was penned* Butler Henderson *has returned to the National Railway Museum in York, where it can be admired today. Ed]*

Notes on the drawings
An example of the first, 1913 batch is shown as outshopped; comparison with the photograph, depicting a Class D11/2 4-4-0 should highlight the many small variations in design and fittings between versions. *[Strictly speaking the tender, reproduced from the Robinson 'ROD' 2-8-0 – see RM June 1985 – should have screw couplings and steam heating pipework depicted – Ed.]*

Type:	Express Passenger
Overall Length:	58'11¼"
Cylinders:	2, 20" x 26" bore/stroke
Boiler Pressure:	180 lbs/sq in
Heating Surface:	1659 sq ft
Grate Area:	26 sq ft
Tractive Effort:	19645 lbs
Mean Weight in Working Order:	109 tons 10 cwt
Coal Capacity:	6 tons
Water Capacity:	4000 gallons
Number Built:	45, 1913-24
Preserved:	1

Caught at King's Lynn on 15 August 1959, Class D16/3 4-4-0 No.62613 awaits departure. Despite an overtly LNER superheated boiler, modified cab and enlarged tender, the engine clearly displays its origin as a GER 'Claud Hamilton'.

Great Eastern Railway 'Claud Hamilton' 4-4-0

OF ALL the motive power proposals initiated by that superlative Victorian mechanical engineer, James Holden, Locomotive superintendent to the Great Eastern Railway from 1885 to 1907, his undoubted masterpiece must be the 'Claud Hamilton' 4-4-0s, engines justly famous not only in Britain but throughout the world in their heyday for rousing performance and enviable stamina in their role as top link express passenger hauliers in the first decade of this century.

By the standards of continuous enlargement in haulage power beginning by then to prevail, these 4-4-0s were comparatively small and light, yet being of the archetypal British express format were highly developed examples of their genre, echoed in several respects by 4-4-0s of many another main line railway in their degree of sophistication. In other words, their lack of sheer size was compensated for by an eminently usable and moreover readily-available power output. Outfitted in the glorious lined royal blue livery applied to top link GER motive power and liberally adorned with burnished copper and brass, together with a polished steel ring on the smokebox door, the 'Claud Hamiltons' were an immensely impressive sight on a premium express: the *Norfolk Coast Express* composed of up to 14 coaches running non-stop 130 miles from Liverpool Street to a tight schedule over gradients towards 1 in 70 in places. Two 'Claud' 4-4-0s were kept in sparkling readiness for that most prestigious of all duties, that of hauling the Royal Train over the lightly-laid North Norfolk line to Wolferton, the station closest to the favourite Royal residence of Sandringham House.

The first of the class was outshopped from the GER Works at Stratford, East London in March 1900. Appropriately numbered 1900 (a choice which dictated that following members of the class were numbered in reverse order, since the GER number system had only reached 1119!) and named *Claud Hamilton* in honour of the Chairman of the GER Board – the sole engine in the class to be named, indeed one of only three GER locomotives ever given names – the new machine was promptly entered for the Paris Exhibition of that year, where it attracted numerous awards for excellence.

Officially dubbed the 1900 Class although quite naturally always identified with the initial engine, the building of the 'Claud Hamiltons' is a somewhat complex story. Basically, batches of ten engines apiece were outshopped each year from 1900 to 1911 inclusive bar 1905, bringing the eventual total to 111 machines – the extra locomotive is accounted for in the original 1900 build, when ten engines emerged over and above the eponymous *Claud Hamilton*, that batch thus comprising 11 constituents. Modifications and updating of equipment were introduced along the way with considerable backdating taking place on older members of the class; some alterations were minor and others radical, including Belpaire fireboxes and eventually superheating, much of which was brought into use under the aegis of Stephen Dewar Holden, son of James who had succeeded to the superintendency (for a much shorter period than his illustrious father) in 1907, midway through the 'Claud' building programme. Astonishingly, and demonstrating the excellence of its then 23-year-old provenance, a batch of ten further 4-4-0s, modernised in detail of course, was undertaken by the newly-hatched LNER in 1923 and known ever since, quite logically, as 'Super-Clauds'.

Until part-way through the 1904 build all the 4-4-0s were equipped with oil-burning apparatus, of a type invented by James Holden, and tenders thus featured oil tanks as opposed to the more traditional coal spaces; eventually, when the cost of fuel oil rose beyond the equivalent price of coal, the oil-firers were converted to coal-burning.

All 111 'Clauds' utilised Stephenson's link motion controlling the inside-mounted cylinders, and as a sign of outward modernity their cabs were spacious and sported twin side windows in the style of the North Eastern Railway: the initial batch was provided with comparatively narrow cabs as shown here in the drawings, subsequent engines having wider cabs spread to all but the width of the running plate, as can be discerned in the photograph. The LNER rebuilt most of the by-then much modified class, many featuring a seeming reversion to round-topped firebox format after years running with Belpaire versions. The original 'Clauds' were reclassified D14 by the LNER, further divisions of the class being D15 (including D15/1 and 2) and D16 (the 'Super-Clauds' and updated rebuilds to that specification; further subdivided D16/1-3).

Several earlier representatives of the class were withdrawn by the mid-1930s, however no fewer than 117 survived into BR hands of which the final engine was removed from service in the early 1960s. GER No.1900 *Claud Hamilton* was withdrawn in May 1947 as LNER No.2500, and whilst a 'Claud' 4-4-0 was earmarked for preservation at Stratford, by cruel mischance it was cut up in error: if any British locomotive was worthy of preservation, a representative of the internationally renowned 'Claud Hamilton' Class 4-4-0 must have been a prime candidate.

Notes on the drawings
These illustrate an example of the 1900 batch, GE Nos.1890-1900, identified by the narrow cab fitted only to engines of that year. Whilst certainly representative of its appearance in GER days the locomotive shown is not in absolutely original guise: initially a single set of Ramsbottom safety valves was supplied (with whistle directly alongside), replaced by the twin sets – and rearranged whistle – depicted shortly thereafter. The tender is a typically squat GER design, to fit the small turntables around the network, fitted with water-scoop apparatus, of which the GER was something of a pioneer. Supplementary views show the 'round shouldered' oil-carrying tender with which the 1900 batch was outshopped, whereas the orthodox coal version comprises the principal drawings. Note the Westinghouse compressor for the air brakes (steam-powered reversers were also installed in the earlier 'Clauds') and the wooden bridge spanning the loco-tender gap to the height of the footplate.

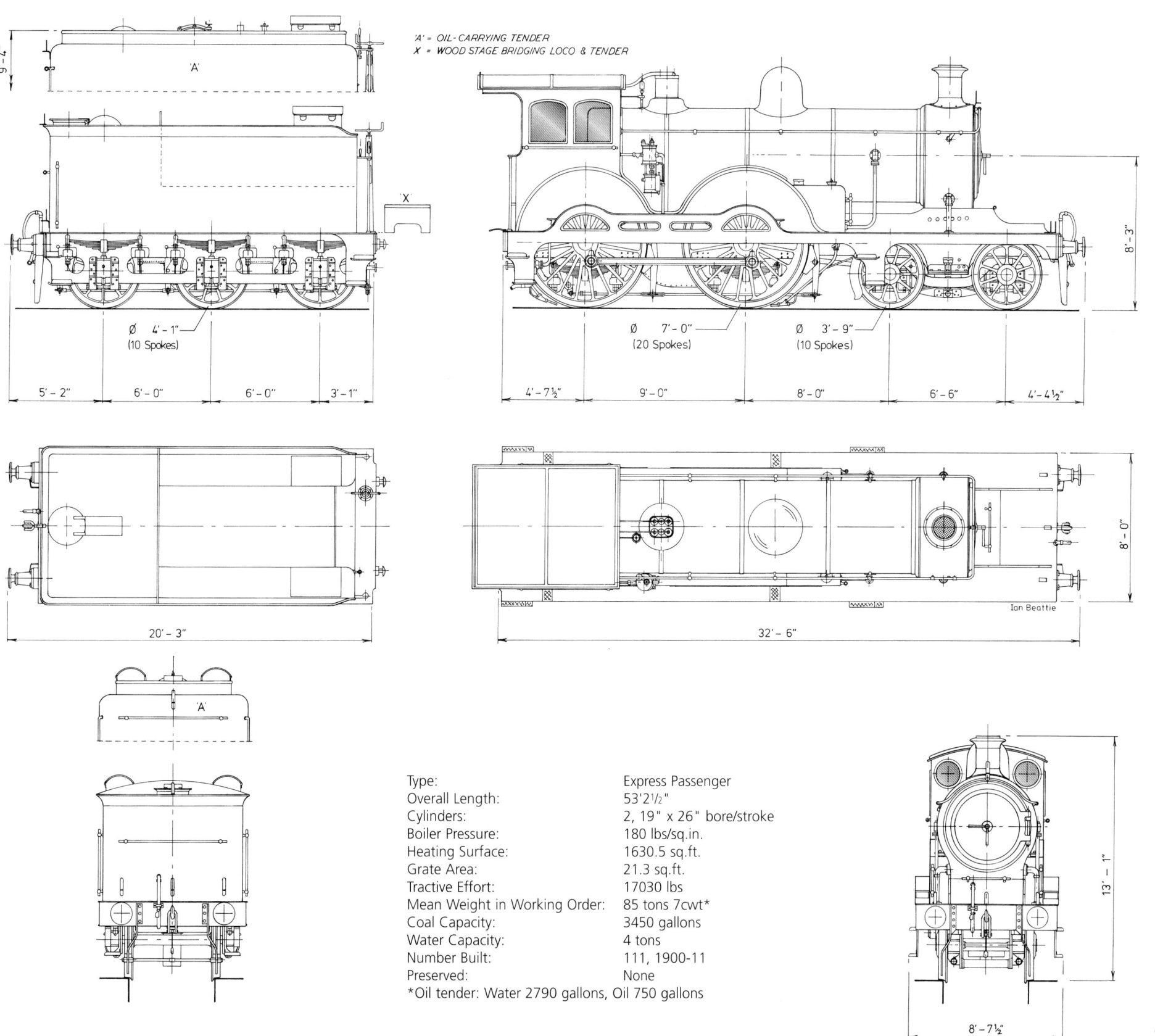

'A' = OIL-CARRYING TENDER
X = WOOD STAGE BRIDGING LOCO & TENDER

Ø 4'-1" (10 Spokes)
Ø 7'-0" (20 Spokes)
Ø 3'-9" (10 Spokes)

Ian Beattie

Type:	Express Passenger
Overall Length:	53'2½"
Cylinders:	2, 19" x 26" bore/stroke
Boiler Pressure:	180 lbs/sq.in.
Heating Surface:	1630.5 sq.ft.
Grate Area:	21.3 sq.ft.
Tractive Effort:	17030 lbs
Mean Weight in Working Order:	85 tons 7cwt*
Coal Capacity:	3450 gallons
Water Capacity:	4 tons
Number Built:	111, 1900-11
Preserved:	None

*Oil tender: Water 2790 gallons, Oil 750 gallons

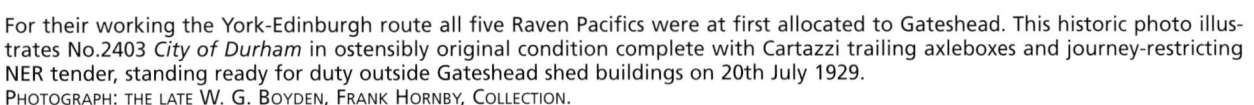

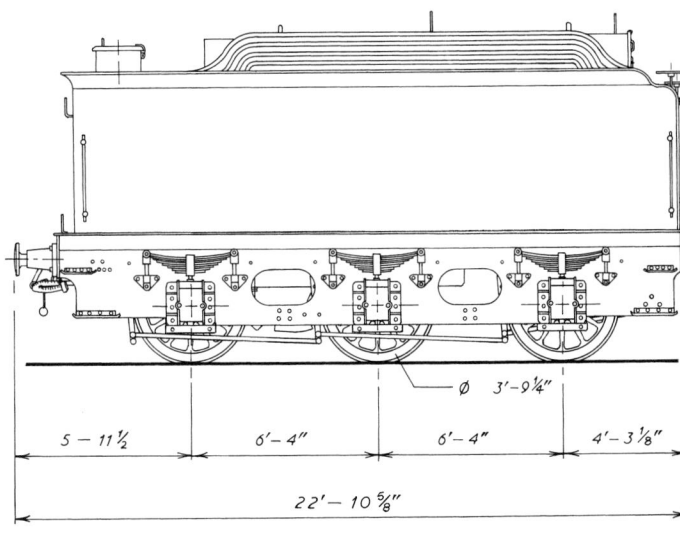

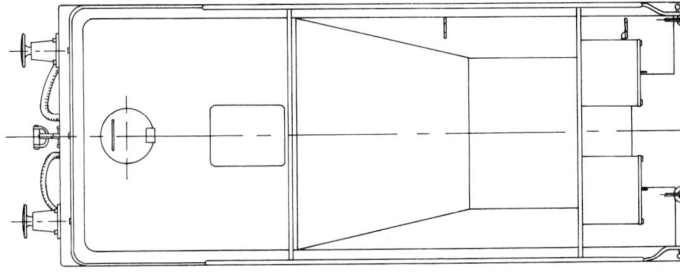

For their working the York-Edinburgh route all five Raven Pacifics were at first allocated to Gateshead. This historic photo illustrates No.2403 *City of Durham* in ostensibly original condition complete with Cartazzi trailing axleboxes and journey-restricting NER tender, standing ready for duty outside Gateshead shed buildings on 20th July 1929.
PHOTOGRAPH: THE LATE W. G. BOYDEN, FRANK HORNBY, COLLECTION.

North Eastern Railway Raven 4-6-2

CERTAINLY it seems an impetuous decision to have made, on the very eve of dissolution. But prestige was at stake. And prestige is a significant factor where a railway's top link passenger operation is concerned, for both the publicity accruing and, in the case of the NER, more subtle motives in the final few months' run up to Grouping. For the powers that be on the NER knew full well that their neighbour and arch-competitor the Great Northern Railway via its brilliant young CME Nigel Gresley was on the verge of issuing a 3-cylinder 4-6-2 locomotive as their flagship, the first of this wheel arrangement since the singleton Great Western *The Great Bear* of 14 years previously.

Not to be upstaged, chief engineer Sir Vincent Raven set to and achieved completion of his Pacific – NER's swansong – in just 8 months, from board approval in March to emergence of No.2400 from Darlington works in November 1922, just under two months before Grouping took place.

Founded in 1854 by union of numerous small undertakings (several established under the auspices of George Hudson, the erstwhile and egregious 'Railway King'), the North Eastern Railway was throughout its independent existence primarily a freight-hauling operation – naturally so being centred on the early industrial heartland of England – yet the company's passenger network assumed due importance as time progressed. Served by a succession of highly competent chief engineers, the NER vaunted many series of excellent express passenger locomotives, culminating in magnificent 3-cylinder simple Atlantics in the early years of this century under the guiding influence of the Worsdell brothers Thomas and Wilson, the latter of whom was succeeded as CME in 1910 by Vincent Litchfield Raven (he was subsequently knighted for his superintendency of Woolwich Arsenal during World War One).

In view of the hurried gestation period Raven's Pacific was basically an inflated Class Z 4-4-2, complete with three cylinders in line abreast in one casting incorporating the valve chests and smokebox saddle; an enormously lengthy parallel boiler – the barrel was 26' long though the tubeplates distanced on 21' owing to the wide firebox being extended into the barrel as a combustion chamber – which (surmounted at the cab end by three conspicuous safety valves) generated the nickname 'Skittle Alley'; and three sets of Stephenson's link motion mounted between the frames, two to one side of the central cylinder and one to the other. All three cylinders driving the leading axle and wheels led to a weak crank axle, not to say a necessarily extended wheelbase (longest of all British 4-6-2s bar Thompson's conversion of *Great Northern*) and thereby the consequent long boiler.

Outshopped in November and December 1922 respectively the initial two Pacifics (though in fact the second was not commissioned into traffic until January 1923) sported trailing wheels having inside radial bearings, a source of trouble through overheating, being close to the firebox, whilst the remaining three engines were given – under Gresley's direction – outside Cartazzi axleboxes in lieu. In all cases the trailing axle supported the very high weight of 20 tons, hardly less than that imposed on the coupled axles.

The less apparent reasons for the double-quick emergence of the Raven 4-6-2 alluded to earlier concerned not only the spur meted out by the GNR version,

50

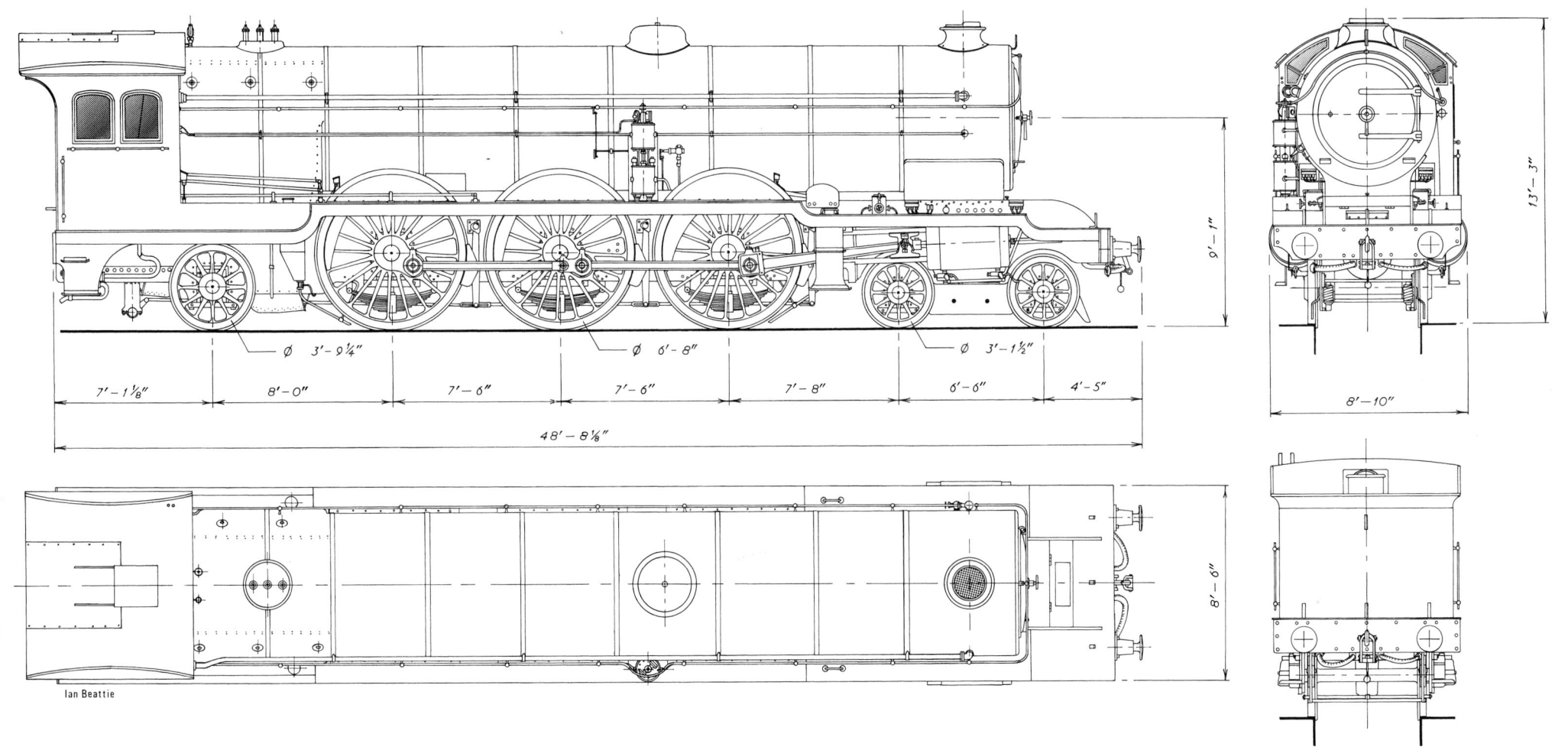

but also to act as an advertisement of NE engineering pedigree when it came to select senior executives for the shortly-to-be-formed LNER Group; to no avail as it transpired. To Nigel Gresley of the GNR went the palm of Group CME. In any event Gresley's was much the better of the two 4-6-2 designs (proved conclusively by comparative tests on the Kings Cross-Doncaster route in 1923). Yet being physically and financially the largest constituent of the LNER, the influence the NER brought to bear in the Group lay greatest in the spheres of works and operation management.

Somewhat hindered by their small capacity tenders, performance in traffic of the five Raven Pacifics – accorded Class A2 in LNER nomenclature – were overshadowed by their GNR-derived A1 contemporaries, even before the LNER/GWR trials in 1925 demonstrated A1 deficiencies in valve technology. The Raven locomotives habitually worked between York and Edinburgh.

In 1929 a reduced-pressure A1 boiler was installed on No.2404 *City of Ripon* (each A2 was named for a city in the NER area) together with an LNER standard 5000-gallon eight wheeled tender – remaining A2s were re-equipped with the latter in 1933-5 – but the resulting improvement in performance was insufficient to justify modifying the other four Raven Pacifics, let alone the heavy cost involved in fitting that upshot of the 1925 trials, long lap long travel valves; and since spare boilers for A2s had not been provided the decision was made to withdraw the engines as their boilers finally wore out beyond economic recovery. All five Pacifics were taken out of service between July 1936 and May 1937.

Notes on the drawings

The drawings depict the prototype Raven Pacific No.2400, the details taken from the works photograph on the engine's completion at Darlington. As built No.2400 featured a regular, rectangular front buffer beam (much as its tender had) which however snagged the platforms at Newcastle and were therefore cut away as shown. Both vacuum and Westinghouse air brake systems were fitted, the air braking removed 1931-33, and in line with NER practice the engines were driven from the right hand side of the commodious cab.

Type:	4-6-2
Overall Length:	72'7¼"
Coupled Wheels:	6'8" dia. 20 spokes
Bogie Wheels:	3'1½" dia. 12 spokes
Trailing Wheels:	3'9¼" dia. 12 spokes
Tender Wheels:	3'9¼" dia. 12 spokes
Cylinders:	3, 19" x 26" bore/stroke
Boiler Pressure:	200 lbs/sq.in
Heating Surface:	2874.6 sq.ft
Grate Area:	41.5 sq.ft
Tractive Effort:	29918 lbs
Coal Capacity:	5½ tons
Water Capacity:	4125 gallons
Mean Weight in Working Order:	148¼ tons
Number built:	5, 1922-4
Preserved:	None

ABOVE: A Darlington-built J39 of 1929 vintage, 0-6-0 No.64810 – matched with a well-coaled, flush-sided 3500-gallon tender – awaits attention in the shed yard at Stratford in former Great Eastern territory on 14 November 1954.

OPPOSITE: the J39s were equally at home on a freight train or a Cleethorpes excursion: No.64835 of 50B Leeds Neville Hill shed poses for its portrait in this undated late 1950s view. PHOTOGRAPH: DOUGLAS DOHERTY.

Gresley Class J39 0-6-0

DESIGNED to the LNER Group Standard 0-6-0, these powerful locomotives and their Scots-based J38 sisters performed admirably until eventual withdrawal.

An early product of Nigel Gresley's fertile genius on his installation as Chief Mechanical Engineer of the newly emergent London & North Eastern Railway was an orthodox 0-6-0 design of archetypal British appearance, nominated the Group's Standard Goods locomotive.

In actuality there were two such 0-6-0 designs: a batch of 35 sporting 4'8" wheels and classified J38 was assembled during 1926, for use principally on steeply-graded lines in Scotland, however initial experience of these perfectly satisfactory hauliers suggested that an increase in wheel diameter could be contemplated readily (together with minor variations in boiler specification) for suitability throughout the widespread LNER empire. Thus was the J39 class created.

Series construction began at Darlington in September 1926 and ran, admittedly discontinuously, until 1941 when 289 examples had been placed in service. All bar 28 emanated from the ex-NER erecting shops, the exceptions being subcontracted to the private builders Beyer Peacock of Manchester in 1936/37.

Much the most numerous class in Gresley's portfolio, original numbering was far from logical and frankly verged on the chaotic, however the LNER's post-World War 2 renumbering scheme tidied matters up properly by assigning numbers 4700-4988 to the J39s in their building sequence – to which in due course BR simply added 60000. Throughout their existence the engines wore black livery, relieved in prewar years by thin red lining.

Somewhat unusually in engines produced specifically for relatively humdrum duties superheating was applied (albeit to a fairly low degree of superheat, since the machines were not intended for ultra-long distance haulage) and vacuum braking apparatus together with screw couplings were mandatory over the class: the burly J39s were therefore thoroughly up to date in their characteristics and, whilst perhaps neither inheriting nor indeed meriting the exceptionally graceful contours of Gresley's more exalted designs, ably met requirements as the Standard Goods class.

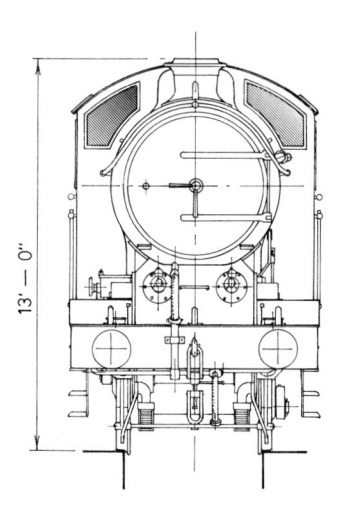

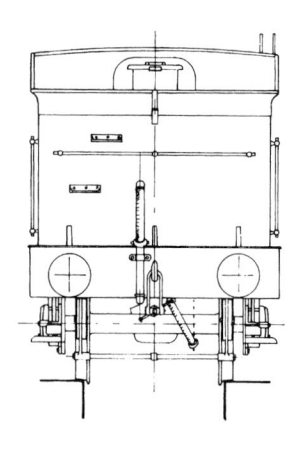

Their tall 5'2" wheels however permitted rostering on fitted freights and especially passenger trains (many J39s carried steam heating pipework in addition), speed upwards of 80 mph being recorded on the latter, with concomitant problems of rapid wear arising in forward axleboxes owing to the lack of a leading carrying axle when such respectable velocities were maintained.

In sum a sound, thoroughly workmanlike design capable of extremely energetic activity, the J39s attracted minimal alteration in appearance or mechanical appurtenance throughout their service lives. All had been withdrawn by the end of 1962 and regrettably none survived for preservation.

Notes on the drawings

Illustrated is a typical J39 0-6-0 as witnessed in LNER and very early BR times. Latterly the locos featured prominent rivetting on smokeboxes and bufferbeams, as depicted in the photo. A variety of tenders were attached including the Group Standard 4200 gallon (shown here) and 3500 gallon types, together with

52

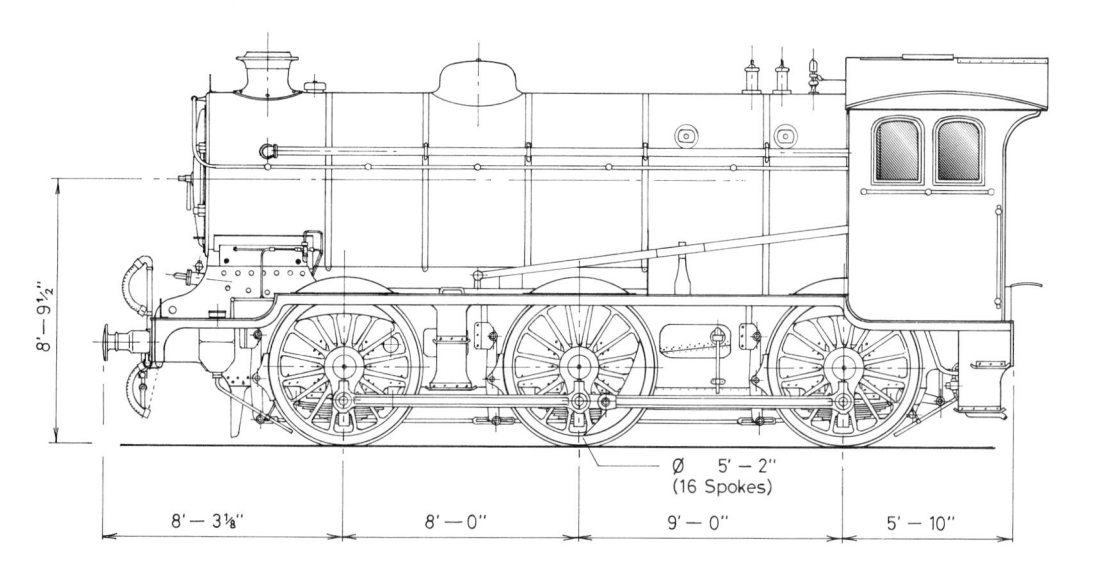

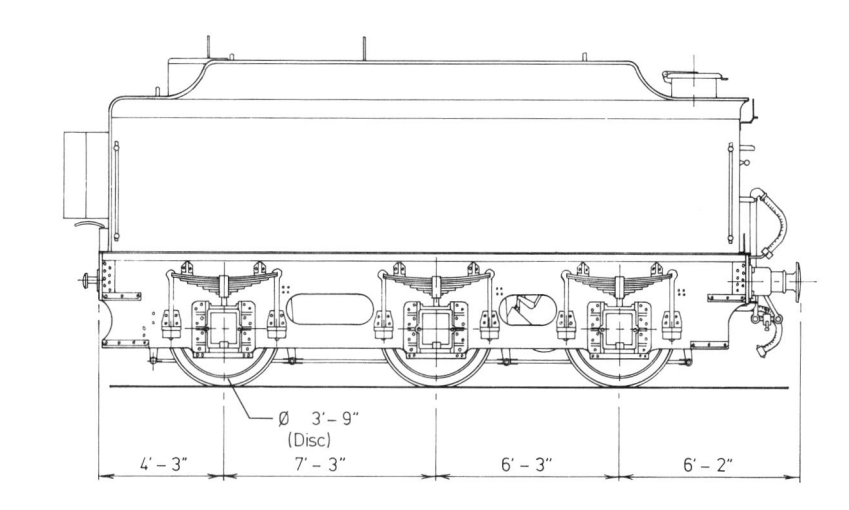

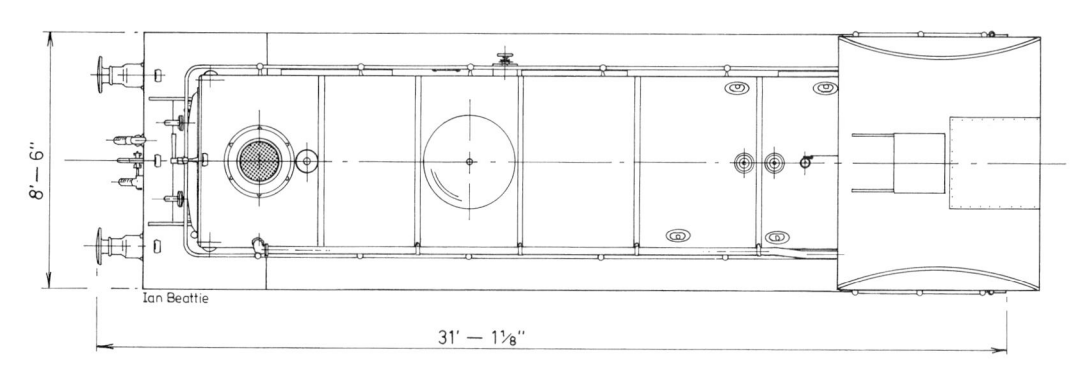

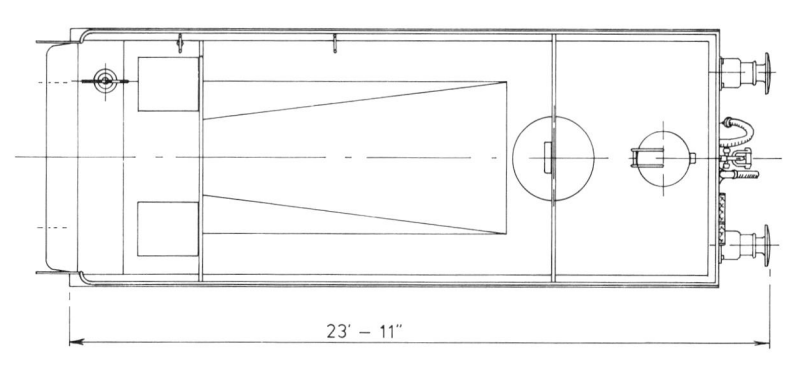

sundry ex-NER versions taken from withdrawn classes. Numerous J39s were equipped with air braking systems, for which the requisite Westinghouse pump was mounted on the right-hand running plate beside the firebox and just forward of the cab (as in all LNER-built engines the J39s were driven from the left side of the footplate). Twin lubricators were likewise quite common fitments.

Type:	Standard Goods
Overall Length:	55'8"
Cylinders:	2, 20" x 26" bore/stroke
Boiler Pressure:	180 lbs/sq in
Heating Surface:	1669.6 sq ft
Grate Area:	26 sq ft
Tractive Effort:	25664 lbs
Mean Weight in Working Order:	110 tons 7 cwt
Coal Capacity:	7 tons
Water Capacity:	4200 gallons
Number Built:	289, 1926-41
Preserved:	None

Nos. 901-906 | Nos. 868-881

Type	Express passenger 4-4-2
Overall Length:	63'0¾"
Cylinders:	2, 20" x 28" bore/stroke
Boiler Pressure:	200 lbs/sq in
Heating Surface:	2256 sq ft
Grate Area:	28.5 sq ft
Tractive Effort:	23500 lbs
Mean Weight In Working Order:	119 tons 16 cwt
Coal Capacity:	7 tons
Water Capacity:	4240 gallons
Number Built:	22, 1906/10/20
Preserved:	None

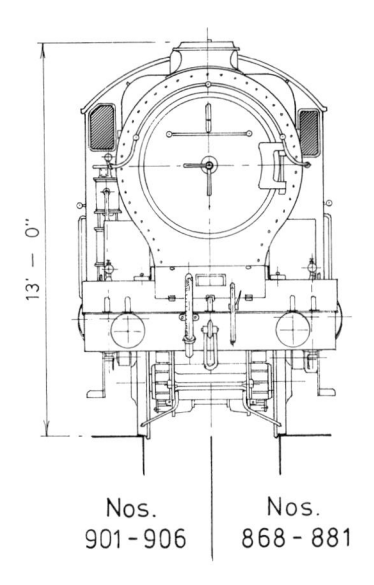

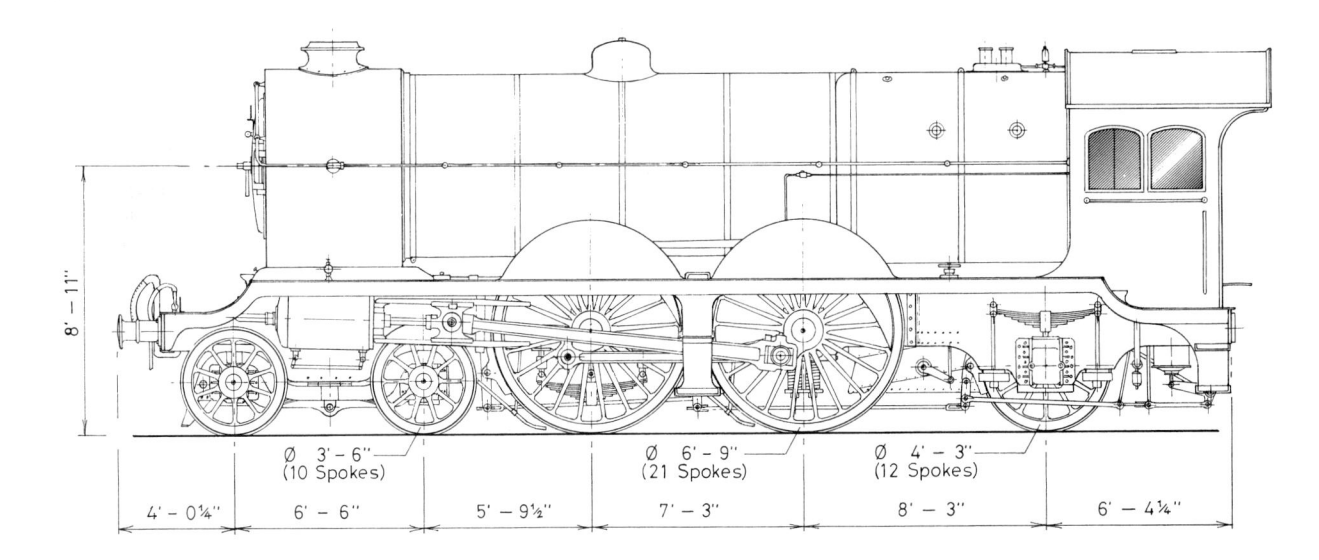

North British Railway Reid 4-4-2

STRETCHING from Aberdeen in the east clear to Mallaig in the far west, encompassing Edinburgh, Glasgow the Border regions and crossing into the English counties of Cumberland and Northumberland, the North British was by a sizeable margin Scotland's most extensive railway. Underpinned by Act of Parliament in 1844, the company in its 75-year history before dissolution upon Grouping underwent many vicissitudes, due not least to the rugged geography which ensured a plethora of hefty gradients throughout the NBR empire; in 1923 the North British Railway handed over some 1300 track miles and an eclectic fleet of 1100 engines on assimilation into the LNER.

At this distance in time from the NBR's heyday the two most celebrated achievements of the company were the magnificent Waverley station, parallel to august Princes Street in the heart of Edinburgh, and the ill-fated bridge across the Firth of Tay which collapsed in December 1879 during a gale, sweeping a passenger train into the river with much loss of life.

The engine concerned in this tragedy (Wheatley 4-4-0 No.224, which was raised, repaired and rendered many further years of service) was typical – if an early example – of the top link roster that confronted William Paton Reid on his appointment as Locomotive Superintendent in 1903. The NBR had depended on 4-4-0s for a long time (akin to inveterate arch rival the Caledonian Railway whose 'Dunalastair' power units constituted the acknowledged benchmark of the genre), however the introduction of bogie passenger rolling stock at the turn of the century complete with ultra-heavy vehicles such as dining and sleeping cars took a mighty toll on the stalwart little engines. A radical redesign was sought.

Given the switchback nature of NBR main lines the advantages of 3-axle traction via the then fairly novel but certainly not untried 4-6-0 wheel arrangement would seem the logical choice; nonetheless Reid acceded to the prevailing fashion for 4-4-2s with his top link offering. Launched in Britain in 1898 by Henry Ivatt of the Great Northern Railway with his 'Klondike' Class (see RM August 1986) the express passenger Atlantic style quickly gained a reputation for high-speed performance with panache and sublime elegance – perfect for any railway's publicity of course – and consequently Reid's variation on the theme duly emerged in 1906.

Outshopped that year from Hyde Park Works, Glasgow, of private manufacturer the North British Locomotive Company – despite the name, no connection with the NBR – were 14 Reid Atlantics, numbered 868-881 and all individually named for Scottish cities, regions or intimate connections thereof. Whilst hopefully eliminating the costly practice of doubleheading (in which they never truly succeeded) the 4-4-2s were intended for premium Edinburgh-Aberdeen and Edinburgh-Perth expresses. Precious little alteration to the infrastructure had been activated beforehand to accommodate these comparatively large machines, a factor that caused initial chaos and much antagonism with the NBR's Chief Civil Engineer, the latter accusing the 4-4-2s of serious shortcomings – poor riding, spreading track and too high a centre of gravity *inter alia* – resulting in their confinement to local duties for a while. Eventually with the assistance of disinterested third parties and in particular Vincent Raven, assistant species, the combination of limited adhesion and tall coupled wheels could well have proved disastrous given the character of NBR main routes. In one sense Gresley over-compensated for this apparent weakness in assigning his vast P2 Class 2-8-2s to Edinburgh-Aberdeen express services in the 1930s!

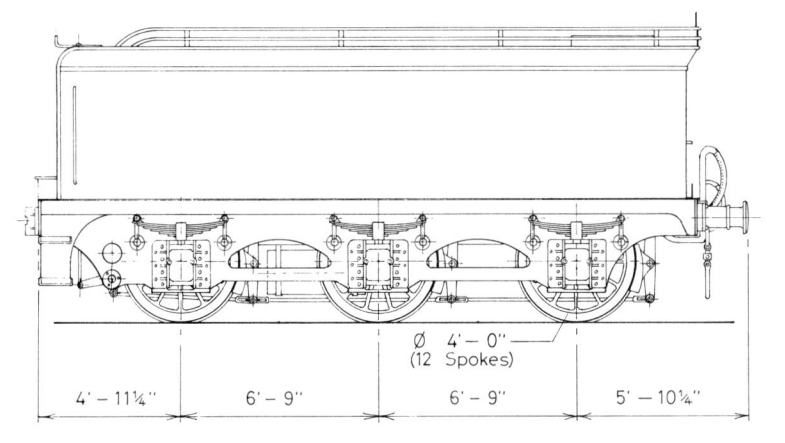

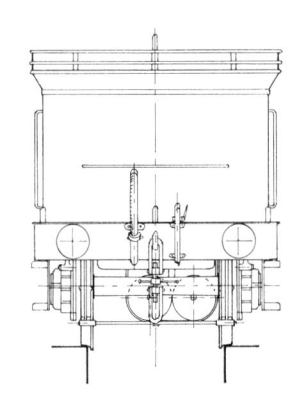

Withdrawals for 21 4-4-2s took place between May 1933 and November 1937; the survivor, No.9875 *Midlothian*, was destined for preservation in the LNER museum at York. Unfortunately the outbreak of World War 2 supervened and the hapless engine was scrapped in November 1939.

Notes on the drawings

Reid's masterpiece is portrayed in the condition it enjoyed in NBR days whilst in original, ie. unsuperheated, guise. Since the two batches, 1906 NBL and 1910 Stephenson, were not identical the front elevation and plan are split along the centrelines to enhance the differences: note the running plate cranked inwards behind the cylinders on Nos.868-881, the wider cab (less roof vent), chimney and much larger dome on the later Nos.901-906.

Both styles featured the characteristic stack of triple safety valves arranged triangularly. It is probable that the 1920-vintage engines, albeit superheated from the outset, bore more or less exact resemblance to the batch built 10 years earlier. Very importantly, please note that the specification table applies to the non-superheated Atlantics.

As can just be discerned in the photos, in LNER times the cylinders sported vertical flat areas shaved off the centrelines to reduce their very considerable outside width over 9') for use over non-NBR routes.

to Wilson Worsdell and later to become chief engineer of the NER, all difficulties were resolved, obstacles removed and the new engines finally acknowledged as undoubted assets.

So useful became the 14 Atlantics that the traffic department requested a further 15 examples, however the NBR's finances at the time would permit a maximum of just 6: the NBL quotation for their supply was rejected in favour of sharper costing from Robert Stephenson & Co of Darlington, who delivered Nos.901-906 in late 1910, the new 4-4-2s again named for Scots connections.

The advantages of superheating – especially in reducing a feverish rate of coal consumption exhibited by the class – became attractive to the powers-that-be and from 1916 the Atlantics entered the NBR's Glasgow-based works at Cowlairs for conversion. Cylinder bores were expanded to 21" whilst boiler pressure was reset at 180 lbs/sq.in. in order to maintain an equivalent tractive effort. Curiously the 6 Stephenson-built engines were excluded from this programme and remained unsuperheated until LNER days. Finally 2 more Atlantics were added to the roster in 1920, under Reid's successor Walter Chalmers, the order on this occasion reverting to NBL; Nos.509-10 were both assembled as superheated locomotives.

Transference of the class into LNER ownership arrived in 1923, when 9000 was added to the NBR numbers and liveries changed to lined apple green. Although the Reid Atlantics must be regarded as successful top link engines, especially when superheated, and certainly were amongst the most handsome of the

The crew aboard No.9876 *Waverley* seem justifiably proud of their mount as all three are recorded for posterity by Walter Boyden at Carlisle Canal shed on 21 July 1929.

Hard-worked Stephenson 4-4-2 No.9902 *Highland Chief* rests cold at Dundee Tay Bridge shed on 17 June 1934. PHOTOGRAPHS: THE LATE W.G.BOYDEN, FRANK HORNBY COLLECTION.

55

Gresley V2 2-6-2

QUITE simply, the V2 was Gresley's most outstanding creation. This at any rate is what the V2 Class's fans would have us believe, and judging the design by the criteria of overall utility, performance and reliability its protagonists must surely be correct, notwithstanding Sir Nigel's perhaps more generally renowned designs the A3s and A4s, as exemplified by *Flying Scotsman* and *Mallard* respectively.

At the start of the 1930s the London & North Eastern Railway began to experience increasing competition from road haulage for its freight handling, with the result that a general speeding-up of such traffic was called for; existing goods locomotives met the order, however when the need for an ultra-fast freight service became apparent not even the otherwise excellent Class K3 2-6-0s *[see overleaf – Ed.]* possessed the necessary stamina or steady running at the high speeds envisaged. Hence an entirely new type of machine was required. The outcome was the V2.

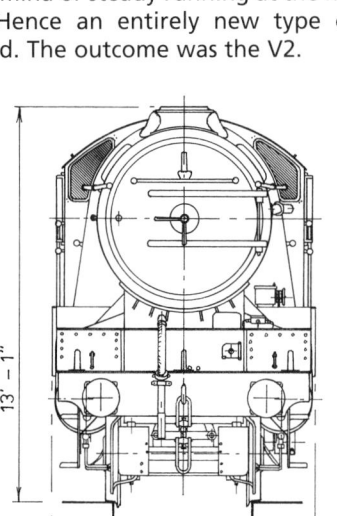

Standing cold at Doncaster shed on 9 September 1954, a relatively clean V2 No.60914 displays BR lined black mixed-traffic livery; the finely-curved running plate lines are a distinctively recognisable Gresley hallmark, featured in most of his locomotive designs. No.60914 was built in June 1940 as No.4885, received a double chimney in August 1958, and was withdrawn in September 1962.

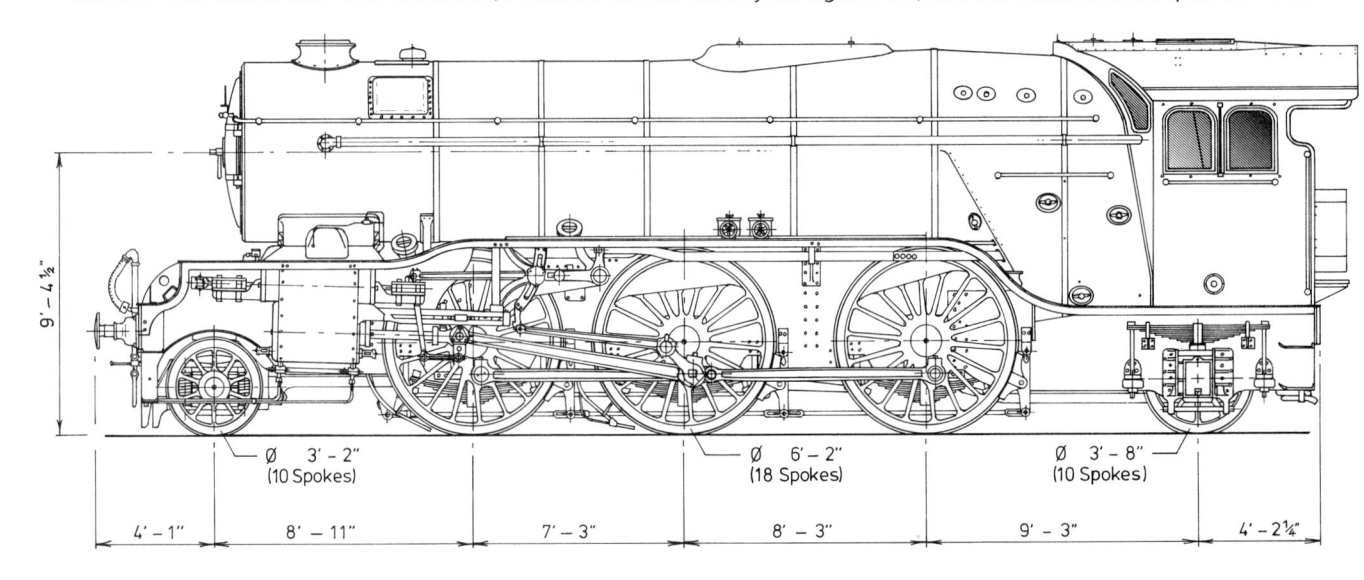

Type:	6-Coupled Mixed Traffic
Overall Length:	66'5½"
Cylinders:	3, 18½" x 26" bore/stroke
Boiler Pressure:	220 lbs/sq in
Heating Surface:	3110.74 sq ft
Grate Area:	41.25 sq ft
Tractive Effort:	33730 lbs
Mean Weight in Working Order:	144 tons 2 cwt
Coal Capacity:	7½ tons
Water Capacity:	4200 gallons
Number Built:	184, 1936-44
Preserved:	1

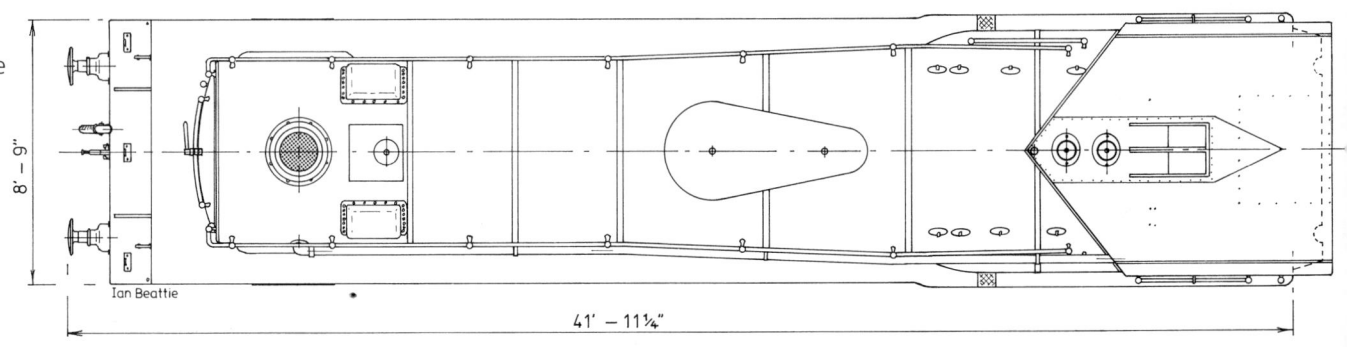

Very similar in appearance to the A3 Pacific but with smaller coupled wheels (pioneered by Gresley's huge Class P2 2-8-2s, which will be studied in these pages anon), an A3 boiler shortened by some 2' and the bogie displaced by a swinging link-controlled pony truck – the latter a source of early concern as to high-speed capabilities, needless as it transpired the initial V2 emerged from Doncaster in June 1936 and was named *Green Arrow*, the title of the rapid freight service for which it was propounded. Just four further V2s followed that year, in order to prove the design. Batches of increasing size began production thereafter, accelerating hugely in the war years; the ex-NER erecting shops at Darlington built the vast majority, the originating Doncaster shops, being involved with production of other classes, contributing only 25 locos to the 184-strong V2 fleet. Assembly ceased in 1944, when the final four engines were completed on the orders of Edward Thompson, Gresley's successor as CME of the LNER, as Pacifics.

In common with the contemporaneous A3 and A4 Pacifics, the V2 sported three cylinders – in this instance combined with the steam chests and smokebox saddle as a single massive casting – of which the centre cylinder was controlled by Gresley's famous conjugated motion, derived from the two outside sets of Walschaert's gear; the sleek, V-fronted cab with its good smoke-deflecting properties was similarly retained, and lateral movement of the trailing axle was restrained by familiar Cartazzi axleboxes. Given that the V2 was designed for high-speed running as well as pulling power, its duties easily encompassed express passenger haulage and hence the application (in pre-war days) of the extremely smart passenger lined apple green livery.

The class was truly outstanding in its appointed mixed-traffic role, coupling steady riding characteristics with high speed potential and immense hauling capacity, plus a surprisingly economical appetite for fuel – a V2 was equally at home competing with a Pacific for top link passenger work as it was slogging away with, say, a hefty unfitted coal train. With a restricted route availability which confined the class generally to main lines, due to a maximum axle load equal to an A3 Class Pacific, though its smaller tender (the LNER standard 6-wheeler) enabled the use of turntables otherwise barred to A3s – the engine lengths of the two designs were surprisingly close – the V2s rendered consistently fast, reliable service throughout their existence. World War II in particular saw many legendary feats of prodigious haulage wrung from these vastly capable 2-6-2s (beyond Gresley's two-strong V4 class the sole tender engines of this wheel configuration in the UK) in which the unassisted lifting of overloaded 26-coach trains was recorded more than once. Wartime indeed sealed the V2s' reputation.

Only eight of the 184 V2s received individual names, of which one was named as late as 1958, within sight of withdrawal. The 2-6-2s were removed from service between 1962 and 1965, with but a single survivor – deservedly the initial engine of the genre, No.4771 *Green Arrow*.

Notes on the drawings
The locomotive is shown as running in LNER years, although no highly evident outward modifications were made over their collective lifespans. Visible riveting tended to become much more evident in the course of time, as did differences in fittings on later batches or where replacements were made, for example in steampipe paths and sheathing, and individual cylinder and smokebox saddle castings in place of the original monobloc. Note the dual Wakefield lubricators, on the left hand side only. *[The P2 2-8-2 was another subject to miss the Drawn & Described treatment – Ed.]*

In a condition typical of steam in its last years, V2 No.60967 accelerates a freight southwards from York: the fireman of the 2-6-2 is watched (somewhat enviously, one suspects) by cameraman Douglas Doherty as he surveys the road ahead along the sleek boiler of his steed. A wartime-built loco (Darlington, 1943), withdrawal came in 1964. PHOTOGRAPH: DOUGLAS DOHERTY.

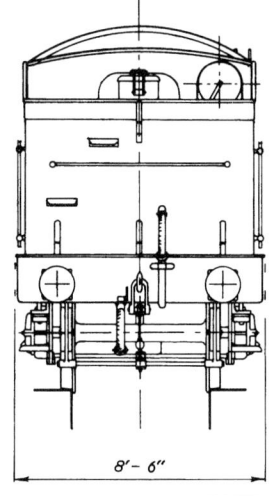

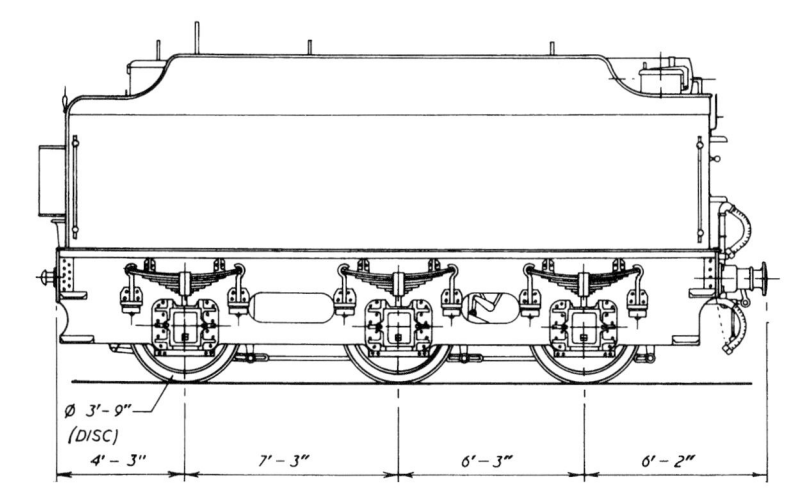

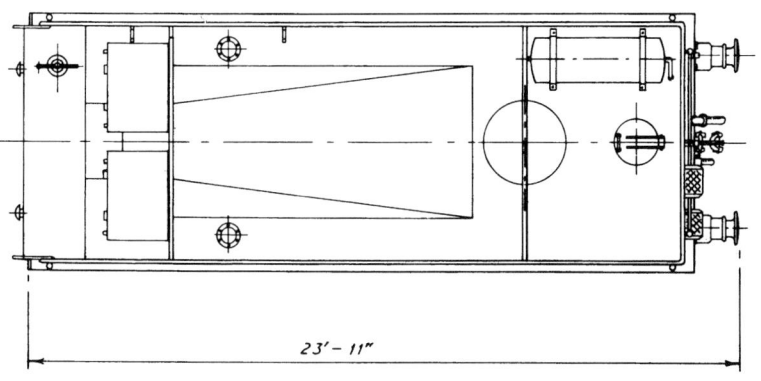

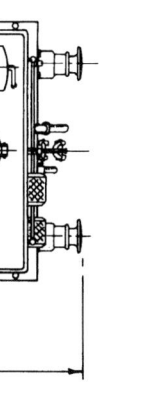

The K3's broad boiler is highlighted in this portrait of 1925-vintage No.61862, in comparatively clean state, coming nicely to the boil on ex-Great Eastern track at Cambridge on 6 September 1953.

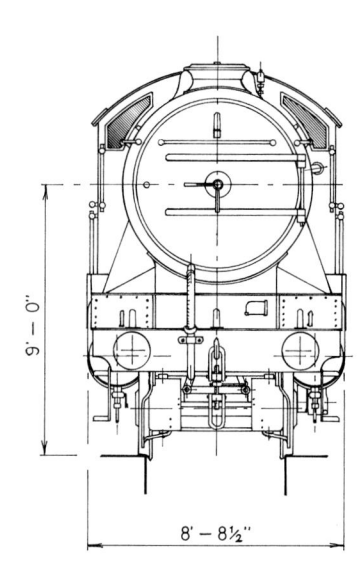

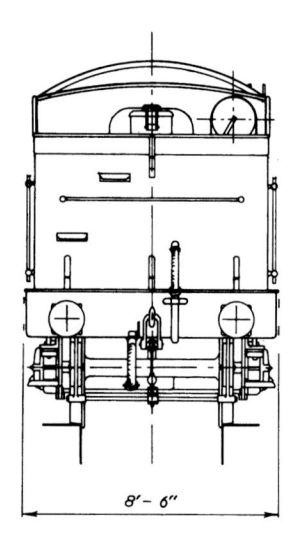

Gresley K3 2-6-0

QUITE EARLY in his career as Chief Mechanical Engineer Nigel Gresley had provided two classes of 2-cylinder 2-6-0s for his employers, the Great Northern Railway. Undoubtedly worthy though these engines were, in some quarters they were considered a mite under-boilered, a label that certainly could not be attached to Gresley's next offering in the same genre.

The launch in 1920 of GNR No.1000, to Class H4, caused considerable fascination due to its then enormous boiler, which spanned a mean 6' in diameter. But beyond this was the less obvious yet equally important provision of 3 cylinders in giving a greatly enhanced power output. Using steel alloy to keep weight down, the twin sets of Walschaert's valve motion controlled the central cylinder's steam chest via Gresley's famous (but in 1920 relatively novel) 'conjugated' gear in avoiding a third, internal set of motion.

Supplied with a cab style originating with Patrick Stirling some 50 years beforehand, therefore superannuated and certainly spartan compared with other companies' methods of crew protection in post-Great War Britain, ten Class H4 Moguls were outshopped from the GNR works at Doncaster in 1920-21 and put to work as mixed-traffic machines. Their passenger-handling proficiency was highlighted very quickly during a major coal strike in 1921, when huge trains were marshalled to minimise use of the precious fuel: running between London and Doncaster on the East Coast Main Line, the new Moguls managed rakes of up to 20 coaches, an unheard-of feat until then.

Upon Grouping in 1923 the erstwhile GNR became a major component of the newly formed London & North Eastern Railway and Gresley was duly appointed CME for the entire Group. Amongst a host of rapid decisions on the locomotive provisions front was an order to restart production of the big Moguls and the first such batch emerged from Darlington (the ex-North Eastern Railway works) in 1924-25. Numerous modifications were instituted over the initial design, most evident of which was a far more generous cab featuring twin side windows and a rearwards-extended roof in the NER fashion.

Further batches between 1929 and 1937 – assembled both in-house and by external contractors – brought the class (in LNE nomenclature retermed the familiar K3) strength to 193, including the GNR builds; the latter engines received NER pattern cabs in 1939. The fleet was subclassified into K3 and K3/2-6 inclusive to take into account detail differences in equipment and tenders attached – however the latter distribution seemed quite haphazard over the 40-year existence of the class.

Immediately successful on such duties as fast fitted freights, the elegant K3s were never strangers to express passenger work (their considerable weight

58

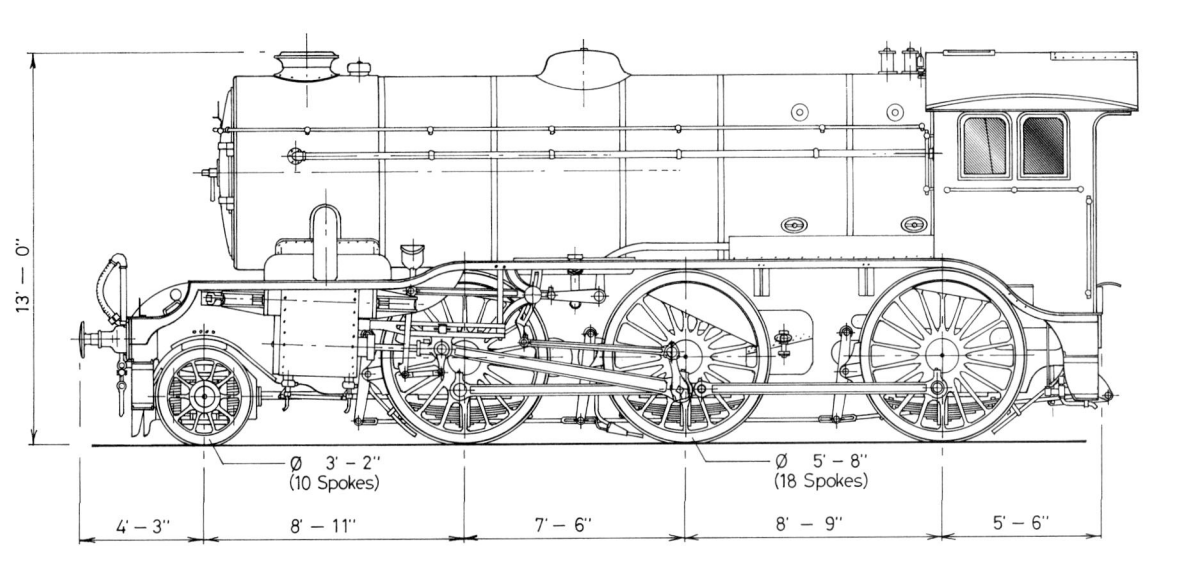

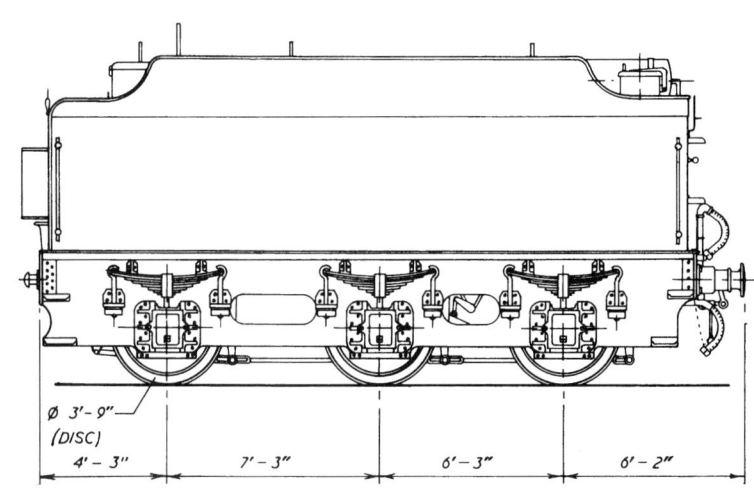

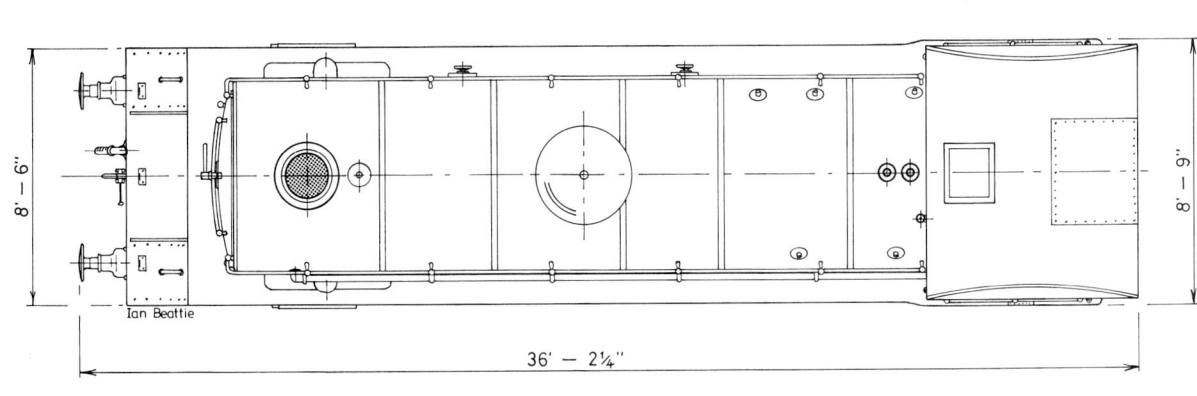

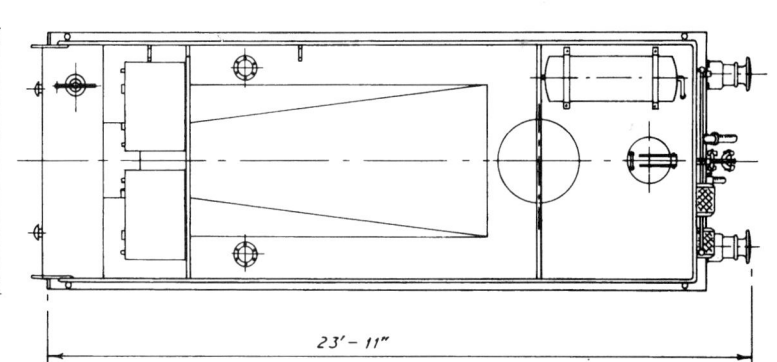

precluded use on any but main or the best-laid secondary lines); bar their green rig in GNR days black livery overall was *de rigueur* throughout their LNE and BR service (BR however applied 'mixed-traffic' lining). Given the nickname 'Jazzers' in the 1920s owing to their reportedly active riding characteristics but, curiously for such a relatively high-profile design, attracting no later epithets, the Moguls were withdrawn between 1959 and 1962 with no survivals for preservation.

A single K3 underwent major conversion during 1945 to 2-cylinder format under the guidance of Edward Thompson as one of his numerous experiments on Gresley engines, in this instance abortive; the unique machine was reclassified K5.

Notes on the drawings

As befits a class that was constructed over nearly 20 years the variety of fixtures and fitments was inevitably considerable; the drawings purport to show a representative K3 2-6-0 when running from the late 1930s onwards. Typical '30s alterations included provision of front footsteps, cutaway corners to the bufferbeam, vertical handrails on the cab front plate, smokebox saddle lagging, access door to the central valves *et al*. Likewise the tender, in this case a later LNER Standard version, typifies those used behind K3s. Please note that the specifications are again merely representative and do not cover the multitude of variations within the class.

Type:	Mixed-Traffic
Overall Length:	59'6"
Cylinders:	3, 18½" x 26" bore/stroke
Boiler Pressure:	180lbs/sq in
Heating Surface:	2308 sq ft
Grate Area:	28 sq ft
Tractive Effort:	30031 lbs
Mean Weight in Working Order:	123 tons 12 cwt
Coal Capacity:	7½ tons
Water Capacity:	4200 gallons
Number Built:	193, 1920-37
Preserved:	None

59

Built at Darlington in May 1947, No.61028 *Umseke* stands alongside Neasden shed buildings awaiting the next turn of duty on 8 April 1955. Note the smokebox-side location of the nameplate and the characteristic 'step' between cab and tender.

Thompson B1 4-6-0

THE DEATH in April 1941 of Sir Nigel Gresley brought into power as Chief Mechanical Engineer of the London & North Eastern Railway a man totally opposed to Gresley's locomotive design precepts – those around which the international reputation of the Group had been established. Edward Thompson was a great believer in simplicity, so that the notions of Gresley's famed 3-cylinder 'derived' valve gear (which in all honesty depended on high-tensile and thus expensive types of steel coupled with accurate assembly and frequent, conscientious maintenance for reliability) was thrown out the window along with those officers of the company who had been 'Gresley men'. It was perhaps fortunate that wartime conditions favoured Thompson's principles, since Gresley's engines had suffered badly from lack of proper maintenance due to depleted staff numbers and intensive working since 1939, and although his age precluded more than 5 or so years as CME Thompson embarked on a bewilderingly ambitious plan for no fewer than ten standard locomotive types of his own design to replace not only surviving pre-Grouping engines but much of Gresley's output as well. His initial design however unlike many of his others not only came to fruition (with a vengeance – 410 built), it turned out to be much the most successful.

One of Gresley's final achievements had been a variety of 2-6-2 3-cylinder machines for replacing elderly pre-1923 general purpose locomotives; but after only two of the prospective V4 Class had been built production was cancelled and effort was channelled into Thompson's substitute. The latter was classified B1 and the first appeared from Darlington works in December 1942; the configuration incorporated existing standard LNER components including boilers and bogies from the B17 'Sandringham' 4-6-0s, somewhat modified cylinders and Walschaert's valve motion from the ex-Great Northern K2 Class Moguls, driving wheels from the V2 2-6-2s, and tenders used were conventional LNER standard 4200-gallon types. From this amalgam of mostly, and ironically, Gresley designed parts emerged the LNER equivalent of the Great Western 'Hall' and the LMS 'Black Five': an uncomplicated mixed-traffic power unit light enough on its axles (17¾ tons) for wide route availability and of the maximum utility from pick-up goods to heavy passenger duty. The B1 was a handsome beast, especially when livened in LNER apple green, although a strange quirk of design was maintained as a sort of 'trademark' in the pronounced drop in tender running-plate level relative to the cab side panels – as though the necessity for a tender had been neglected in the planning stage.

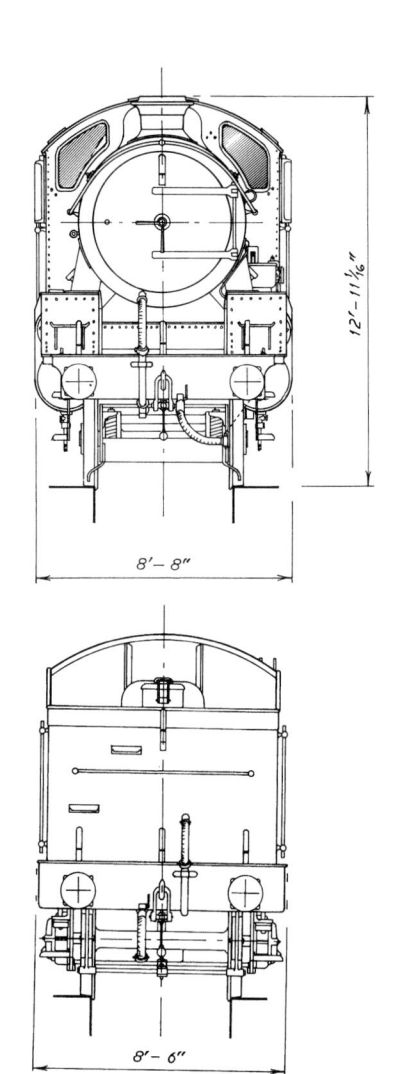

Numerous varieties of obsolescent motive power were displaced, throughout the LNER empire, by the ubiquitous B1s, amongst which were the once top link Atlantics of GCR, GNR, NBR and NER origin. The initial 40 Thompson 4-6-0s were erected at Darlington and these received names from species of South African antelopes (hence the sometimes-quoted 'Antelope' class nomenclature); the frames of these particular engines were shorter by 2⅛" behind the rearmost coupled wheels (making engine length 36'10⅛" – see

60

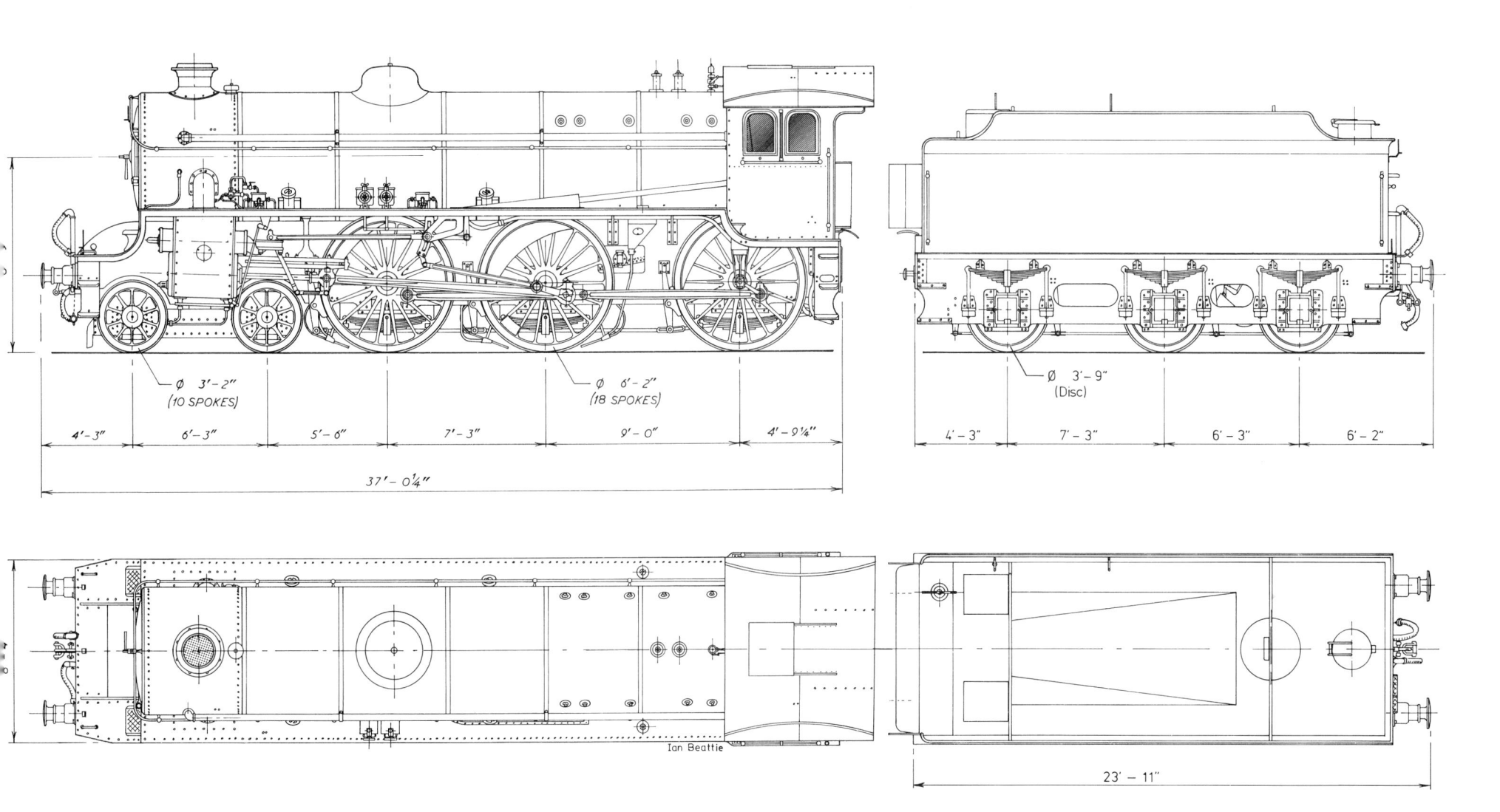

drawings). The succeeding 18 engines were named for Directors of the LNER and thereafter no further names were applied, the exception being No.61379, christened *Mayflower* in 1951 since this engine regularly served Boston, Lincs., with this town's connections with Boston, Massachusetts and hence the Pilgrim Fathers whose vessel was the *Mayflower*.

Of the 410 machines outshopped over all but 10 years – initial assembly was comparatively slow, during the war years, but accelerated rapidly after 1945 and into BR days until supersession by BR Standard 4-6-0s in 1952 – the great majority was provided by private builders the North British Locomotive Company of Glasgow, the remainder being assembled 'in-house' at Darlington and Gorton.

Much varied and useful work was performed by these simple, powerful engines over the entire LNER network (and succeeding BR regions) including the north of Scotland, for which area sixteen B1s were issued with squatter chimneys and lowered cabs matching the reduced loading gauge mandatory there. Renowned for free-steaming and easy controllability, the 4-6-0s never exhibited good riding qualities and as they became older and more careworn the B1 footplate became ever more of a boneshaking experience. Beyond No.61057, broken up following an accident at Chelmsford in 1950, the class remained intact until withdrawal commenced in 1962; by the end of 1967 all 409 had disappeared from revenue service. Two survived the cutting torch, No.1264 and No.1306, the latter being named *Mayflower* (from the plates transferred from condemned No.61379) and which currently enhances the Nene Valley Railway; the former is preserved on the Great Central Railway.

Type:	4-6-0
Overall Length:	61'7³⁄₈"
Bogie Wheels:	3'2" dia. 10 spokes
Coupled Wheels:	6'2" dia. 18 spokes
Tender Wheels:	3'9" dia. disc
Cylinders:	2, 20" x 26" bore/stroke
Boiler Pressure:	225 lbs/sq in
Heating Surface:	2020 sq ft
Grate Area:	27.9 sq ft
Tractive Effort:	26878 lbs
Mean Weight in Working Order:	123¼ tons
Coal Capacity:	7½ tons
Water Capacity:	4200 gallons
Number Built:	410, 1942-52
Preserved:	2

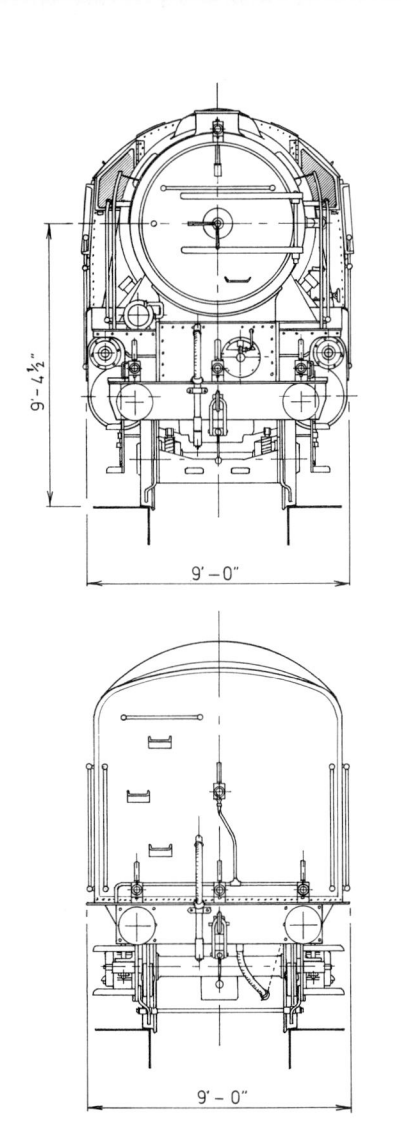

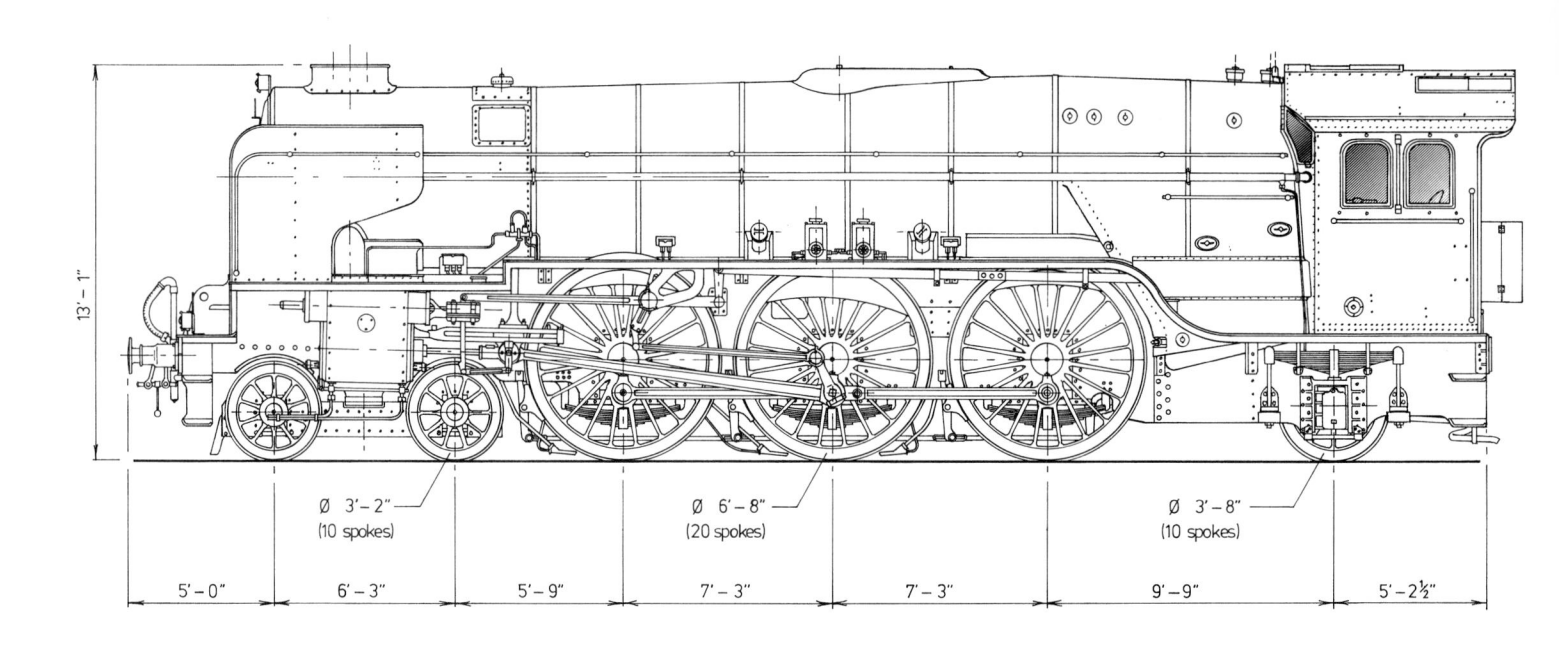

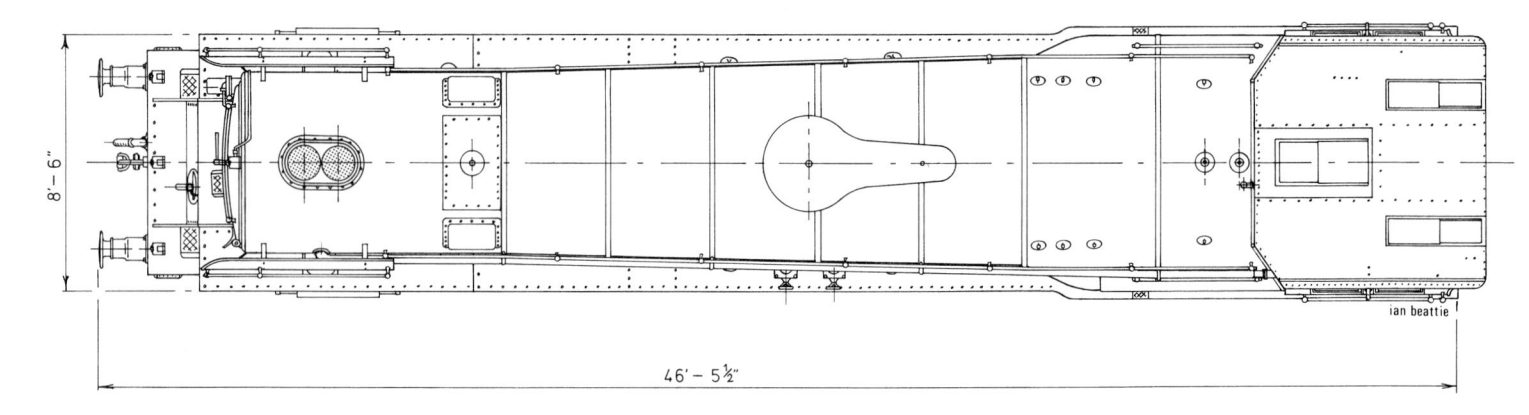

Peppercorn A1 4-6-2

ON HIS appointment as CME of the London & North Eastern Railway in 1946, Arthur Peppercorn delayed outstanding orders on Doncaster and Darlington erecting shops for 16 and 23 premium Pacific locomotives respectively, that his predecessor Edward Thompson had instigated, to allow a rapid if not radical redesign.

Sir Nigel Gresley's death in April 1941 had brought Thompson to the fore, at a period when wartime exigencies were beginning to bite hard into the thorough maintenance schedules demanded by Gresley 3-cylinder engines for reliable performance: an enigmatic character, Thompson sincerely detested Gresley's precepts based on conjugated valve motion and introduced the simpler, much easier to maintain 3-cylinder designs having 3 separate sets of valve gear. The fact that Thompson's 4-6-2 engines were ungainly and overlong in the wheelbase caused Peppercorn's reappraisal.

Unlike the former CME Peppercorn was very much a 'Gresley man' and surrounded himself with ex-Gresley engineers who had been metaphorically put out to grass after the events of 1941; however he did not reinstate Gresley's conjugated motion but rather cleaned up and made much more elegant Thompson's Pacific blueprint. Two Pacifics were the outcome, sharing the same Diagram 118 boiler, divided drive and three individual sets of valve motion: the A2 with 6'2" coupled wheels, and A1 with 6'8" wheels being slightly longer overall.

Outshopping of A1s commenced in August 1948, directly following the last of the 15 A2s, the 49th being delivered in December 1949 thus although a pure LNER design they were all built after nationalisation; all were eventually named, in a mixture of themes. Originally streamlining á la A4 was to be applied and the LNER directors had allotted funds for this, but the newly formed Railway Executive countermanded this order in the then prevailing spirit of austerity. Peppercorn retired on the last day of 1949 as CME of British Railways' Eastern and North Eastern Regions and unfortunately died not long thereafter, so he witnessed little of the excellent and spirited work undertaken by his exceptionally frugal and free-steaming Pacifics, principally on the East Coast Main Line. Nominally more powerful than the famed A4s, the A1s were less prone to wheelslip but gained a reputation, albeit lowkey, for giving a rougher footplate ride than Gresley 4-6-2s. Unlike the specialised corridor tenders, those attached to A1s were steam-braked and could not be interchanged with the former, therefore the streamlined A4s remained in charge of Kings Cross-Edinburgh non-stop workings.

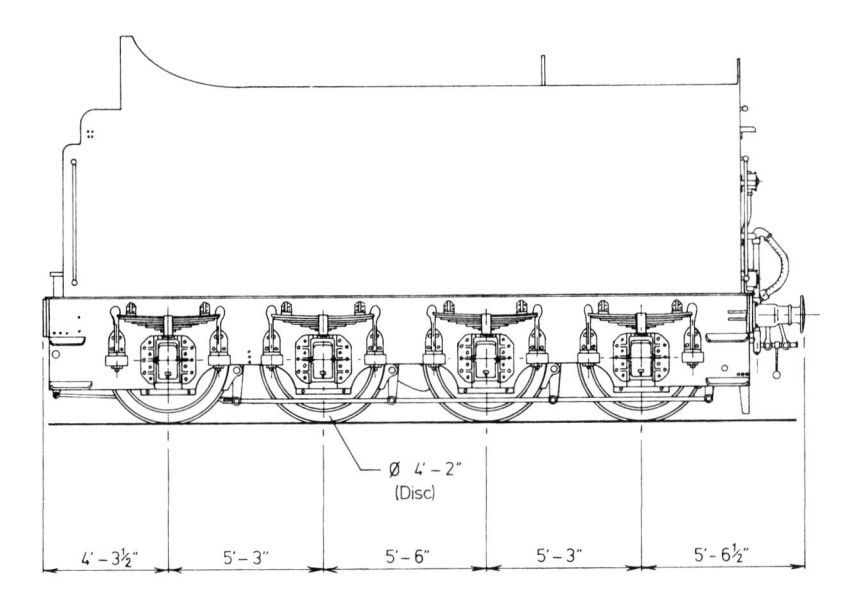

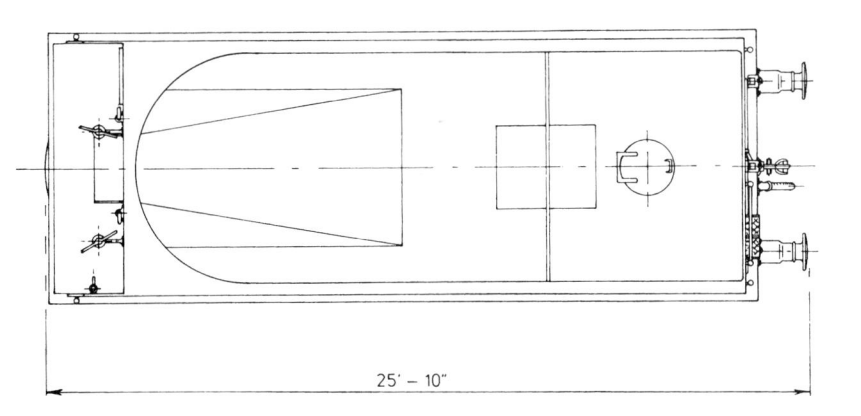

Top: built at Doncaster in April 1949, No.60125 *Scottish Union* indicating signs of very hard work, rests cold on shed at its birthpace on 7 May 1960. No.60125 was removed from traffic in July 1964.

Above: captured in steam amongst the confines of Kings Cross shed is No.60118 *Archibald Sturrock*, awaiting its return to home at Copley Hill, Leeds (37B) later on in this October 1956 day. Photograph: Norman Browne.

Little in the way of modifications were applied during the A1 class's life beyond lipped double chimneys, more classical than the 'stove-pipe' style originally fitted; high-capacity Wakefield 7Z lubricators were prominent atop the left-hand running plate. Five engines were equipped, expensively, with roller axle bearings that proved very successful, however overall the A1s were the most economical of all multi-cylinder 4-6-2s (and several 4-6-0s) in service and their minimal maintenance ensured their popularity with shed staff; they averaged the highest daily mileage of any contemporaneous British locomotive, a measure of crews' esteem too.

Classified in power category 8 by BR, the tough A1s were withdrawn between October 1962 and November 1965, strangely without an example preserved (unlike the numerically much smaller A2 class from which 60532 *Blue Peter* survives) following short but hard-worked existences. *[As this book was in preparation, steady progress was being made in the A1 Project's aim to build a new A1 – Ed.]*

Notes on the drawings
The A1 shown is much as outshopped, including a flush-sided tender (prominently riveted versions were also used). Cylinders inclined at 1 in 50. Note the 'stove-pipe' dual chimney, and the drain piping from the ejector pipe which debouched on to the rear wheel's Cartazzi axlebox – this caused an occasional hot-box and the outlet was subsequently extended to below the frame. Electric lighting was standard.

Type:	Express Passenger 4-6-2
Overall Length:	72'11¾"
Cylinders:	3, 19" x 26" bore/stroke
Boiler Pressure:	250 lb/sq in
Heating Surface:	3141 sq ft
Grate Area:	50 sq ft
Tractive Effort:	37400 lbs
Mean Weight in Working Order:	164 tons 10 cwt
Coal Capacity:	9 tons
Water Capacity:	5000 gallons
Number Built:	49, 1948-49 (50th under construction)
Preserved:	None

Section 4
Southern Railway (and constituents)

Locomotive	Page	Locomotive	Page
London, Brighton & South Coast Railway 4-6-4T	64-65	London & South Western Railway M7 0-4-4T	74-75
Maunsell N15x 4-6-0	66-67	Maunsell Class V 'Schools' 4-4-0	76-77
LBSCR 'Terrier' 0-6-0T	68	Bulleid 'Leader' 0-6-6-0T	78-79
Bulleid Light Pacific (original condition)	69-71	SECR/SR N Class 2-6-0	80-82
South Eastern & Chatham Railway Class H 0-4-4T	72-73	Beattie 2-4-0WT	82-83

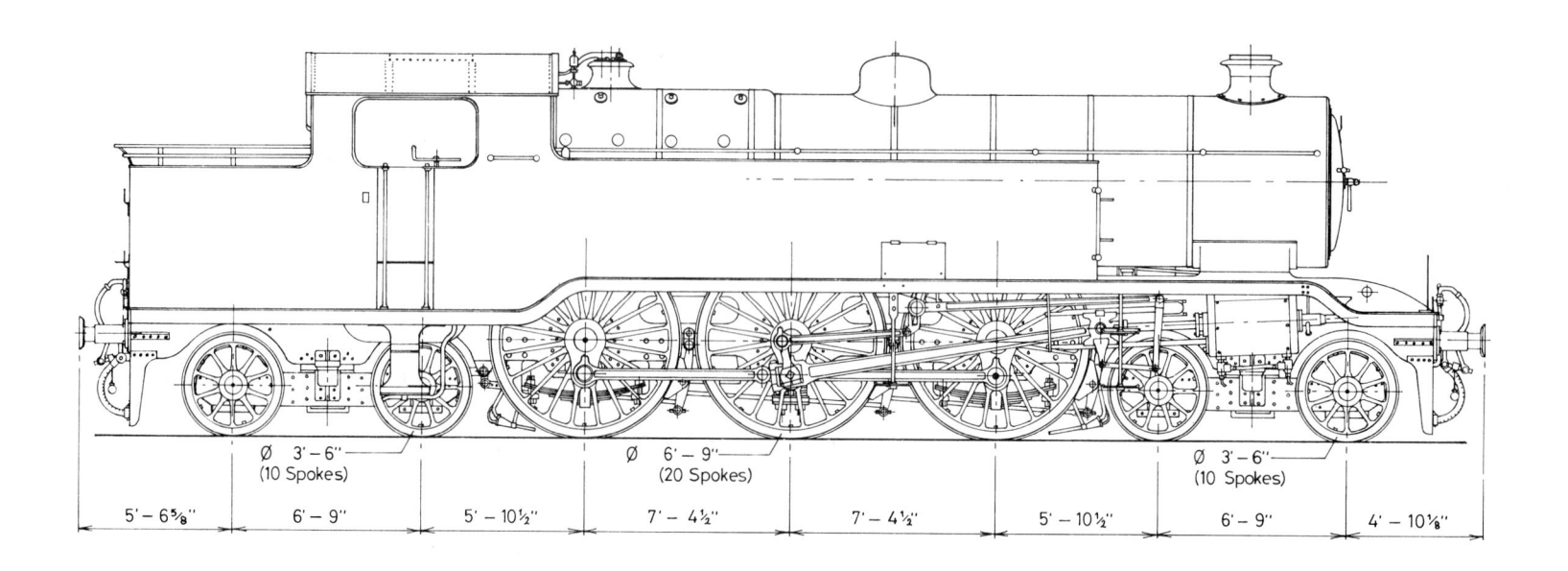

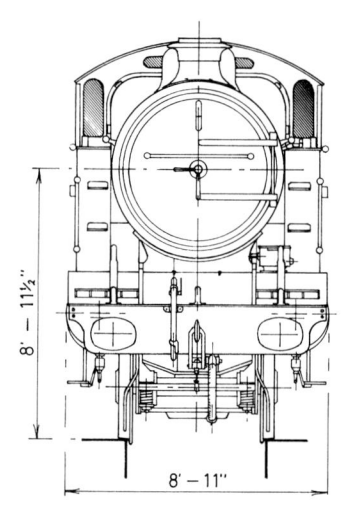

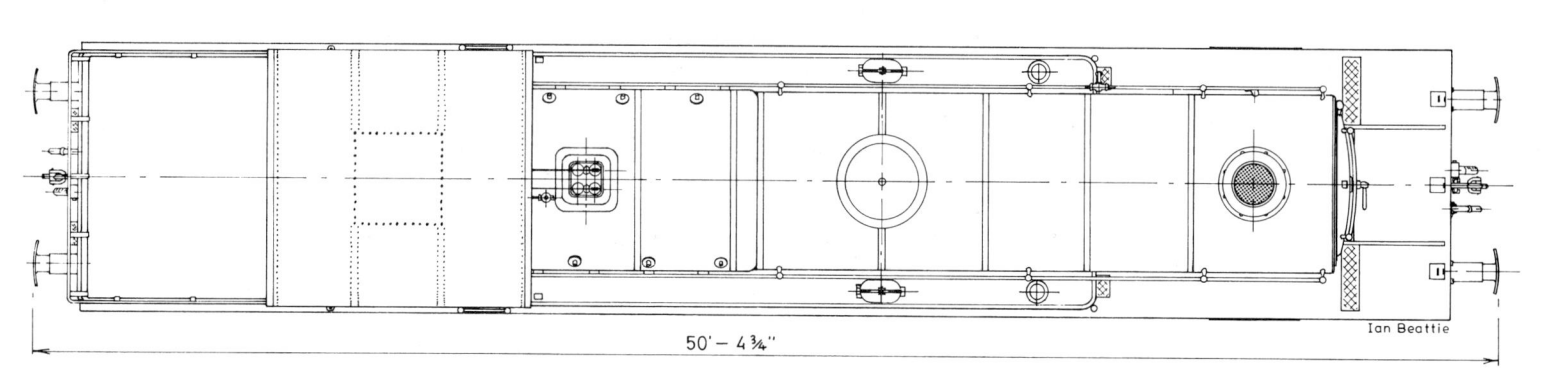

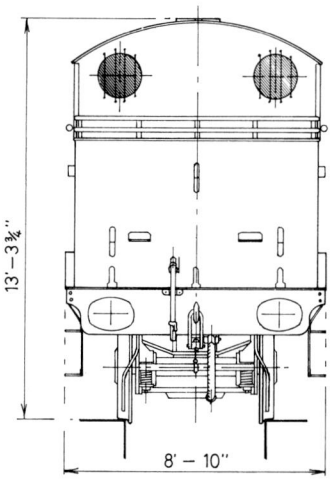

Ian Beattie

64

LBSCR 4-6-4T

IN FITTING tribute to the 75th anniversary of the end of World War I this month *[November 1993 – Ed.]*, we consider here a class containing a designated War Memorial Locomotive of that era.

In relation to its small geographical size the London, Brighton & South Coast Railway saw a high proportion of its workforce lost in enemy action between 1914 and 1919: the last in the line of Colonel Lawson Billinton's immense 4-6-4 tank engines, 1922-built No.333, was with due solemnity named *Remembrance* and the sacrifice of 532 employees commemorated by tablets affixed to both side tanks.

One of the very few 4-6-4 designs witnessed on Britain's railways, the hefty LBSC tanks were essentially uprated variants of locomotive superintendent Billinton's previous twin 4-6-2Ts (see RM December 1982) and constituted the final indigenous handiwork of this autonomous railway before being engulfed by the act of Grouping in 1923; as top link express hauliers these engines owed their existence to the fact that the Brighton system consisted of short-distance main line routes, which obviated the necessity for tender engines with their enhanced water cartage.

Constructed to meet a directive for a much speeded-up service between London and Brighton (a distance of 51 miles station to station) – although in actuality the timetable never did undercut the customary top link 60 minutes, then or since – the first of the Class L Baltics emerged from Brighton Works in April 1914. Numbered 327 and christened *Charles C. Macrae*, the prototype underwent rigorous trials in service whilst the second engine was under construction: No. 327 exhibited some more or less minor shortcomings, most serious of which was a derailment, apparently due to water sloshing around uncontrollably in the massive side tanks. Filling of these was thereafter restricted to a height of only some 1'3" which, by lowering the engine's centre of gravity (in company with a well tank slung under the boiler – plus the conventional bunker tank – to maintain the necessary water capacity), cured this potentially lethal tendency to hop rails. No.328, the second 4-6-4T, was outshopped in September 1914, after which there was a hiatus in production due to the Great War.

Five further Baltics made their appearance in 1921-22; numbered 329-333 respectively, these engines incorporated minor boiler changes to which the specification table herewith refers – and joined their earlier counterparts in sporting the striking LBSC dark umber livery of the period, bar No.333 *Remembrance* which entered service in late 1922 wearing 'photographic grey', paintwork it retained until repainted olive green by the Southern Railway during the 1920s (as were of course all its classmates).

The official LBSC photo of No.333 *Remembrance*, which certainly captures the massive stance of this superb machine. The inset shows the memorial tablets carried on each tankside.

Much the most powerful of the Brighton motive power roster and as such the Company's premium express engines, the imposing 4-6-4Ts with their symmetrical wheelbase could be used equally well chimney– or bunker-first – in practice however, as befitted their exalted status, trains were (almost) invariably drawn chimney-forwards. Especially associated with the 'Southern Belle' service between London and Brighton (after electrification renamed 'Brighton Belle', still much lamented over 20 years after its demise), to which train the Baltics' excess power over the earlier 4-6-2Ts enabled attachment of additional Pullman coaches as a standard feature, Billinton's swansong products ruled the rails until the ex-LBSC main lines were electrified under SR auspices in 1933.

Only three 4-6-4Ts were named (beyond the two already mentioned, No.329 carried the title *Stephenson*), however on their withdrawal from premium traffic in 1933 the class was rebuilt into 4-6-0 tender format, retaining a considerable proportion of original components including boilers, cylinders, valve gear and the distinctively shaped running plates. In this guise, and reclassified N15x, all seven received names – of pioneer locomotive engineers – except (SR) No.2333 which continued as the official War Memorial engine for its originating railway. Redistributed throughout the much extended SR network, although the process of rebuilding had somehow contrived to sap their awesome power, the class finally became extinct in 1957.

Notes on the drawings

The locomotive shown is in the condition extant during late Brighton and early Southern years. The cylinders were inclined at 1 in 24; note that the outside-mounted Walschaert's valve gear controls valves set between the frames inboard of the cylinders via rocking levers, the whole so contrived due to the supposedly economic use of 3-class cylinders.

Comparatively few alterations were instituted during the tanks' short life, being performed by the SR generally to meet composite Group standards – for example, chimney height and cab roofs were modified to the overall SR loading gauge; clack valves appeared on the boiler centreline forward of the side tanks; and vacuum braking apparatus was installed alongside the habitual LBSC air brake.

The position of the water filler caps shown is conjectural, as no photos or drawings have been found to indicate their true location. *[In fact they were over the centre of the expansion link, hinged at the front not the rear, and round-ended not squared – Ed.]*

Type:	Express Passenger
Cylinders:	2, 22" x 28" bore/stroke
Boiler Pressure:	170lbs/sq in
Heating Surface:	1816.5 sq ft
Grate Area:	26.7 sq ft
Tractive Effort:	24180 lbs
Mean Weight in Working Order:	98 tons 5 cwt
Coal Capacity:	3½ tons
Water Capacity:	2686 gallons
Number Built:	7, 1914-22
Preserved:	None

In commendably clean BR mixed-traffic lined black livery, N15x No.32329 *Stephenson* poses on Basingstoke shed with another Brighton *emigré* in former South Western territory, E4 0-6-2 No.32502, on 2 April 1955. PHOTOGRAPH: PHILIP J. KELLEY.

Maunsell Class N15x 4-6-0 (rebuilt LBSC 4-6-4T)

THE EARLY history of these handsome machines has already been considered *[on the preceding pages – Ed.]*. Service under the Southern Railway banner remained initially much as before the act of Grouping, however electrification of the Eastbourne and Brighton routes in the early 1930s as part of ongoing SR policy fundamentally undermined the Baltics' reason for existence. A thorough technical appraisal of the redundant machines showed them to be in fine physical fettle overall which, coupled with the Southern's antipathy towards large passenger tank engines (the fatal derailment at Sevenoaks in 1927 involved a 'River' Class 2-6-4T), convinced Chief Mechanical Engineer Richard Maunsell that their conversion to tender format should result in ideal augmentations and enhancements to the hugely successful but fully stretched 'King Arthur' 4-6-0 fleet.

Accordingly rebuilding was sanctioned and the seven Baltics duly metamorphosed into 4-6-0s between 1934 and 1936; allocated to London-Southampton services, the refurbished engines utilised almost all their original fittings and fixtures including major items such as frames (necessarily modified to suit) and boilers, wheels, cylinders and valve motion. Cylinders were linered down by 1" to 21" diameter and boiler pressure raised to 190 lbs/sq in, giving a figure for tractive effort slightly but not significantly lower than previously; attached were 5000-gallon bogie tenders.

Of the original seven only three had sported names, of which two (*Stephenson* on No.2329 and No.2333 *Remembrance*) were carried over to the rebuilds. Suggested by the ex-GWR and ex-SECR engineer Harry Holcroft, inventor in concert with Nigel Gresley of conjugated 3-cylinder valve gear, the remaining 4-6-0s commemorated pioneer locomotive engineers, namely: No.2327 *Trevithick*, No. 2328 *Hackworth*, No.2330 *Cudworth*, No.2331 *Beattie* and No.2332 *Stroudley*.

Somehow during the rebuilding process much of the sparkle and panache that characterised the Baltics were lost – a mystery considering the re-employment of so much original componentry – which unfortunately did not do justice to those illustrious names chosen for the 4-6-0s. The engines were disliked by crews and could barely approach let alone equal 'King Arthurs' in performance.

Shortly after the Second World War, in which some of the 'Remembrance' 4-6-0s (by which the class was also known) were leased to the GWR for goods working, Maunsell's successor Oliver Bulleid's famous lightweight Pacifics began to emerge in significant numbers on the SR and then, following nationalisation in 1948, the Southern Region of British Railways, resulting in the unloved 4-6-0s becoming largely superfluous. Their sphere of operation grew wider as time passed, being steamed for sundry duties far beyond – and beneath – their once-designated express passenger role; withdrawals commenced in 1956, with No.32331 *Beattie* the last to disappear during 1957.

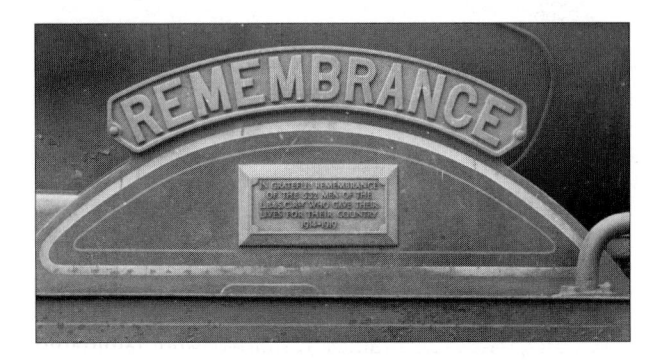

Treatment of the war memorial after rebuilding. PHILIP J.KELLEY.

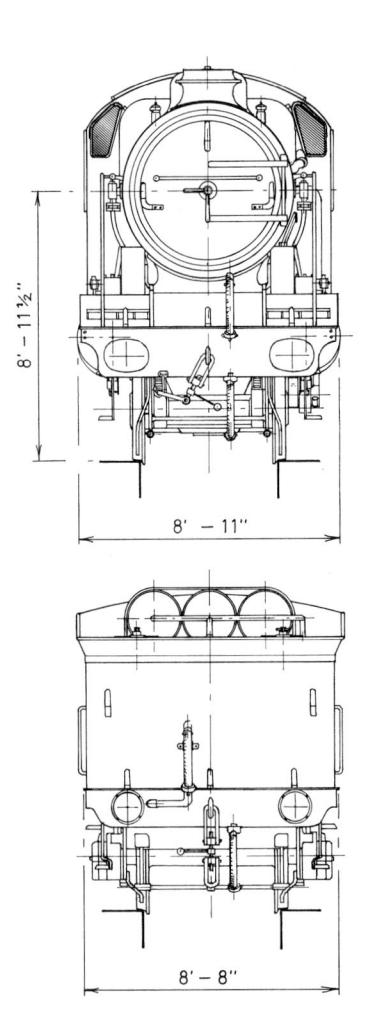

Notes on the drawings
The Class N15x 4-6-0 is shown in mid-1930s guise complete with smokebox mounted superheater anti-vacuum 'snifting' valves – these were removed under Bulleid's regime as CME – though in truth the engines remained virtually unaltered throughout their career. Smoke deflectors were fitted from the outset: frame, smokebox and saddle detail concealed by the deflector is marked in the side elevation by dashed lines.

Comparison with the LBSCR 4-6-4T drawings

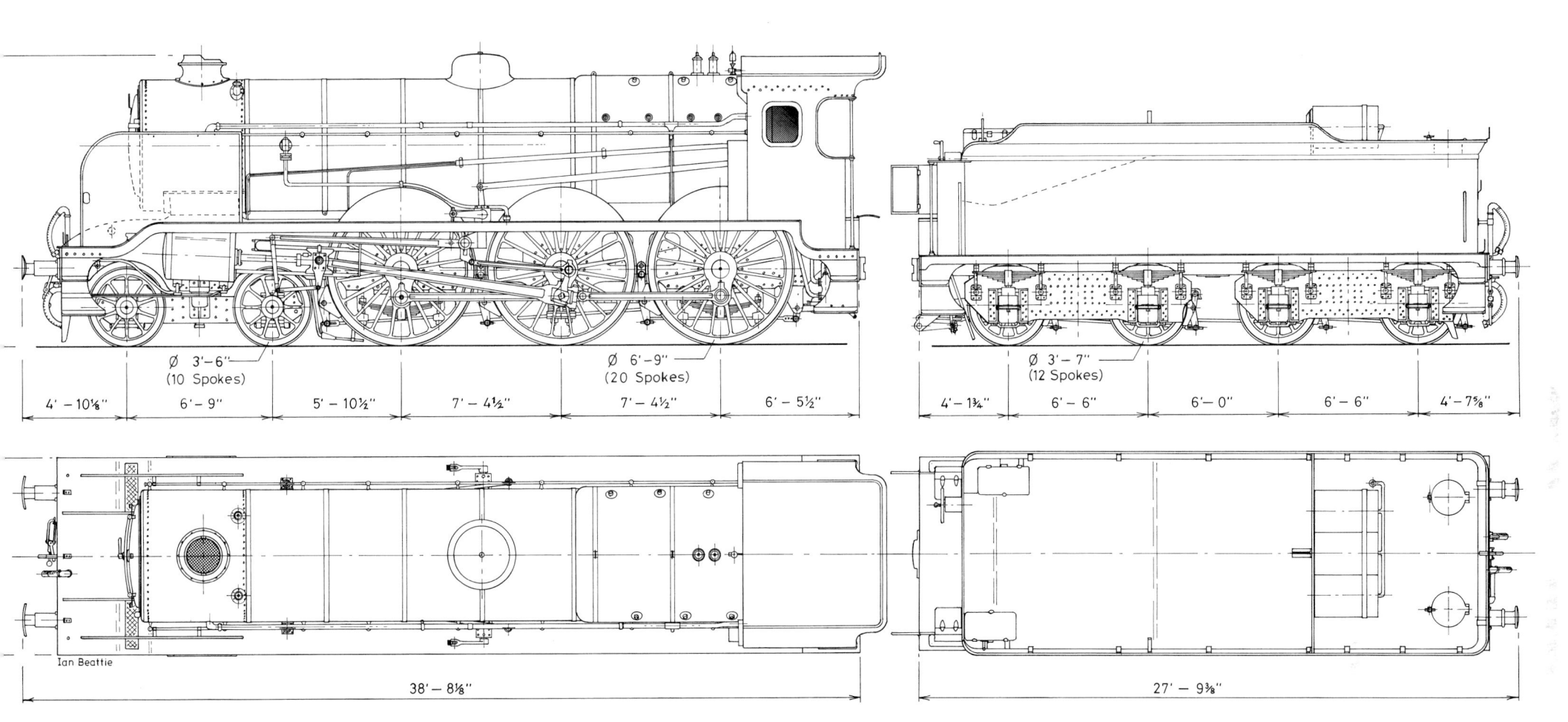

Left: a crisp shot enhanced by low sun of 'Remembrance' Class No.32330 *Cudworth* pausing momentarily at Clapham Junction in 1954. PHOTOGRAPH: NORMAN BROWNE.

The London & South Western-style 5000-gallon tender of Urie design was adapted to suit the N15x Class, notably in the installation of triple vacuum reservoirs set directly behind the coal plate; the dashed lines in the profile view depict the bunker/tank division and water filler location.

Type:	Express Passenger
Overall Length:	66'11¾"
Cylinders:	2, 21" x 28" bore/stroke
Boiler Pressure:	180 lbs/sq in
Heating Surface:	1816.5 sq ft
Grate Area:	26.7 sq ft
Tractive Effort:	23324 lbs
Mean Weight in Working Order:	130 tons 13 cwt
Coal Capacity:	5 tons
Water Capacity:	5000 gallons
Number Built:	7, 1934-6
Preserved:	None

illustrates how relatively little was added or subtracted in the conversion to tender format; the frame and running plate were modified accordingly and new cab attached of course, however the bogie was heavily reworked, with sideframes reshaped and laminated suspension substituted for the original helical springs.

67

LBSCR 'Terrier' 0-6-0T

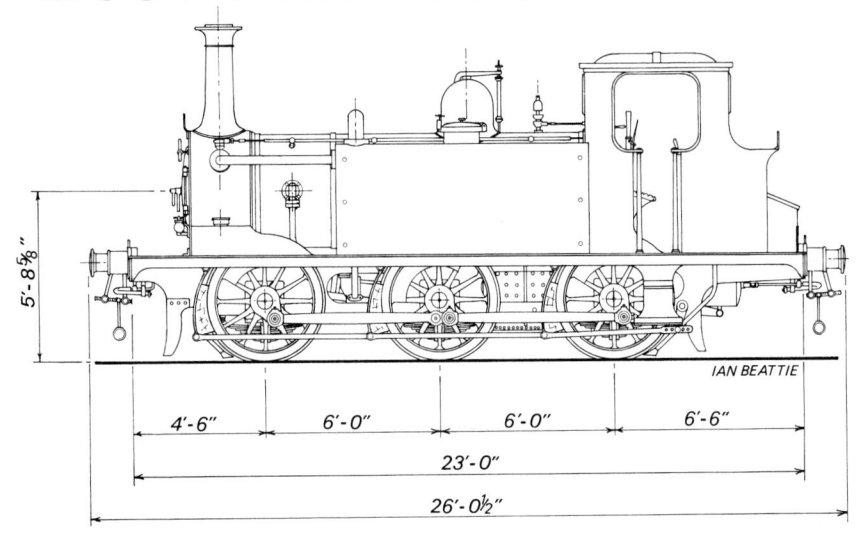

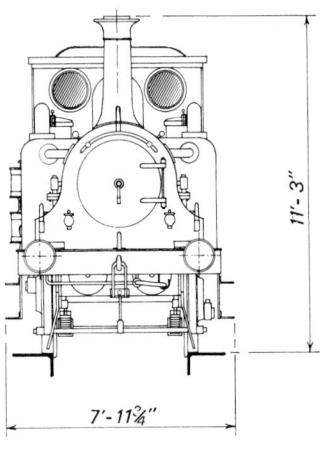

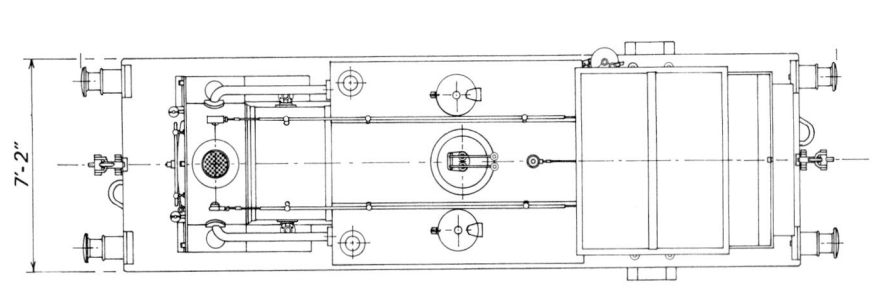

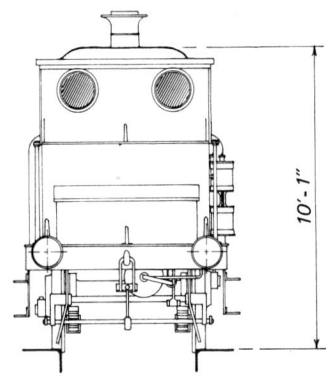

CALLED 'Terriers' for, like their canine namesakes, they were small, dapper and extraordinarily agile, these remarkable creations of the small dapper (but by most accounts not so manoeuvrable) William Stroudley, Scots locomotive superintendent of the London, Brighton & South Coast Railway from 1870 to 1889, lay positive claim to the title 'most famous British tank locomotives'. Originally designed for use on the poorly laid and viciously graded East and South London Railways' lines, the 50 members constituting the Class A rapidly spread beyond these confines into the dominions of the LBSCR and later the SR, being found in every role open to such hardy, powerful little engines blessed in addition with unlimited route availability.

Outshopped from the LBSCR works at Brighton in seven batches from 1872 to 1880, all 50 'Terriers' were named after localities (not necessarily on LBSCR territory, or indeed served by any railway), and dressed overall in Stroudley's inimical 'improved engine green' livery enhanced by some of the most comprehensive lining-out witnessed on any British railway. The locomotives were renumbered in 1902 and their names discarded in 1905. The drawings show a 'Terrier' in as-built condition complete with wooden brake blocks and low-set buffers; also shown is the Westinghouse train brake gear not fitted at first but eventually installed throughout the class. Valve gear events were controlled by Stephenson's link motion acting on a steam chest cast between the steeply inclined (1 in 11) cylinders, and feedwater was fed to the boiler clack-valves via pumps worked off the crossheads.

Scrapping began in 1901, when the most venerable of the class had given approaching 30 years' service, and in following years several 'Terriers' were sold out of LBSCR service, to minor railways amongst other undertakings. The year 1911 saw rebuilding of the truncated LBSCR fleet with new boilers and extended smokeboxes, the engines then being reclassified A1x; only two examples survived thereafter in original guise, having been sold away before the conversion programme, and one remains today amongst the ten preserved 'Terriers' – an astonishingly high survival rate for a class completed more than a century ago, ample testimony not simply to their undeniably appealing character but also to Stroudley's design prowess.

No.10 *Sutton*, from the K&ESR, participates in the Morden (Northern Line) depot centenary celebrations on 3 November 1990.

Type:	0-6-0T
Cylinders:	2, 13" x 20" bore/stroke
Boiler Pressure:	140 lbs/sq in
Heating Surface:	518 sq ft
Grate Area:	10 sq ft
Water Capacity:	500 gallons
Mean Weight in Working Order:	24 tons
Number Built:	50, 1872-1880
Preserved:	10

Bulleid 'West Country/Battle of Britain' 4-6-2

APPOINTED CME to the Southern Railway during autumn 1937 in succession to Richard Maunsell, Oliver Bulleid had spent most of his working life as assistant to Nigel Gresley on first the GNR and then, following grouping, the LNER. Born in New Zealand of a Devonian family, Bulleid was trained on the Great Northern at Doncaster, under the eye of the redoubtable H.A.Ivatt (whose daughter he married); his long-term loyalty to the GNR might have seemed stultifying in any lesser person, however Bulleid's sublime technological instinct combined with his idiosyncratic character created an engineer of rare insight and inventiveness. The directors of the SR certainly did not invite Bulleid to assume the responsibilities of Chief Mechanical Engineer on mere speculation.

In his 11-year tenure Bulleid created basically four locomotive designs alone for the SR, yet their impact was enormous. The Q1-class goods 0-6-0s were extraordinary to look at, yet proved much the most powerful of their type; the unique 'Leader' concept was radical (too much so in the end); but the major achievements of his technical prowess and for which Bulleid is best remembered were the two 4-6-2 designs, the 'Merchant Navy' and 'West Country/Battle of Britain' or 'light' Pacifics.

Sharing a highly distinctive shape of boiler cladding – Bulleid would never countenance the description 'streamlined'; he insisted his Pacifics were 'airsmoothed' – that inevitably gave rise to nicknames ('Spam Can' is an enduring epithet) and many novel mechanical details, the two versions were hugely successful and acted without peer as the top link fleet in Southern England until the end of steam.

Whereas the 'Merchant Navy' class of 30 engines, introduced in 1941, were obviously express passenger machines (though Bulleid contrived against all the odds in the austere atmosphere of wartime Britain to have such grandiose engines built, by classifying them as 'mixed-traffic') the somewhat smaller Light Pacifics that followed four years later were deliberately scaled-down to work secondary routes in a true mixed-traffic role, though the emphasis was chiefly on passenger haulage. First off the line emerging from Brighton works in June 1945, liveried in Bulleid's favoured malachite green paintwork, another achievement since wartime black remained mandatory on all railways for many more months, was No.21C101 *Exeter*. This identification used the French style, where 2 = two leading axles, 1 = one trailing axle, and C = three coupled axles followed by the individual locomotive number.

The locomotives sported three cylinders, 'boxpok'-style wheels all round developed by Bulleid in association with steel manufacturers Firth Brown to give enhanced support for tyres over orthodox spoked wheels, and inside valve gear of Bulleid's own devising which comprised a chain-driven variation on Walschaert's linkage fully enclosed in a sealed case incorporating an oil bath. Also provided was a Lemaître multiple blastpipe arrangement with wide chimney

'Battle of Britain' No.34109 *Sir Trafford Leigh-Mallory* poses for the camera at Ilfracombe (commemorated by 34017) in June 1960.

No.34055 *Fighter Pilot* has an M7 for company on Bournemouth Central shed on 28 June 1961. PHOTOGRAPH: DOUGLAS DOHERTY.

that Bulleid had previously applied to older SR classes with considerable success (notably the 'Lord Nelson' 4-6-0s, whose performance was transformed thereby, in concert with redesigned front ends) and a well thought-out cab behind the 'airsmoothed' casing. Thus the Light Pacifics proved powerful, free-steaming and very adaptable engines, if – initially at least and not surprisingly given so much innovatory equipment – cursed with plentiful teething troubles to boot.

Named after habitations and geographical features to be found in their intended area of service, 66 engines were classified 'West Country' (building was shared between Brighton and Eastleigh from 1945 to 1950); almost contemporaneously and in a typically Southern blaze of publicity, capitalising on an event then still fresh, a further 44 locomotives were named after RAF personalities, places, squadrons and aircraft involved in the Battle of Britain of summer 1940. Hence the famous 'Battle of Britain' sub-class, which in all other respects was identical with the 'West Country' Pacifics: building took place in 1946-51 at the ex-LBSCR erecting shops at Brighton. Of the combined total, 40 were outshopped under the aegis of BR after nationalisation. Whilst the definitive shape of the boiler casing had been defined by the time of their outshopping, the Light Pacifics were subjected to considerable smoke-deflector and front-end casing modifications in arriving at the optimum smoke-lifting format; cabs were quickly altered since the original design provided unacceptably minute and virtually useless front windows – the guise shown in the drawings is that fitted originally to most BR engines and retroactively to all 'BB'/'WC' 4-6-2s; the wedge-shaped front window has a demonstrably large and effective surface area.

As originally built, the classes gave sterling service so long as frequent and efficient maintenance was observed, but they were not easy to drive and required sympathetic handling from footplate crews. Heavy coal consumption and a distinct proneness for slipping when starting were the principal penalties of an excellent overall performance. Ultimately the complex mechanical arrangements hid high operating costs (for example, in time the valve gear, which had been designed in the manner described in order to squeeze into the confined space between the frames occupied by the central cylinder and the bulbous tapered boiler, not only leaked oil but suffered chain stretch that upset valve timing) caused BR to undertake a draconian programme of rebuilding. Whereas all 'Merchant Navy' 4-6-2s were so dealt with, 50 of the 110 Light Pacifics escaped rebuilding, for the programme was curtailed owing to the imminent withdrawal of steam traction. Withdrawals were enacted between 1963 and 1967, from which no fewer than ten unrebuilt 'West Country' and 'Battle of Britain' Pacifics have been rescued for preservation.

Notes on the drawings

These illustrate a representative Bulleid Light Pacific complete with final cab style; the lines on the boiler casing depict the major panels involved in its construction (but by no means all panels involved), secured by rivets or bolts of far too small a size to be displayed adequately in 4mm scale. Note the effective 'clasp' braking system, the tender brakes operated unusually from the rear of the frames (the wheels were Bulleid-Firth-Brown boxpok too). For once the boiler pitch is purely academic; note that the smokebox door axis does not correspond with it. The electric lamp system was initial equipment but apparently little-used (the turbo generator for same is lodged beneath the cab), the conventional brackets atop the lamps being preferred. Not easily visible is the frame-mounted splasher over the rear bogie wheel, protecting the piston rod and slide-bar. The dashed lines on the tender profile outline the coal area, tank top, filler and air reservoirs.

I have included two sets of nameplates and badges,

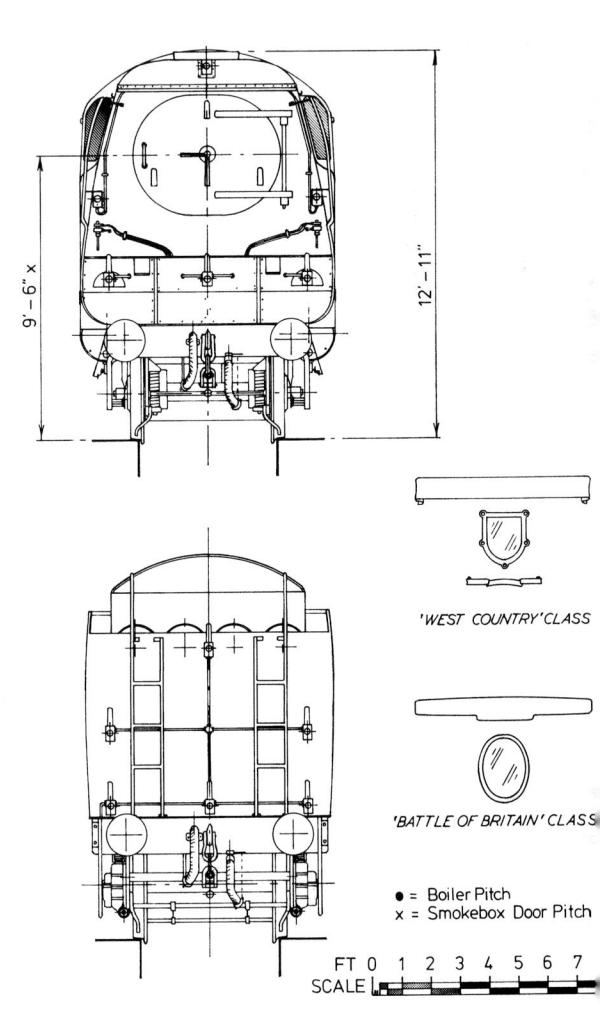

LEFT: closeup of the nameplate from 'Battle of Britiain' series No.34054. Family or Squadron crests were carried on 'BB's; town or county crests where applicable/available were carried on the 'WC's.

RIGHT: a comparison between original and rebuilt Light Pacifics at the London end of Bournemouth Central on 3 July 1964. Passing through the centre roads with an Up Channel Islands boat train is rebuild No.34093 *Saunton*; awaiting the right-away with the 5.10pm to Waterloo is No.34038 *Lynton*.
PHOTOGRAPHS: DOUGLAS DOHERTY.

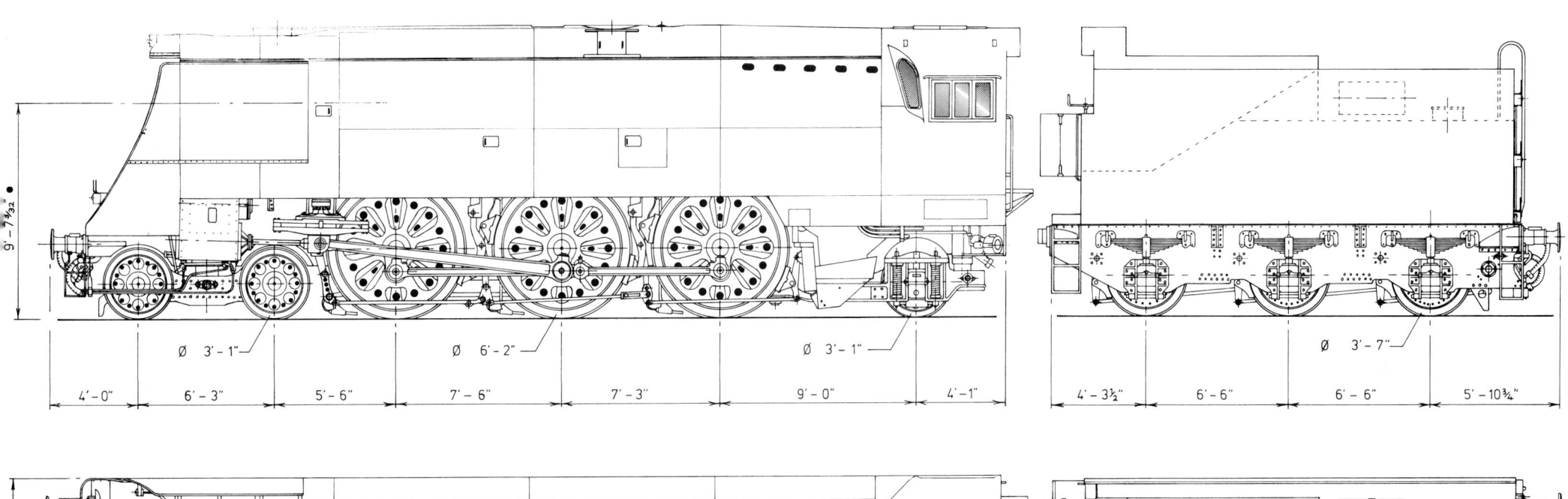

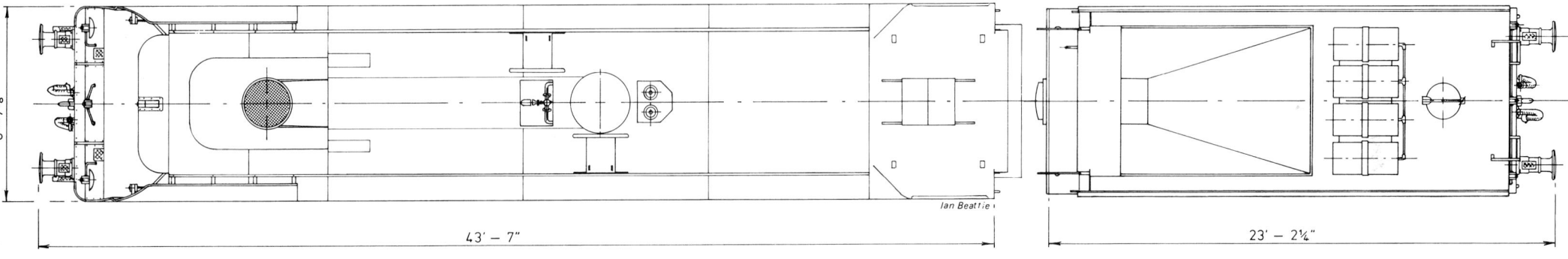

corresponding to the two classes: the nameplates varied in length according to the name they carrried so those shown are representative only. On 'West Country' engines the class name was found in the small scroll-like plate beneath the badge, and on 'Battle of Britain' 4-6-2s the class name was placed on the main nameplate below the individual name.

Type:	Passenger Locomotive
Overall Length:	67'4¾"
Cylinders:	3, 16⅜" x 24" bore/stroke
Boiler Pressure:	280 lbs/sq in
Heating Surface:	2667 sq ft
Grate Area:	38.25 sq ft
Tractive Effort:	31000 lbs
Mean Weight in Working Order:	128 tons 12 cwt
Coal Capacity:	5 tons
Water Capacity:	4500 gallons
Number Built:	110, 1945-51
Preserved:	10 (in unrebuilt form)

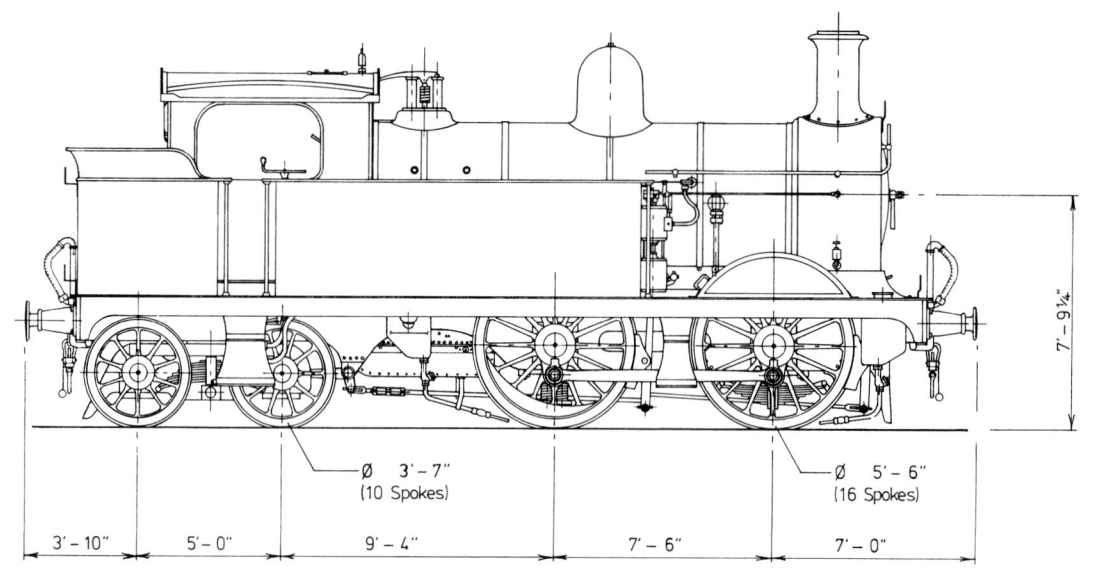

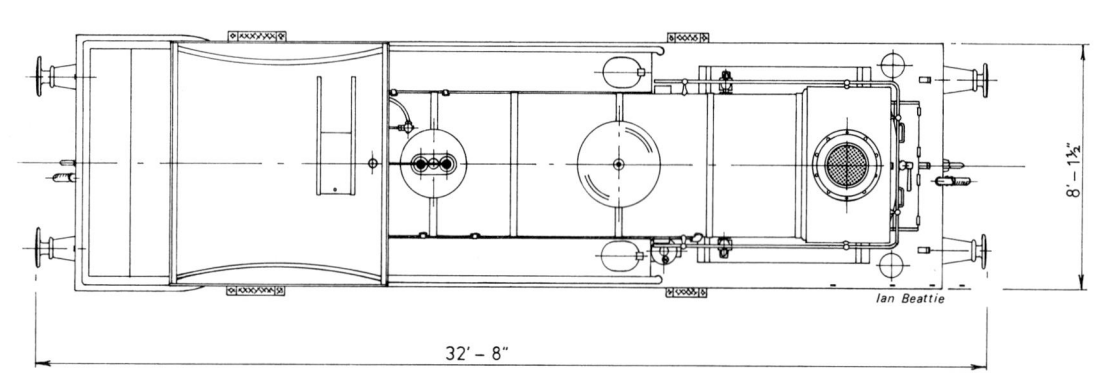

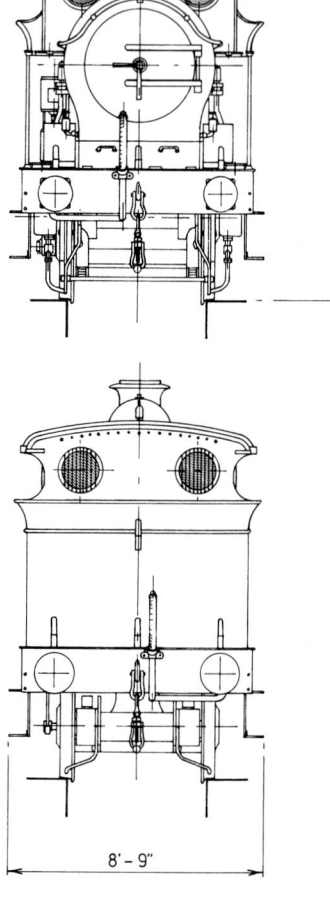

SECR H Class 0-4-4T

LOCOMOTIVE Superintendent to the South Eastern & Chatham Railways Management Committee from 1898, Harry Wainwright was by all accounts a flamboyant man with a strong character; yet after his resignation his staff and those with whom he had come into contact – for instance train crews – remembered curiously little of his personality.

Whilst not wielding the influence of say, Dugald Drummond, Wainwright undoubtedly contributed crucially to the success story of the SECR. As has been recounted previously in this series (see RM May 1984, Class D 4-4-0) the SECR was not a single entity, rather a working partnership of two companies, the South Eastern and the London, Chatham & Dover Railways, whose intense rivalry over similar and often identical routes in South London and the Kent area contrived to ruin each other, financially and in reputation, towards the end of the Victorian age.

Wainwright modernised the locomotive and rolling stock fleets by providing a succession of excellent and thoroughly researched designs that helped transform the twin companies' former public notoriety into a model of reliability and punctuality. But he resigned in 1913, ostensibly for health reasons though more probably due to personality clashes. The momentum of his first years as superintendent had stagnated, to the point where the need for more engines and stock became desperate: the SECR Board turned to Inchicore in Ireland and persuaded the highly able Richard Maunsell to replace Wainwright. But that's another story.

One of the most effective of Wainwright's manifold designs was the ubiquitous H Class four-coupled tank engine, which typically of such mundane little workhorses went about their business with little glamour yet with an enviable purposefulness and chronometrical reliability for nigh on 60 years. Their versatility is witnessed by the sheer numbers involved: 66 were outshopped from the SECR works at Ashford in numerous batches from 1904 beyond Wainwright's era into 1915 (perhaps apocryphal, it is said that on his appointment in Wainwright's stead Maunsell discovered that though 66 had been commissioned only 64 were on the engine roster, the last having been outshopped in 1911: he insisted that the complete order be fulfilled as envisaged).

Numbered seemingly at random, the SECR 0-4-4Ts were amongst the best of their type, albeit unpopular with the Board of Trade for a propensity towards instability (much more apparent than proven), and as their weight shows were in fact quite large, substantial machines. Indeed they were surprisingly similar in power and overall size to the contemporary LSWR M7 Class 0-4-4Ts (see RM June 1982 *[and overleaf – Ed.]*), in comparison with which some knowledgeable commentators of the period favoured Wainwright's design. In SECR and SR days most Class H engines worked in the London suburban area on commuter trains though they were common throughout the SECR region; in later years they wandered far beyond their erstwhile boundaries to work push-pull trains on branch lines and empty coaching stock duties at major stations.

Driven from the right hand side of the curiously shaped cab – to throw off rainwater away from the crew – all engines were fitted with vacuum brakes in accordance with their *metier*, passenger working; additional air braking was installed on 13 engines, on which the Westinghouse pump nestled against the left front tank plate, matching the steam-reverser on the right hand side. In SECR times a select few were equipped for push-pull work, however they proved so useful on suburban traffic that the equipment was quickly removed and the duties rostered to 0-6-0Ts in lieu. In BR days many of the H Class tanks were assigned to push-pull traffic and the necessary fittings were installed, as shown in one of the photos. Their inside cylinders were controlled by Stephenson's link motion, and although not evident from outside the smokeboxes contained Stone's patent spark-arresting device. Two engines were scrapped in 1944, the remainder passing into BR hands on nationalisation: general withdrawal took place between 1951 and 1964, the final representative of this sturdy and hardworking class being preserved. In its metamorphosis as SECR No.263, this fine locomotive is part of the very catholic Bluebell Railway collection.

Notes on the drawings
These depict a typical Class H 0-4-4T in pre-Grouping condition: little real outward change was evidenced from outshopping to scrapping in most instances. Note the unusual transverse-opening cab roof vent, the feedwater clack valves set below the boiler centre-line, and different sizes of buffer heads front and rear (the rear being larger to obviate any chance of buffer locking: in SR years and beyond the engines appear to have been refitted with equally-sized buffers all round).

Type:	Suburban Passenger Tank
Cylinders:	2, 18" x 26" bore/stroke
Boiler Pressure:	160 lbs/sq in
Heating Surface:	1104.26 sq ft
Grate Area:	16.66 sq ft
Tractive Effort:	16800 lbs
Mean Weight in Working Order:	53 tons 18 cwt
Coal Capacity:	2¼ tons
Water Capacity:	1200 gallons
Number Built:	66, 1904-15
Preserved:	1

TOP RIGHT: No.31306 poses with another H on Bricklayers Arms shed circa 1957. PHOTO: THE LATE LES PICKERING, PER BOB BROWN.

RIGHT: push-pull fitted No.31193 in the bay at Maidstone West with a Tonbridge train on 17 March 1956. PHOTO: PHILIP KELLEY.

LSWR M7 0-4-4T

AT THE TIME Dugald Drummond laid down plans for the M7 on the London & South Western Railway, the use of the 0-4-4 wheel arrangement for passenger tank locomotives was still comparatively novel. During the 1880s Stroudley's 'Gladstone' class of 0-4-2s had demonstrated just how stable were locomotives sporting large leading coupled wheels at speed – in the conditions then prevailing – and the neighbouring LSWR had followed this lead by providing two classes of 0-4-4T (O2 and T1) for suburban work off the drawing board of locomotive superintendent William Adams, late of the GER.

The undoubted success of this format in LSWR usage prompted what is often regarded, alongside his 'Greyhound' 4-4-0s, as Drummond's finest work. In any event it was unquestionably his first for the Company. Like so many extremely able railway engineers, Drummond was an uncompromising Scot, with an austere but fair-minded disposition who nevertheless evoked steadfast loyalty from his superficially cowed subordinates.

Fundamentally the design of the M7 sprang from and was an enlarged version of Adams' T1 0-4-4T, yet leavened by Drummond's previous experience with his 0-4-4Ts for the CR and NBR respectively. Besides being his initial LSWR engine Drummond introduced a left-hand driving position on to the traditionally right-hand orientated LSWR, a move unpopular at first but eventually accepted by crews in the light of the M7's tidy and reliable performance characteristics.

Intended for suburban and secondary line passenger working particularly in and around London, the M7s in due course became widely dispersed throughout the LSWR and thereafter the SR dominions. They worked alongside the smaller, lighter (47-ton) Class O2 0-4-4Ts and the precursive T1s, being joined in SR days by ex-SECR Class H 0-4-4Ts of similar size and weight.

A measure of the M7's utility is indicated by the number outshopped and by the protracted period of production, during which time little in the way of modification was needed: 105, between 1897 and 1911. Early on in the M7's collective career, variations were wrought in water injection equipment. Drummond specified his own, patented system of feedwater heater (displayed in the drawing, though more often found on the RH side of the locomotive) and pump, which were replaced by straightforward injectors and boiler-side clack valves as shown in the photograph of No.30039.

Still in LSWR days, several M7s were modified by fitting of rejigged smokeboxes accompanied by removal of the leading, smokebox-flanking sand boxes. Simultaneously a number of these altered engines were shortened by 1'3" in the front overhang, ie. the distance from front buffer face to the leading wheel centreline, the overall length being thus adjusted to 35'0".

In July 1921 No.126 was adapted by Drummond's successor as CME (the title had changed during Drummond's incumbency) Robert Urie by installation of a standard Eastleigh superheater. This in turn necessitated an elongated smokebox that spoiled the hitherto trim contours of the original engine, and caused an over-heavy front end. A rear-slung counterbalance weight was added which then made the engine too heavy for suburban work – a Catch-22 situation exacerbated by nil returns from the superheater tests. No.126 was withdrawn from service in 1937 and stored.

In general the M7 0-4-4Ts were regarded as thoroughly practical, willing and well-found workhorses nicely suited to passenger operation over lesser routes. In later SR years and under BR management a considerable proportion of the M7 roster was assigned to branches in the South-West where the engines' sure-footedness and stable riding ameliorated the often severe gradients and curves of branch lines thereabouts.

Two single events brought public fame, however temporary, to the otherwise unremarked 0-4-4Ts. In 1923 No.58 was selected to haul the Duke and Duchess of York, later TM King George VI and Queen Elizabeth, on the first stage of their honeymoon journey, from Waterloo to Bookham.

By contrast No.672 aroused instant attention at Waterloo in 1948 by disappearing suddenly and without warning down a lift shaft connecting the terminus to the underground Waterloo & City Line. The crew leapt to safety but the unfortunate locomotive proved irrecoverable and was therefore cut up in situ.

ABOVE: pictured 'at home' on the ashpits of Fratton shed, Portsmouth (70F), M7 No.30039 poses for its portrait on 10 May 1959.

RIGHT: No.30132, one of the converted batch *sans* wingplates and above-board sandboxes, waits on Reading Southern shed on 23 April 1961, with tenders of Maunsell Moguls for company. PHOTOGRAPHS: PHILIP J. KELLEY.

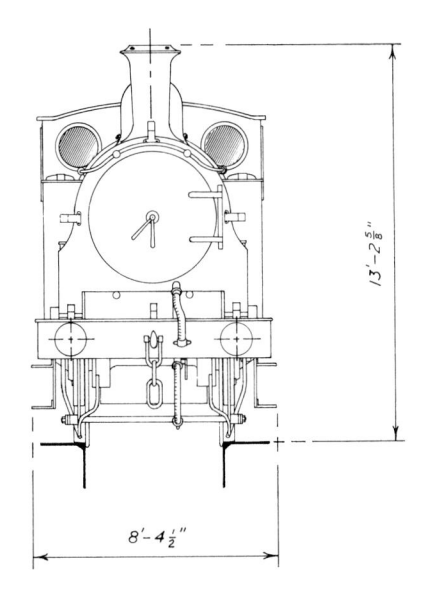

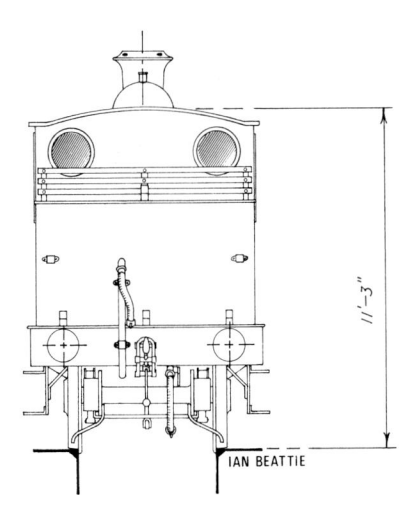

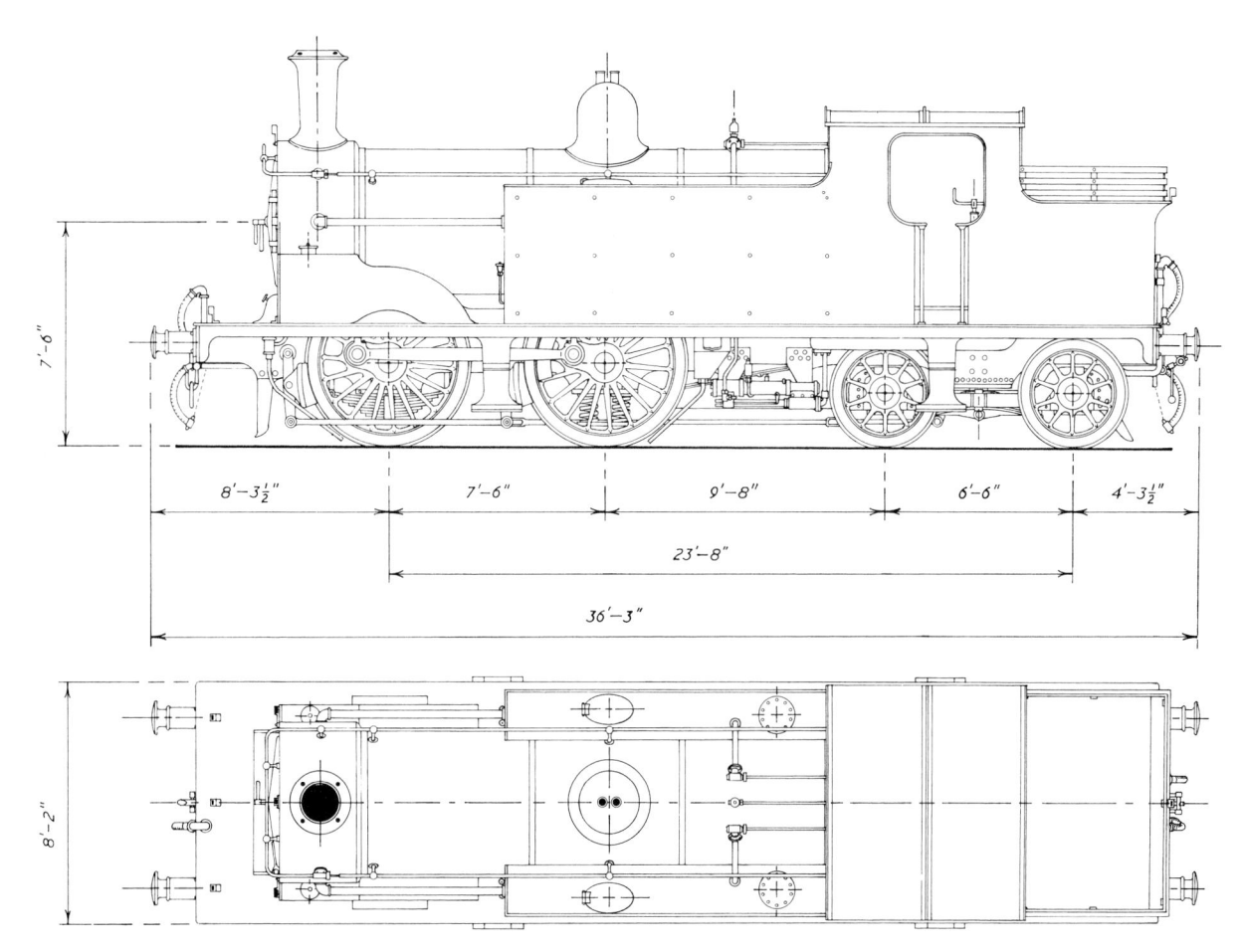

This was the first of the class to be scrapped, but its 104 *confrères* followed suit between 1957 and 1964, with two surviving for posterity.

Type:	0-4-4T
Coupled Wheels:	5'7" dia. 18 spokes
Bogie Wheels:	3'7" dia. 10 spokes
Cylinders:	2, 18½" x 26" bore/stroke
Boiler Pressure:	175 lbs.sq.in.
Heating Surface:	1191 sq.ft.
Grate Area:	20.35 sq.ft.
Water Capacity:	1300 gallons
Coal Capacity:	3 tons
Mean Weight in Working Order:	60 tons 4 cwt
Nominal Tractive Effort:	19750 lbs.
Number Built:	105, 1897-1911
Preserved:	2

First of the 1932 build, Class V No.30910 *Merchant Taylors* stands serenely exuding power and grace at Newhaven, 12 April 1958.

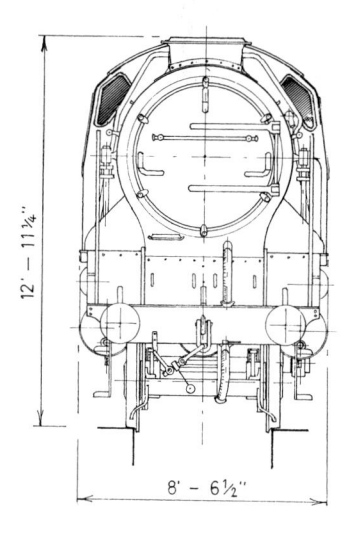

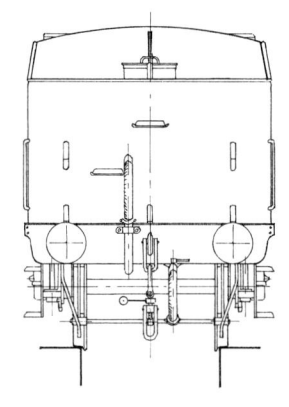

Class V 'Schools' 4-4-0

THE SEVENTH son of a Dublin solicitor, Richard Edward Lloyd Maunsell (1868-1944) forged for himself a brilliant career as a locomotive engineer *par exellence* which culminated in his tenure as Chief Mechanical Engineer of the newly formed Southern Railway in 1923, a post he held with characteristic flair until retirement in October 1937. Amongst the many superb designs with which his name is indelibly associated one in particular, the Class V 'Schools' 4-4-0, is generally regarded as Maunsell's masterpiece.

Not only did this 4-4-0 exceed its operating brief, it was exceedingly popular with engine crews, who were legendarily quick to condemn any machine that exhibited the minutest shortcoming. It was also the heaviest, most powerful, last (excepting the VS Class for the GNRI) and arguably most successful of its type in Britain – a vivid statement bearing in mind that British railways were virtually ruled by 4-4-0s for decades. Yet the 'Schools' story began as a classic compromise.

Several routes in the SR's busy Eastern section (comprising the former SECR domain) were restricted as to width of stock, none more so than the line between Tonbridge and Hastings which was limited to an absolute outside measurement of 8'6½" by numerous ultra-narrow tunnels thereon.

This precluded the use of premium express machines such as 'King Arthur' and 'Lord Nelson' 4-6-0s, the usual motive power being 4-4-0s of sundry antiquity and competence within this area of considerable and moreover increasing railborne activity. In consequence a traffic order for a power unit capable of working 400-ton trains at an average speed of 55mph and built within the strictures of the Hastings line was outlined to Maunsell in the mid-to-late 1920s, the time the 'Lord Nelsons' were abuilding (see RM February 1993).

Maunsell's riposte to this dichotomous set of requirements was inspired. He devised a sturdy yet comparatively long 4-4-0 frame into which was worked 3 cylinders, fed by a shortened 'King Arthur' boiler that in turn was allied to a round-topped firebox for a low cab height. Many components were common to the 'Lord Nelsons', including wheels, cylinders and their individual sets of Walschaert's motion, and the bogie. Compact 6-wheel tenders sported sloping side panels matching those of the cabs in meeting the Hastings loading gauge.

The outcome was triumphant. From the outset the engines performed superbly, not simply on ex-SECR routes but on express haulage over tracks the preserve of 'Nelsons' and later the Bulleid Pacifics. All 40 4-4-0s were outshopped from the principal SR erecting shops at Eastleigh, near Southampton, with the initial 10 emerging in 1930 and numbered 900-909, the remainder following in batches between 1932 and 1935 and given the numbers 910-939. In a felicitous campaign by the SR publicity department the new engines were named for public schools (by no means all in the SR empire), with most naming ceremonies being arranged at the relevant schools for maximum effect.

Oliver Bulleid succeeded Maunsell as CME of the Southern network, and in 1938 instituted experiments with Lemaître multijet blastpipes and altered valve porting; 3 'Schools' engines were thus adapted, fitted with exceptionally ugly plain chimneys at first. Results were reasonable enough to cause a wholesale conversion of the class to this format (fortunately including a much more more stylish built-up, lipped stack), however the arrival of war in September 1939 halted the process after 20 engines had undergone the refit. After the war a rethink concluded that the expense no longer warranted conversion and the unmodified 4-4-0s worked out their careers without change in this respect.

On Nationalisation in 1948 the Southern Region of BR came into being; the 'Schools' were renumbered by adding 30000 to their SR identities. In time they were repainted into BR lined express green from Bulleid's bright malachite livery (they were originally outshopped in Maunsell's lined olive green) and continued

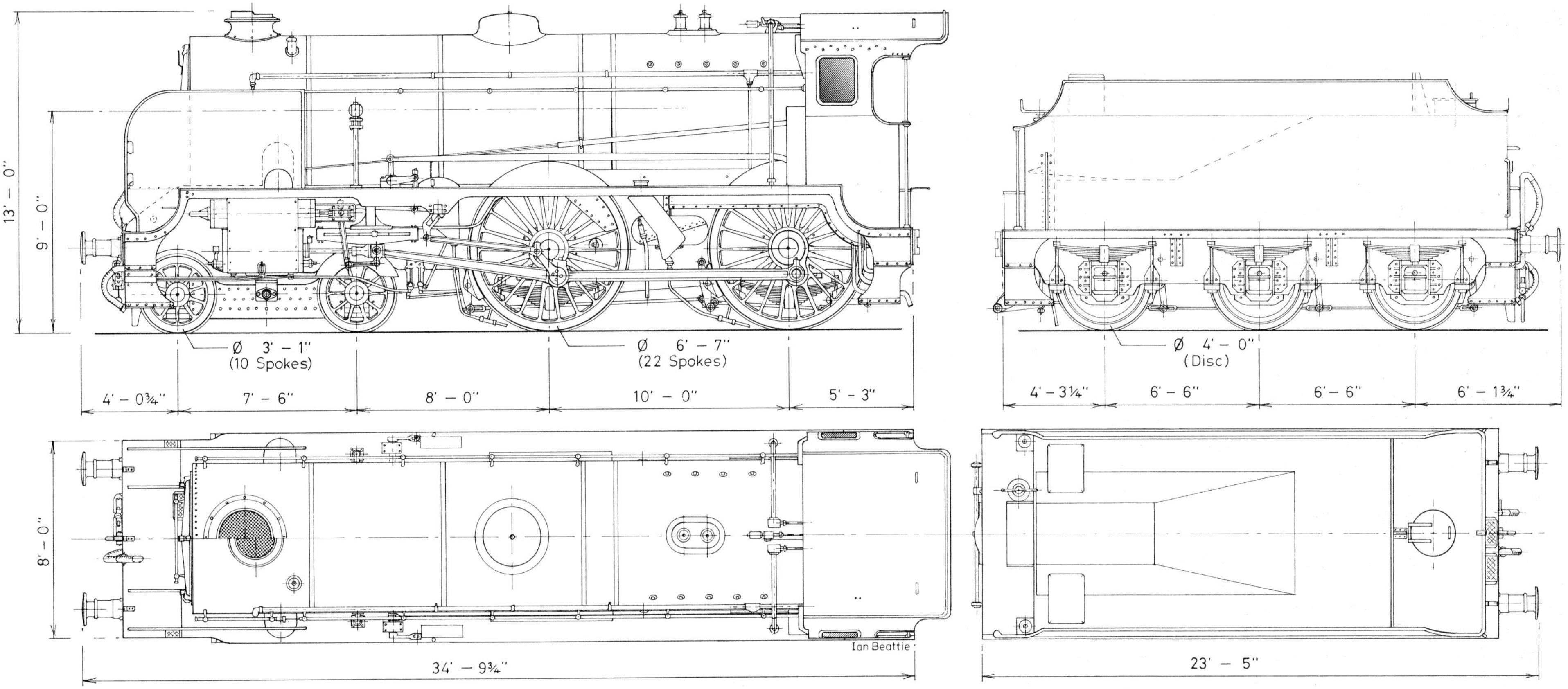

to render lively account wherever and on whatever kind of work they were allotted. Mass withdrawal of the class was enacted in 1961-62 as electrification and the diesel revolution took hold with a vengeance on the SR; fortunately 3 of these powerful, dependable and elegant 4-4-0s were rescued for preservation – strangely all from the 1934 batch.

Notes on the drawings

The views here represent overall a typical 'Schools', however it should be noted that the first ten engines of the class – of 1930 vintage – exhibited some divergences in fitments compared with the later builds. These chiefly comprise outshopping less smoke deflectors (fitted retroactively, and when new to the later batches), a V-shaped bogie sideframe illustrated here in view A and identical to that of 'Lord Nelson' 4-6-0s, superseded by a "horizontal" style of frame shown in the main side elevation. Another important item was the 'low-window' cabside style found on the first engines, see part-view B.

The very large-diameter chimney added to Lemaître-fitted 'Schools' is depicted in full in the front view (note loss of snifting valves, excised by Bulleid) and in a 'split' plan view alongside the standard stack for comparison (the 'Bulleid' chimney is positioned much further forward on the smokebox). The standard stack is present in the side elevation, which also demonstrates that it sat somewhat taller than its successor.

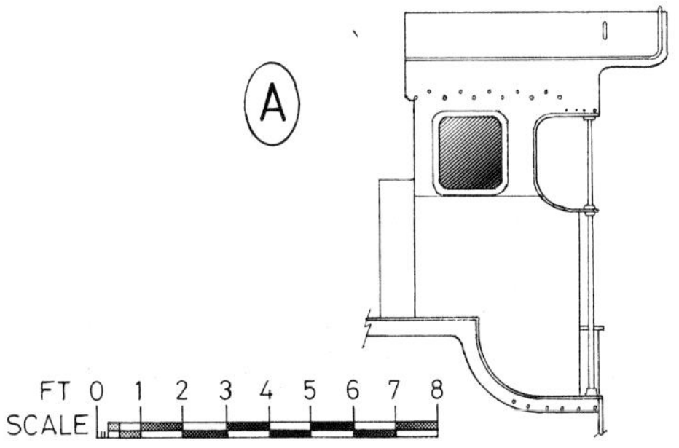

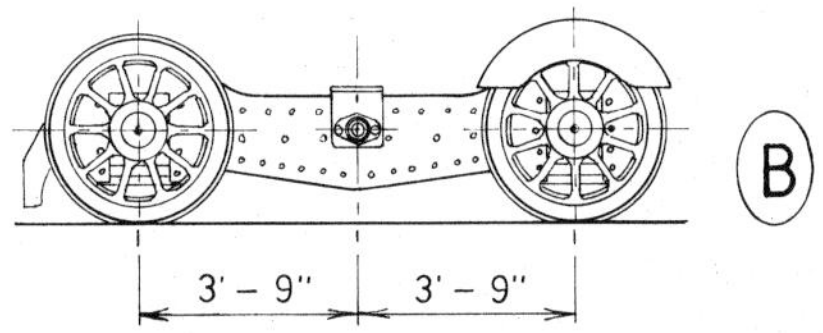

Finally on the locomotive, visors were added to both front cab spectacles (shielding the latter against falling soot in tunnels) but which were absent on Nos.900-909.

The tender herewith is that normally attached to the 'Schools', with the proviso that many featured 12-spoked wheels (of the same diameter) in lieu of the disc variety shown; a unique raised-sided, self-trimming tender ran with No.932 and latterly with No.30905; and on occasion a 'Schools' was to be found hauling a Maunsell/Urie bogie tender.

Type:	Express Passenger
Overall Length:	58'9¾"
Cylinders:	3, 16½" x 26" bore/stroke
Boiler Pressure:	220 lbs/sq in
Heating Surface:	2049 sq ft
Grate Area:	28.3 sq ft
Tractive Effort:	25130 lbs
Mean Weight in Working Order:	109 tons 10 cwt
Coal Capacity:	5 tons
Water Capacity:	4000 gallons
Number Built:	40, 1930-35
Preserved:	3

Bulleid 'Leader' 0-6-6-0T

ARGUABLY the most extraordinary and certainly the most revolutionary steam locomotive ever to hit British rails, the celebrated 'Leader' project emanated from the fertile mind of Oliver Vaughan Snell Bulleid, CME to the Southern Railway from 1938 and previously assistant to Sir Nigel Gresley on the GNR and LNER.

That Bulleid evinced idiosyncratic notions of loco design was self evident in his ugly but immensely powerful Q1 0-6-0 and the magnificent if flawed 'Merchant Navy' and lightweight Pacifics, however even in comparison with these astoundingly individual products his 'Leader' concept was simply, unbeatably unique. Bulleid had reconsidered the principles and desiderata of mixed-traffic engine construction and use from the ground up and concluded that a heavy tank loco, having a top speed of 90mph and able to cover most SR lines, together with its full weight available for adhesion plus a twin-cab format to obviate wasteful turning, with lower maintenance demands and hence greater availability than hitherto generally found, was the ultimate answer.

Bulleid's powers of persuasion must have been formidable, for in 1946, a time of severe austerity and depletion due to the recently concluded world war, the SR Board authorised the construction of five such tank locos (a further thirty were projected to complete the class); in view of the sheer plethora of engineering novelty involved this was a courageous decision indeed, although several preliminary experiments into sundry aspects of the design had been more or less successfully conducted employing conventional revenue-earning locos as guinea pigs. The first 'Leader', No.36001, emerged from Brighton works in June 1949 and trials commenced.

Ostensibly akin to a diesel locomotive, its slab-sided body hid a reasonably orthodox boiler that fed steam to two three-axle bogies, each containing three cylinders controlled by sleeve valves, the associated Walschaert's valve motion – adapted by Bulleid and much as fitted to his 4-6-2s – being chain-driven from the central bogie axle onto which all three pistons drove. Coupling to the outer axles was made via a unique asymmetrical chain-driven arrangement, which whilst not indescribable (!) is nevertheless more helpfully explained by examination of the drawing herewith. Wheels were of Boxpok style developed by Bulleid in co-operation with the steel manufacturers Firth Brown of Sheffield, of the same size as used on the Q1 Class. All moving parts between the bogie frames were enclosed on oil baths, in the (unfulfilled) quest for lower servicing requirements and thus improved availability.

Shortly after No.36001 was outshopped Bulleid retired; he was 67, beyond statutory retirement age, but more importantly his free spirit was alien to the precepts of the newly nationalised BR; he went on to design a turf-burning engine for the CIE. Intensive trials of the 'Leader' were undertaken between frequent bouts of works attention, for teething problems were legion – though whether initially greater than expected for such a radical design is a matter for conjecture – which unfortunately multiplied stratospherically as time passed, to the point where the authorities were compelled to call a halt to the ever-mounting drain on funds that constant repairs to No.36001 imposed. In November 1949 work was ordered to cease on the remaining four 'Leaders' under construction at Brighton. At this time the second engine was within two days of completion and the third well advanced (assembly of the remaining two had not begun); the partially-finished machines were put in storage for several months before being cut up.

So unreliable had No.36001 become by this stage that Brighton works gave up the ghost and the engine transferred to Eastleigh in mid-1950 for a fresh approach. The famous ex-NER dynamometer coach was borrowed and a series of test runs instituted. These were a failure since 'Leader' *inter alia* steamed poorly, problems arose with the firebox and a crank axle fractured (that from the stillborn No.36002 was substituted but also broke – the fault was attributed to the

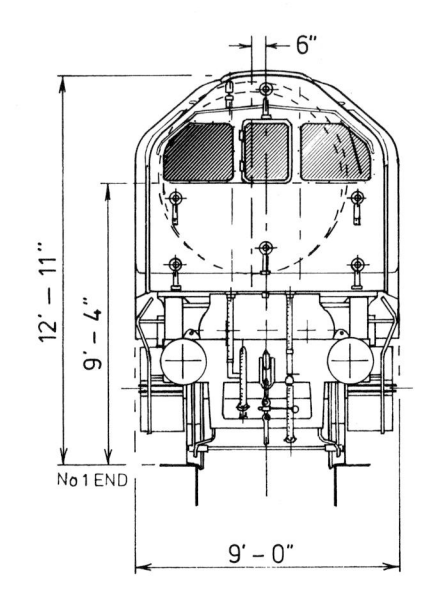

Type:	Mixed Traffic
Cylinders:	6, 12¼" x 15" bore/stroke
Boiler Pressure:	280 lbs/sq in
Heating Surface:	2841 sq ft
Grate Area:	43 sq ft
Tractive Effort:	26336 lbs
Mean Weight in Working Order:	130 tons 10 cwt
Coal Capacity:	4 tons
Water Capacity:	4000 gallons
Number Built:	3, 1949 (see text)
Preserved:	None

In this rare and historic photo, Norman Browne captured 'Leader' No.36001 in motion, undergoing trials whilst attached to the veteran ex-NER dynamometer coach and passing under the signal gantry at the southern end of Eastleigh station, on 23 August 1950, the engine sporting its habitual lined 'works grey' livery. PHOTOGRAPH: NORMAN BROWNE.

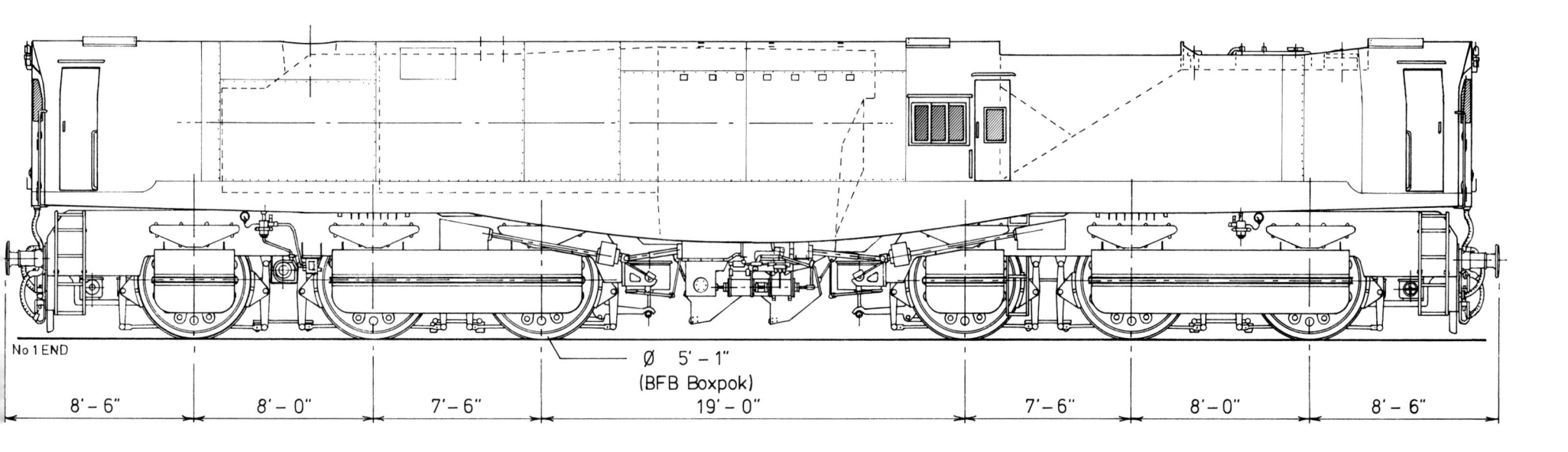

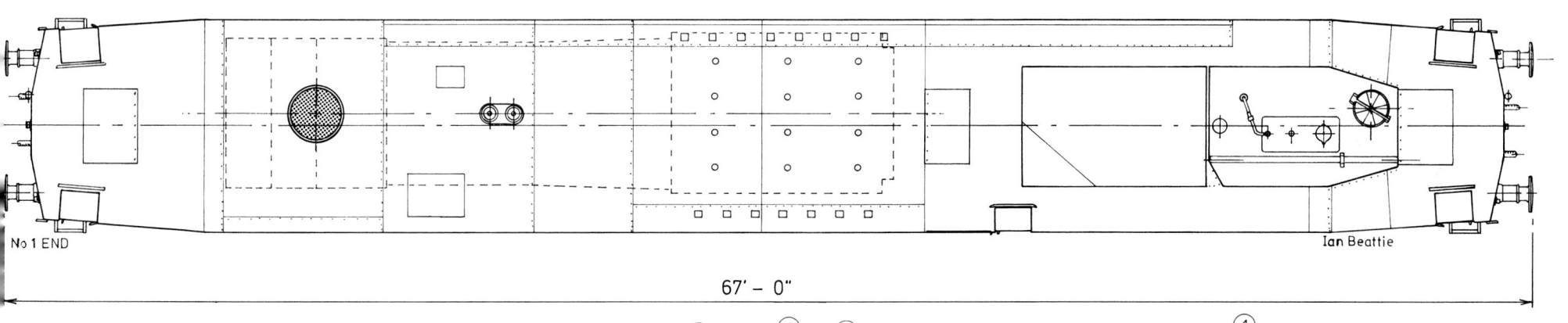

asymmetric drive). The engine proved grotesquely overweight, far beyond its designed weight ceiling and obviating any minor or branch line work had success attended it in other respects; the fireman's isolated work station was unpopular, both with the locomen's trade union and as a safety measure – a loco crew was a team at base – and unbearably hot to boot. Further testing became ever more desultory until in November 1950 the authorities finally ceded total defeat and No.36001 was withdrawn: it was scrapped at Eastleigh in 1951. So ended a brave but ultimately too radical an idea, yet the annals of British steam would have been very much the poorer had the 'Leader' 0-6-6-0T never existed.

Notes on the drawings

The opposite side of the loco to that shown is substantially similar but lacks the windows and door to the fireman's station shown here. Note that the boiler, indicated by dashed lines, is offset by 6" from the loco's longitudinal centreline (to provide corridor access between cabs), the cause of major balancing problems only partially overcome by selective ballasting.

The dashed outlines to the right of the fireman's station denote the coal bunker, tank breather, filler and TIA water treatment container. No.2 end is identical to No.1 except that the whistle and screen wiper are transposed (see plan view). The firebox washout access holes in the body were covered by individual sliding shutters.

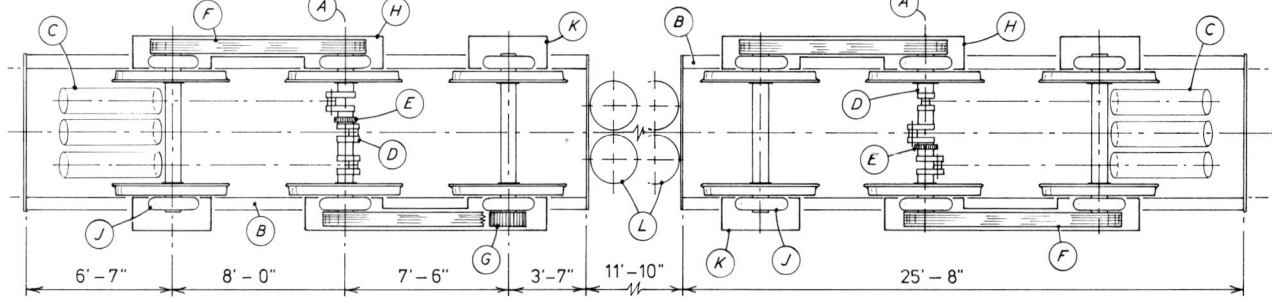

A – Bogie Pivot Line
B – Bogie Frame
C – Cylinders (inclined 1 in 8)
D – Crank Axle
E – Valve Motion Drive Sprocket
F – Drive Chain
G – Drive Sprocket
H – Chain Cover
J – Axlebox
K – Axlebox Cover
L – Brake Cylinders

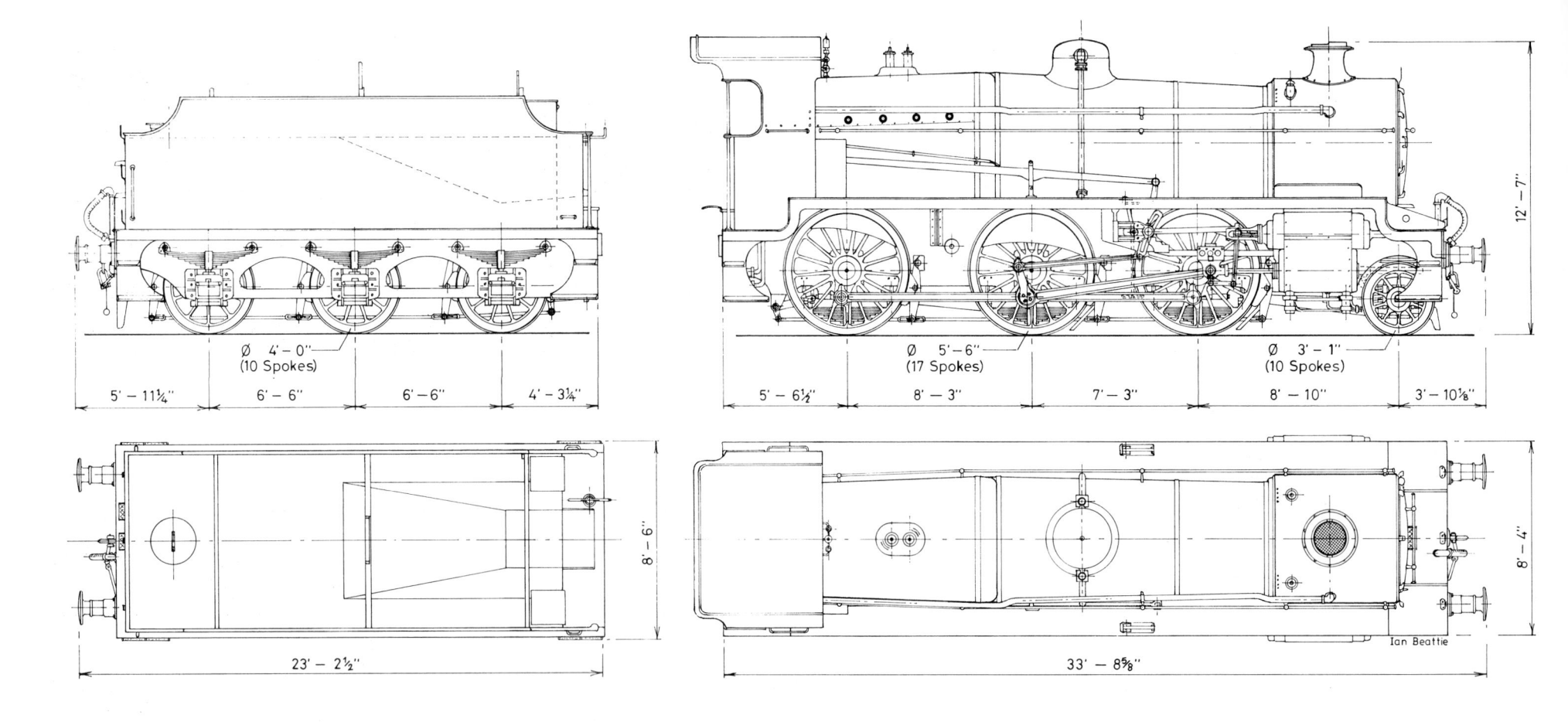

Maunsell N and N1 Class 2-6-0

WHILST generally considered a Southern Railway locomotive the N Class Mogul was in fact a South Eastern & Chatham Railway product with crucial input via the GWR. This thoroughly versatile mixed-traffic design was initiated before the Great War by SEC chief engineer Richard Maunsell, in response to the requirement for a sufficiently powerful machine to alleviate the extensive – and expensive – practice of double-heading.

The Swindon connection occurred with the arrival of Harry Holcroft at Ashford, Kent; a wholehearted Great Western man and a brilliant engineer still not given his rightful due, Holcroft brought the GW attributes of tapered boiler and long-lap valves (amongst others) to the SEC headquarters, with the first fruits apparent on the new Mogul. Delayed by wartime exigencies, the prototype emerged in July 1917, attired in the then customary grey livery.

Destined to remain the sole example for almost 3 years, 2-6-0 No.810 underwent much testing and experimentation, chiefly on the freight workings for which the design was essentially proposed. The exceptional competence and utility of the Mogul became widely recognised on the commissioning of 15 engines, numbered chronologically to 825, up to the point of Grouping in January 1923. An experimental exception was made in the case of No.822, which was equipped with 3 cylinders, the central cylinder being controlled by Holcroft's conjugated valve motion derived from the outside-mounted sets of Walschaert's gear.

The ubiquity of the Mogul prototype had meanwhile attracted Government notice. The design was selected for replication at the Woolwich Arsenal, the huge ordnance manufactory whose workforce, following the hectic war years of intensive armaments production, was facing redundancy; the plan envisaged initial assembly of 100 locomotives from brought-in sets of parts. All this presupposed the expected nationalisation of Britain's railways (in which the 2-6-0s would form a standard class), however in the event the act of Grouping was substituted in lieu and, none of the emergent Groups expressing interest in acquiring the Moguls, production at Woolwich ceased in 1922.

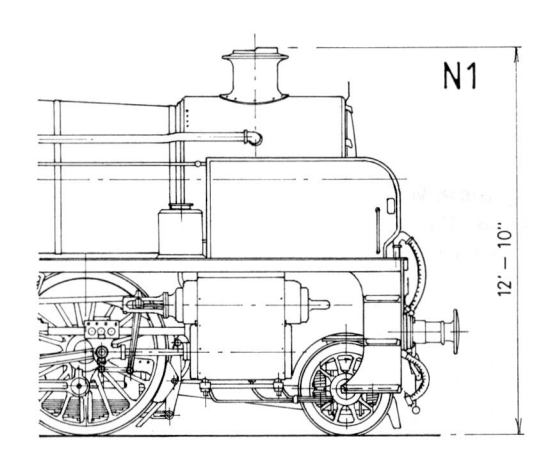

The newly formed SR Group purchased therefrom at bargain rates parts for 50 2-6-0s, which were duly erected at Ashford in 1924 and 1925 – the resulting N Class Moguls were numbered 826-875 and were virtually indistinguishable from the SECR-built versions.

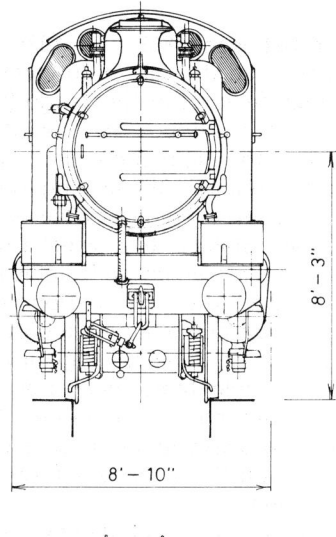

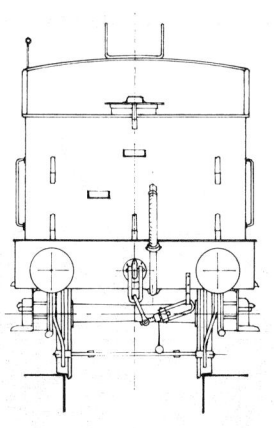

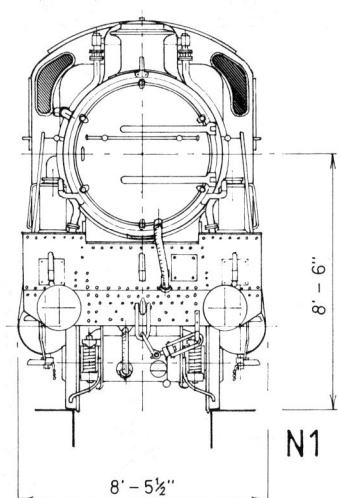

derived right-hand driving of their forebears. Used throughout the SR system and all types of duty from semi-fast passenger to pick-up goods, the ubiquitous Ns were particularly remarkable in the west of England, where their all-pervading usefulness was only sapped (but certainly not negated) by Bulleid's amazing Light Pacifics *[see RM April 1989 and elsewhere in the volume – Ed.]* from the late 1940s onwards.

Tremendous feats of strength and endurance were performed during World War II by the Ns, whose ability to haul remarkably heavy trains with the lightest maintenance merely underscored their legendary versatility. Withdrawals took place in 1962-66 with a singleton set aside for preservation: 1925-vintage No.31874 is currently a stalwart of the Mid-Hants Railway.

Turning to the 3-cylinder N1 derivatives, the solitary No.822 of 1922 was joined in 1930 by 5 classmates (erected, as was customary, at Ashford) which differed in featuring 3 sets of Walschaert's valve gear in place of Holcroft's invention: No.822 was rebuilt to conform thus in 1931. Set against the inevitable increase in maintenance the operational advantages occasioned by the 3-cylinder layout were all but nullified – anyway the contemporaneous U1 3-cylinder Mogul was a rather better proposition – given the N's known strengths. All N1s were withdrawn in late 1962 with no survivals.

During their collective lifetime the N Moguls were subjected to sundry experiments and modifications. The main experiments were of little lasting value and not of vital interest here, however many fitments changed the appearance of the Ns quite markedly. Smoke deflectors made their debut on Ns in 1933 and all the 2-6-0s – including N1s – were so equipped as they passed through shops. Piston tail rods were a feature of all but the final batch of Ns, these being removed when front footsteps were acquired (although one or two engines ran for a time with both items simultaneously in place) together with the central steps formerly mounted on the motion brackets. The twin superheater anti-vacuum valves visible on smokeboxes behind the chimneys, colloquially called 'snifting' valves, were removed under Bulleid's aegis. A planned programme of replacement cylinders and reworked front ends under BR management was abandoned after only a handful of engines when the prospect of early withdrawal became imminent.

Notes on the drawings
The main illustrations display an N Class 2-6-0 in typical right-hand driving guise complete with front footsteps (note piston tail rod and central step shown in dashed lines). The tender is a 3500-gallon version with which

With a further batch of 15 engines outshopped from Ashford in 1932-34 and numbered 1400-14, the class strength reached its maximum of 80. Unlike the preceding engines, the last series employed left-hand drive (the SR standard format) as opposed to the SECR-

Important and fondly-remembered adjuncts of the SR's west of England scene, a 1924-built N Mogul pauses nosily at Barnstaple Junction with a van train in June 1960. An archetypal 'Woolworth' (a celebrated nickname, wittily corruped from 'Woolwich') heading an archetypal train, No.31844 was taken out of service in 1963. PHOTOGRAPH: NORMAN BROWNE.

most of the class were furnished; the 1932-34 batch sported a 4000-gallon variant. In later days the buffer beam usually sprouted visible rivet heads, as in the photo.

The front and part-side views of the N1 variation show the relevant contrasts with the parent 2-cylinder Mogul. Note that the boiler is pitched 3" higher (the U1-type chimney taller by a similar amount) though the frames, cab and running plates retain the original N dimensions. Steam heating is depicted, though not all N1s were so fitted. Note also that the shifting valves have gone, and smoke deflectors are in situ. Finally the cabfront spectacles are not the same as the N, taking into account the raised boiler/firebox unit.

Type:	Mixed Traffic
Overall Length:	57'6⅝"
Cylinders:	2, 19" x 28" bore/stroke
	(N1: 3, 16" x 28")
Boiler, Pressure:	200 lbs/sq in
Heating Surface:	1728.6 sq ft
Grate Area:	25 sq ft
Tractive Effort:	26000 lbs
Mean Weight in Working Order:	98 tons 13 cwt
Coal Capacity:	5 tons
Water Capacity:	3500 gallons
Number Built:	80, 1917-34
	(N1: 6, 1922-30)
Preserved:	1 (N1: 0)

On the Mid-Hants Railway, No.31874 approaches Alresford with a train from Ropley in the days before extension of the 'Watercress Line' to Alton. PHOTOGRAPH: JOHN CHALCRAFT.

LSWR Beattie 2-4-0WT

THREE ECCENTRIC little well tanks survived their 82 fellows by more than 60 years because their inherent stability and light weight was of premium value in the running of a short mineral branch in the depths of Cornwall, until displaced first by ex-GWR pannier tanks and ultimately by Class 08 diesels; the branch closed in 1983. Thus can the story of the famous Beattie tanks be encapsulated in a few words. But there was far more to them than this simple, bald epitaph.

Joseph Beattie in his capacity as locomotive superintendent of the London & South Western Railway designed a series of 2-4-0 tank locomotives to operate the burgeoning suburban traffic running into and out of Waterloo, the LSWR terminus in London, a task calling for reliable machines possessing good accelerative powers. Outshopped by Messrs. Beyer, Peacock of Manchester between 1863 and 1875, 85 distinctive 2-4-0WTs answered the call to duty with considerable gusto. Unusual features of the design (but in common with other Beattie products) included Allan valve gear – very similar to Stephenson's but having straight instead of curved links – the leading, carrying axle suspended by four sets of springs to Beattie's design which imparted superb stability to a wheel arrangement that all too often induced an uncomfortable lateral pitching movement, and Beattie's own version of feed pumping via a steam driven pump mounted on the left running plate ahead of the cab (or, originally, the spectacle plate). Beattie's inimitable feedwater heating device was however not used in this instance – its presence was distinguished by a second, rather smaller chimney outlet mounted atop the smokebox forward of the conventional chimney.

Joseph Beattie was succeeded by his son William in

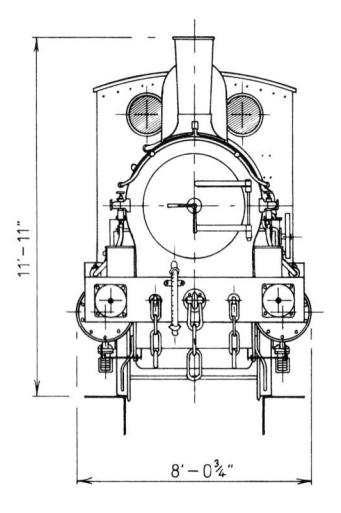

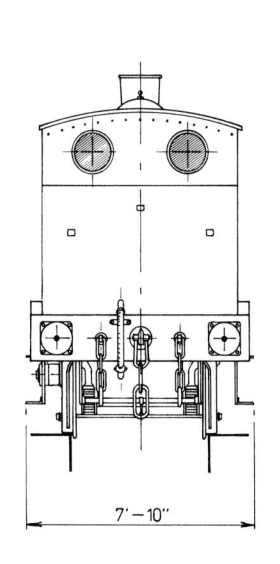

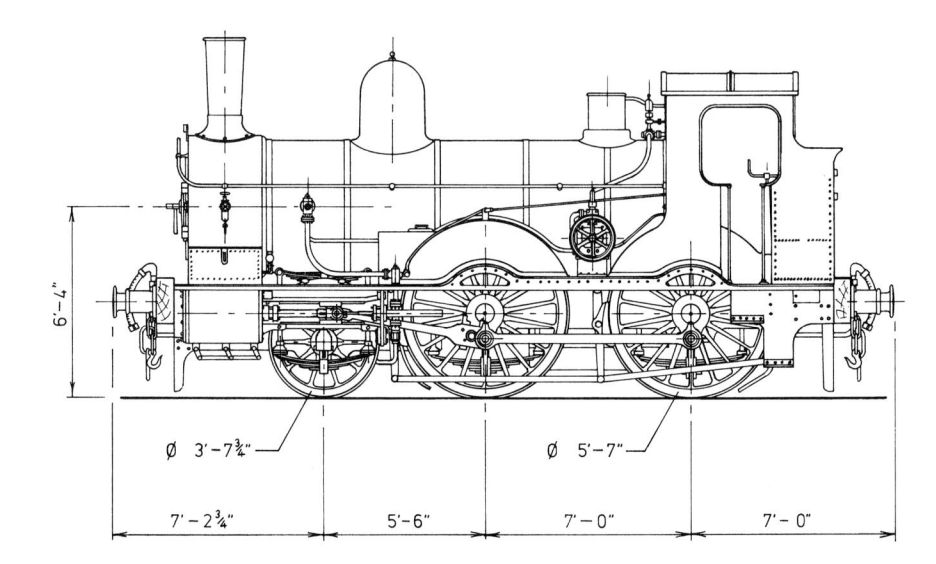

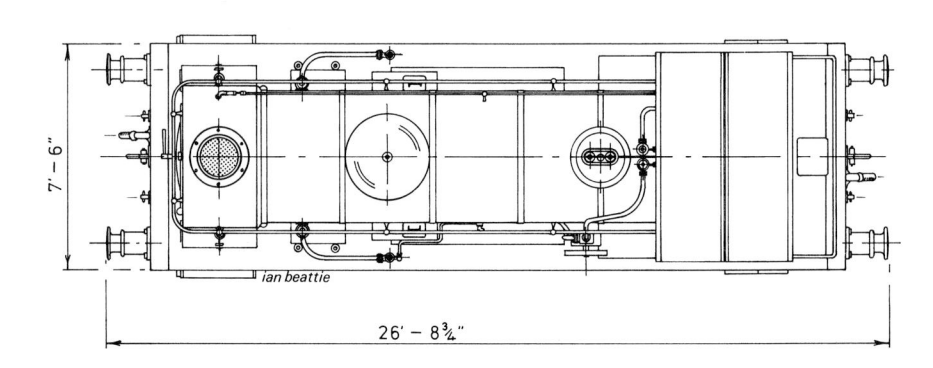

82

motive power for effective operation; the Beattie tanks were ideal for this purpose and Nos.298, 314 and 329 (eventually BR Nos.30587, 30585 and 30586 respectively) remained there for 64 years, until withdrawal in 1962. Over the years all three were rebuilt several times, finally ending up as shown in the photo, with Drummond boilers (note the characteristic chimney, and safety valves in steam dome). Two are preserved today, one by the National Collection on loan to the Dart Valley Railway at Buckfastleigh as a static exhibit and the other as a working engine by the Quainton Railway Society near Aylesbury, and the third (the only one with square splashers over the coupled wheels; no 30586) was cut up shortly after withdrawal.

Notes on the drawings

The four principal views relate to a 2-4-0WT as rebuilt by William Adams, undertaken as a class from 1884 to 1892, with his archetypal fitments: stovepipe chimney, large steam dome and shrouded Ramsbottom safety valves. Beattie's famous feedwater 'donkey pump' was retained, as were the unique front axle suspension arrangements.

Two supplementary views represent the 2-4-0WT as delivered by Beyer, Peacock in 1863: the dissimilarities to the rebuilt version(s) are self-evident but note that the rear axle has no visible spring.

When photographed by Frank Hornby at Quainton Road on 12 April 1971, No.30585 (*née* LSWR No.314) was a sprightly 97 years young, having emerged from the Gorton factory of Beyer, Peacock in 1874. Note the Drummond fitments, as mentioned in the text. It's still there at the Buckinghamshire Railway Centre, carrying its duplicate list number 0314.

Type:	2-4-0 Well Tank
Cylinders:	2, 16½" x 20" bore/stroke
Boiler Pressure:	160 lbs/sq in
Heating Surface:	847 sq ft*
Grate Area:	14.8 sq ft*
Water Capacity:	550 gallons
Tractive Effort:	11050 lbs*
Mean Weight in Working Order:	37 tons 16 cwt*
Number built:	85, 1863-75
Preserved:	2

*In Final Condition

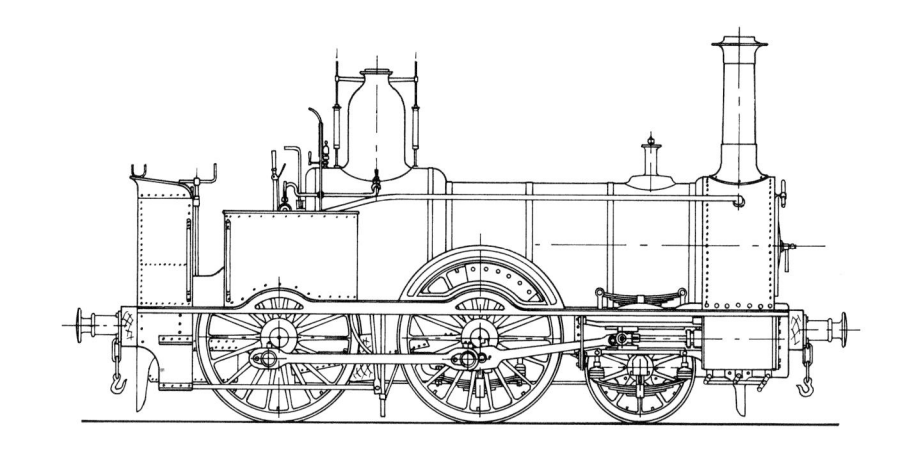

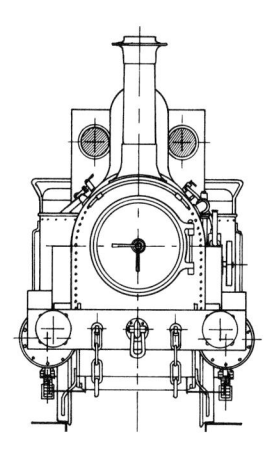

1871 (despite the synonymity I am not related – so far as I am aware), whose exploits on the LSWR are best drawn about with a shade and whose most successful activity was to perpetuate many of his parent's designs, including the 2-4-0WT, thus the three survivors are often hailed as W.G.Beattie's in as much as they were built in 1874-75.

As the 19th century drew towards a close the ever-increasing burdens on the suburban fleet necessitated more powerful constituents, so that the well tanks were replaced in service by Adams' excellent 4-4-2Ts (see RM August 1983) which in turn were succeeded by Drummond's evergreen M7 0-4-4Ts (see RM June 1982 *[and elsewhere in this volume – Ed.]*). Withdrawals of the small four-coupled tanks began therefore in 1888 and all had disappeared from revenue service by 1898, bar three.

The Bodmin-Wadebridge line, long isolated from other rail systems but physically connected to the LSWR in the 1890s, served a major china-clay quarry at Wenford Bridge via a constricted, twisty and lightly laid branch that required particularly nimble yet stable

Section 5
British Railways

Locomotive	Page	Locomotive	Page
Standard Class 3 2-6-2T	84-85	Class 08 and 13 shunter/Tinsley yard hump shunter	96-97
Standard Class 4 2-6-4T	86-87	BR/Sulzer Type 2 (TOPS Class 25)	98-99
Standard Class 9 2-10-0	88-89	BR/AEI AL1/Class 81 electric	100-101
Standard Class 5 4-6-0	90-92	BR Class 52 'Western' diesel hydraulic	102-103
English Electric 'Deltic' and production BR Class 55s	93-95		

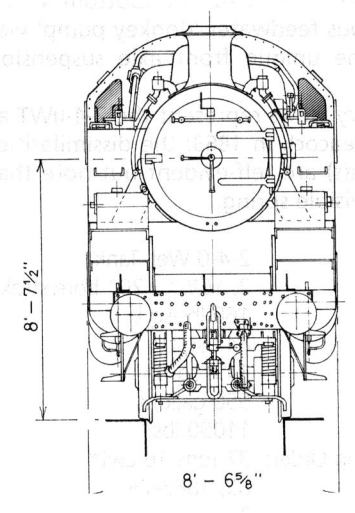

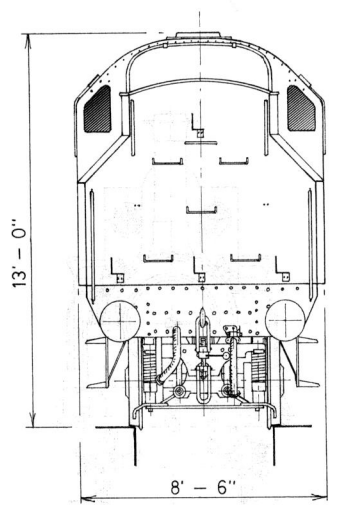

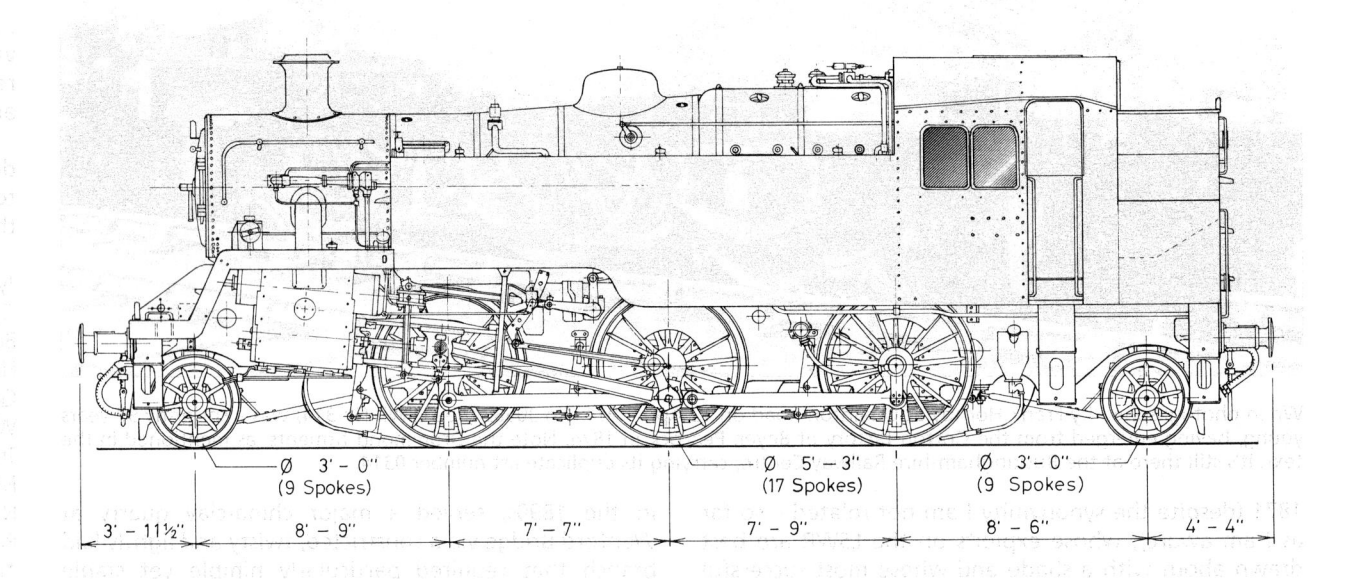

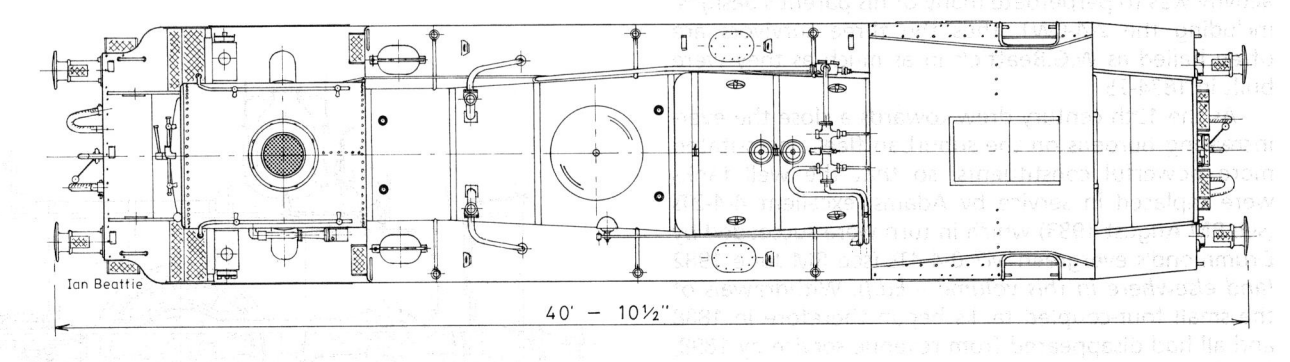

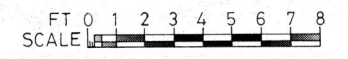

Standard Class 3 2-6-2T

CONCEIVED to run over those branch and cross-country routes denied to Standard Class 4 engines due to axle loading – specifically the 2-6-0s and 2-6-4Ts, whereas the sister 4-6-0s were considered main line hauliers – yet evincing considerably more power than the ubiquitous Class 2 types of all denominations (from BR Standards back in age to pre-Grouping designs), those erstwhile stalwarts of minor workings, the Standard Class 3 Prairie tanks enjoyed but brief utility in the British Railways scheme of things.

As was true of all Standard varieties, a particular engineering and building facility was made responsible for concept, detail design, manufacture and maintenance: the Class 3 tank was duly assigned to the hugely capable staff at the ex-Great Western works at Swindon, nerve centre of BR's Western Region since nationalisation in 1948.

Easily recognisable as a member of the BR Standard family having such characteristic traits as tall running plates linked to steeply inclined fillets (alongside and under the smokebox). Stanier/LMS-pattern wheel style and highset cylinders controlled by Walschaert's valve motion, the Class 3 tanks carried a boiler intimately derived from the GW No.4 type used by such luminaries as 'Large Prairies' (see RM August 1993 *[and the GW section herein – Ed.]*) and 56xx 0-6-2Ts (featured here in May 1994 *[and ditto – Ed.]*). With suitably shortened barrels, much enhanced superheaters and – most obviously externally – domes, these revised boilers were categorised BR6.

Production commenced at Swindon in 1952 and numbers allotted were from the 82xxx range beginning with 82000 attached to the first of the line. In all 45 engines were outshopped – 20 in 1952, the remainder in 1954-55 – and were numbered chronologically. An additional 18 locos had initially been planned within the 1954-55 batch, 10 for the Western Region and 8 for allocation to the North Eastern Region, but in the event the order was curtailed and No.82044 remained the final example of its class.

At the outset 25 2-6-2Ts went to the Western and the remainder to the Southern Regions, although in time the class spread somewhat further afield. They were much used at first for light-to-medium passenger and freight services on branch or cross-country routes (the author well remembers them at his childhood home of Budleigh Salterton, on the SR Sidmouth Junction-Exmouth branch, where the Class 3s intermingled with the ubiquitous LMS Ivatt Class 2 2-6-2Ts). However the superbly free-steaming, free-running BR Prairies fell victim to improvements in permanent way technology which allowed Class 4 types to tackle their duties with greater efficiency. The death-knell was ultimately sounded by at first a trickle and then a deluge of diesel multiple units in the wake of BR's much-vaunted Modernisation Plan; the excellent but ultimately outmoded 2-6-2Ts were withdrawn between 1964 and 1967 without survival for preservation, their senselessly short, seriously uneconomic 10-12 year lives all too typical of BR Standard history.

Notes on the drawings

Given such brief careers precious little in the way of changes was made to the BR 2-6-2Ts, the most striking being a change of livery on numerous WR-allocated engines from mandatory lined black livery (BR's code for mixed-traffic engines), applied to all 45 class members during assembly to Brunswick passenger green in the mid- to late 1950s; several received lining-out too. Another instance of Swindonisation was the eventual fitting of a handrail atop the boiler forward of the dome (see the photo) to most if not all WR Class 3s.

Please note that in the drawings pipe runs are omitted for clarity from the prominent lubricators mounted above the cylinders - some of the relevant pipework can be discerned beneath the smokebox in the photo. The vertical lubricator splash shields shown are unique to the BR Class 3 Prairies and distinguish them quickly from similar-looking engines of BR and LMS provenance. Note also that the dashed lines in the front view display the steampipes (located behind the lubricators) and those in the side elevation (i) the raised platform between the frames just forward of the smokebox, (ii) the coal space in the hopper-style bunker aft of the cab. The lamp brackets shown are of WR type.

Resplendent in pristine fully lined green livery, 1955-vintage BR Class 3 2-6-2T No.82039 stands outside Swindon Works on 3 November 1957, in full steam evidenced by safety valves lifting and cylinder cocks ajar. The 'SC' plate on the smokebox door indicates that No. 82039 sports a self-cleaning smokebox, common throughout the class.

Type:	Mixed-Traffic Prairie Tank
Cylinders:	2, 17½" x 26" bore/stroke
Boiler Pressure:	200 lbs/sq in
Heating Surface:	1226.46 sq ft
Grate Area:	20.35 sq ft
Tractive Effort:	21490 lbs
Mean Weight in Working Order:	74 tons 1 cwt
Coal Capacity:	3 tons
Water Capacity:	1500 gallons
Number Built:	45, 1952-55
Preserved:	None

Standard Class 4 2-6-4T

IN COMMON with the other designs of locomotive that constituted the British Railways Standard range, the lifespan of the Class 4 2-6-4 tanks was rendered tragically and uneconomically short by the overwhelming impetus of diesel and electric traction. Too many of these hitherto extremely useful hauliers ended their service on empty coach stock movement, goods shunting and the like, a ludicrous fate for machines of such size and power.

In early policy deliberations for proposed BR Standard locomotives the well-proven and highly regarded LMS Stanier and Fairburn 2-6-4Ts amply met the required desiderata – indeed the latter versions continued to be built for a while after nationalisation – however they proved over-large for the newly formulated loading gauge ensuring suitability throughout Britain's rail network. A new design was duly commissioned.

Each Standard proposal was assigned to a specific design office, to formulate the overall design irrespective of the provenance of individual components (from boilers downwards in scale) or at which erecting shops building was to take place; each design was thus an amalgam of standardised details emanating from various sources. The four offices involved corresponded with major railway works inherited from the Groups – Swindon, Derby, Doncaster and Brighton – and Brighton was made responsible for the Standard 2-6-4T.

The outcome was hardly radical. It was revealed as very similar to the aforementioned LMS counterparts but modified with smaller cylinders and uprated boiler pressure to achieve an equivalent tractive effort; classified BR5, the boiler used was almost identical to the LMS design but featured BR standard mountings and fittings. Unique to the new engines was the incorporation of curved flanks, very evident in front and rear views (in coachbuilding parlance 'barrel-sided'), quite distinctive alongside their vertically-sided forebears.

No fewer than 155 2-6-4Ts were assembled altogether over a period of six years, the huge majority at the Brighton works of the former LBSCR; however two batches were completed at Derby (the initial 10 engines of the class in 1951, and 5 more in 1954-5), plus a single batch of 10 outshopped from Doncaster during 1954. All wore the ex-LNWR style, mixed-traffic lined black livery which suited these machines particularly well. Identity numbers allotted were 80000-80154.

Allocated to all Regions bar the Western at first, though the engines' utility was such that the WR was not long denied, like their LMS progenitors the BR 2-6-4Ts' forte was suburban passenger work, for which purpose their free-steaming and fine riding characteristics combined with hearty acceleration and a wide performance range not only made them ideal but – equally as important – endeared them to their crews. Fleet withdrawal took effect between 1962 and 1967.

Deservedly one of the best and most popular BR Standard classes, this is reflected in the large number of survivors (though truth be told this was due to the vagaries of scrapping disposal: it was fortunate that the celebrated Woodham Brothers' yard at Barry acquired a sizeable proportion of the fleet from BR...) which continue to impress as powerful yet resourceful prime movers on today's preserved railways.

Notes on the drawings
There are some very minor, almost insignificant variations between the sundry batches, however the illustrations depict a 'typical' BR 2-6-4T as found throughout the UK. Some early examples sported fluted coupling rods, though the majority were equipped with plain 'fish-bellied' rods as shown and to which the early engines eventually conformed; note that two styles of return crank fixings were used, square-shanked clamp as in the drawings and 4-bolt as per No.80137.

ABOVE: discovered awaiting its next turn of duty, with a full head of steam and in a reasonably clean state bar filthy tank sides, the massive, four-square stance of Brighton-built (in 1956) 2-6-4T No.80137, neatly captured near the coaling ramp at Neasden shed, Eastern Region, on 3 March 1957.

OPPOSITE: main line-ticketed No.80079 was captured in lively fettle during the Exeter Rail Fair in May 1994, when in company with sister No.80080 the Brighton-built locomotive was running rail trips on the Barnstaple branch. The 2-6-4T entered traffic in March 1953, and in common with '80 was an 'escapee' from Barry yard. PHOTOGRAPH: ANDREW BURNHAM.

Type:	Mixed Traffic Tank
Cylinders:	2, 18" x 28" bore/stroke
Boiler Pressure:	225 lbs/sq in
Heating Surface:	1606 sq ft
Grate Area:	26.7 sq ft
Tractive Effort:	25515 lbs
Mean Weight in Working Order:	86 tons 13 cwt
Coal Capacity:	3½ tons
Water Capacity:	2000 gallons
Number Built:	155, 1951-6
Preserved:	15

87

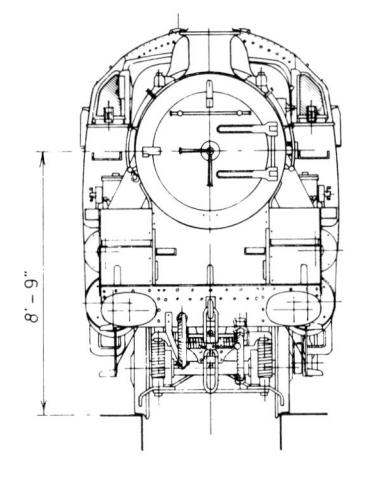

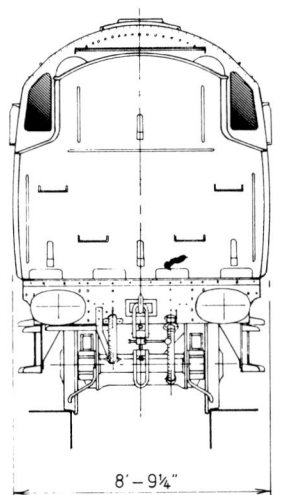

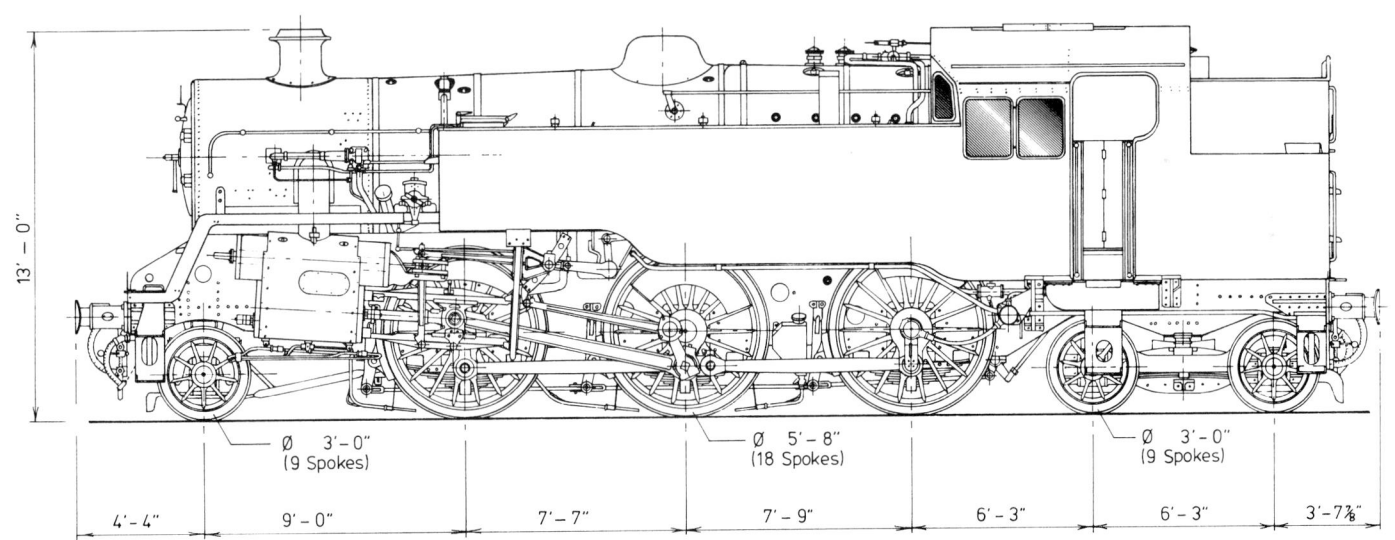

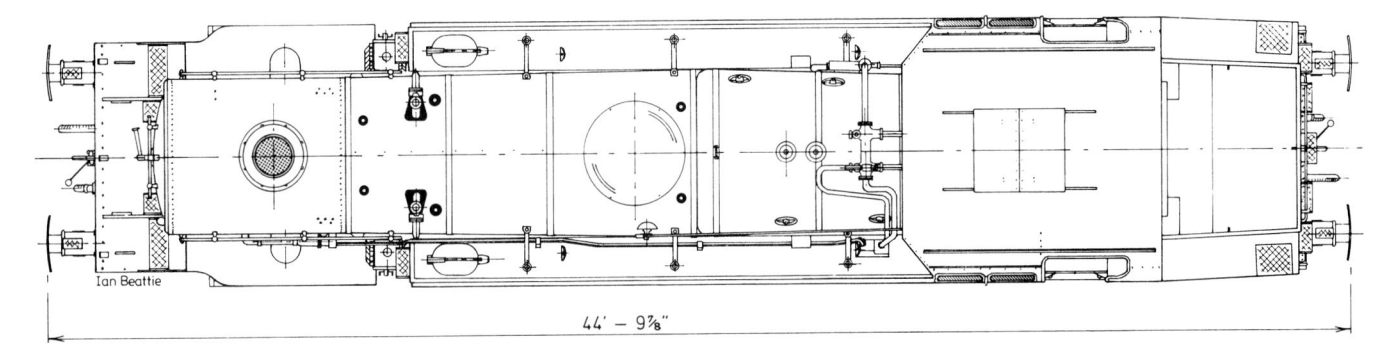

ABOVE: with her crew looking out for the official photographer, No.92105 lifts 27 loaded iron ore tipplers away from Storefield, near Kettering, in this undated view. Another 9F lurks in the distance with a similar train. PHOTOGRAPH: BR LONDON MIDLAND REGION.

OPPOSITE: 1955-built No.92050, with BR1C tender, stands in steam ready for its next working at Willesden on 14 December 1958.

Standard Class 9F 2-10-0

FINAL, most famous and probably the best of the 12 BR Standard locomotive designs that emanated from a panel of engineers presided over by Robert Riddles on behalf of the British Transport Commission, the body set up to run the transport systems nationalised in 1948, the Class 9 ten-coupled freight locomotive was originally planned as a 2-8-2, since this wheel arrangement allowed a desirably large grate area. However the improved adhesion of a ten-coupled engine together with the acknowledged accomplishments of Riddles' wartime Austerity 2-10-0 persuaded the panel to adopt this format whilst incorporating as many proven Standard components as possible.

The outcome was the familiar, ebullient 2-10-0 still much in evidence on today's BR and preserved railway networks, thanks to the several preserved 9Fs (chief amongst which is the last 2-10-0 built No.92220 *Evening Star*, part of the National Collection and which annually undertakes a heavy programme of main line steam duties).

With its boiler pitched very high enabling the firebox to clear the rear wheels, and steeply sloping cylinders – for platform clearance purposes – reminiscent of the LMS Horwich Crabs *[see RM December 1992 – Ed.]*, the big freight engines were outshopped from both Crewe and Swindon works over a period of seven years; the 9Fs quickly became legendary for their supreme free-running characteristics which, coupled with fine controllability was the ideal for freight haulage where smooth, nicely judged progress was vital in the days of loose-coupled goods trains.

The locomotives were occasionally diagrammed for passenger work, most memorably on the erstwhile Somerset & Dorset route between Bath and Bournemouth, at which they proved outstandingly successful, notwithstanding their relatively small wheels and lack of steam-heating apparatus: an unofficial maximum of 90 mph was witnessed on one occasion. Their easy steaming that led to such active performance aggravated what was the design's only major defect, a tendency towards excessive cylinder wear – this drawback effectively banned the 9Fs from passenger duties after a time.

During the course of the production span several important additions to specification were applied to various 2-10-0s, principal of which was the introduction in 1955 of ten engines equipped with Franco-Crosti boilers *[see RM February 1997 – Ed.]*, supposedly to enhance steam production; however the claims made for these 'double-barrelled' devices (which were pitched from rail level at a British height record of 9'11¾") were not met in practice and they were converted to orthodox guise in 1959. Following successful trials with double-chimneyed 9F No.92178, 68 further engines were built from new with such chimneys installed and four were eventually modified from conventional single-chimney status: one engine was further altered by the use of a Giesl ejector, but test results were inconclusive and in any case the demise of steam power was too close by then to warrant any real development in this arena – which also accounted for the sudden cessation of the double-chimney installation programme.

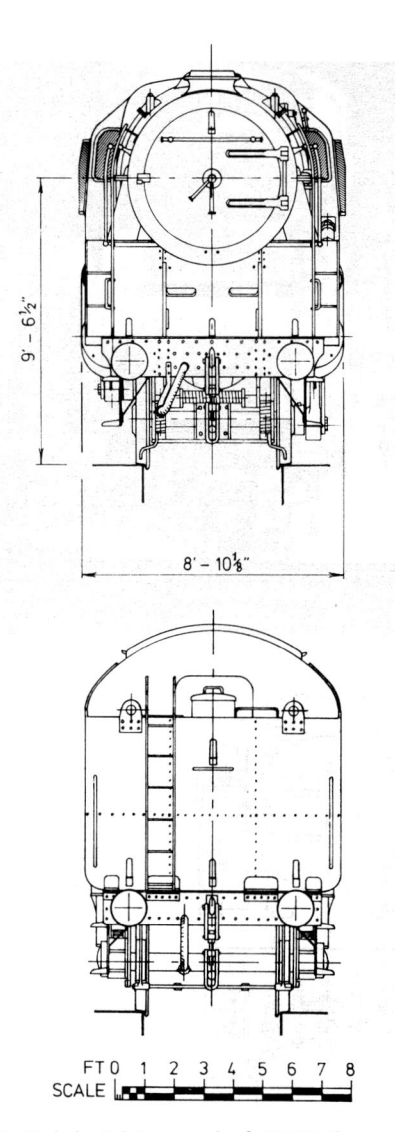

Altogether five types of BR Standard tender went towards equipping the 251 9Fs. That type illustrated here is the BR1C variety. 2-10-0 No.92167 was originally linked to a type BR1K tender incorporating a mechanical stoker (to the American Berkeley patent) to relieve much of the fireman's task in keeping the massive firebox filled; this tender was dimensionally identical to that shown here though the coal and water capacities differed. The three 9Fs so fitted eventually abandoned the stoking facility and were re-equipped with conventional BR1C tenders.

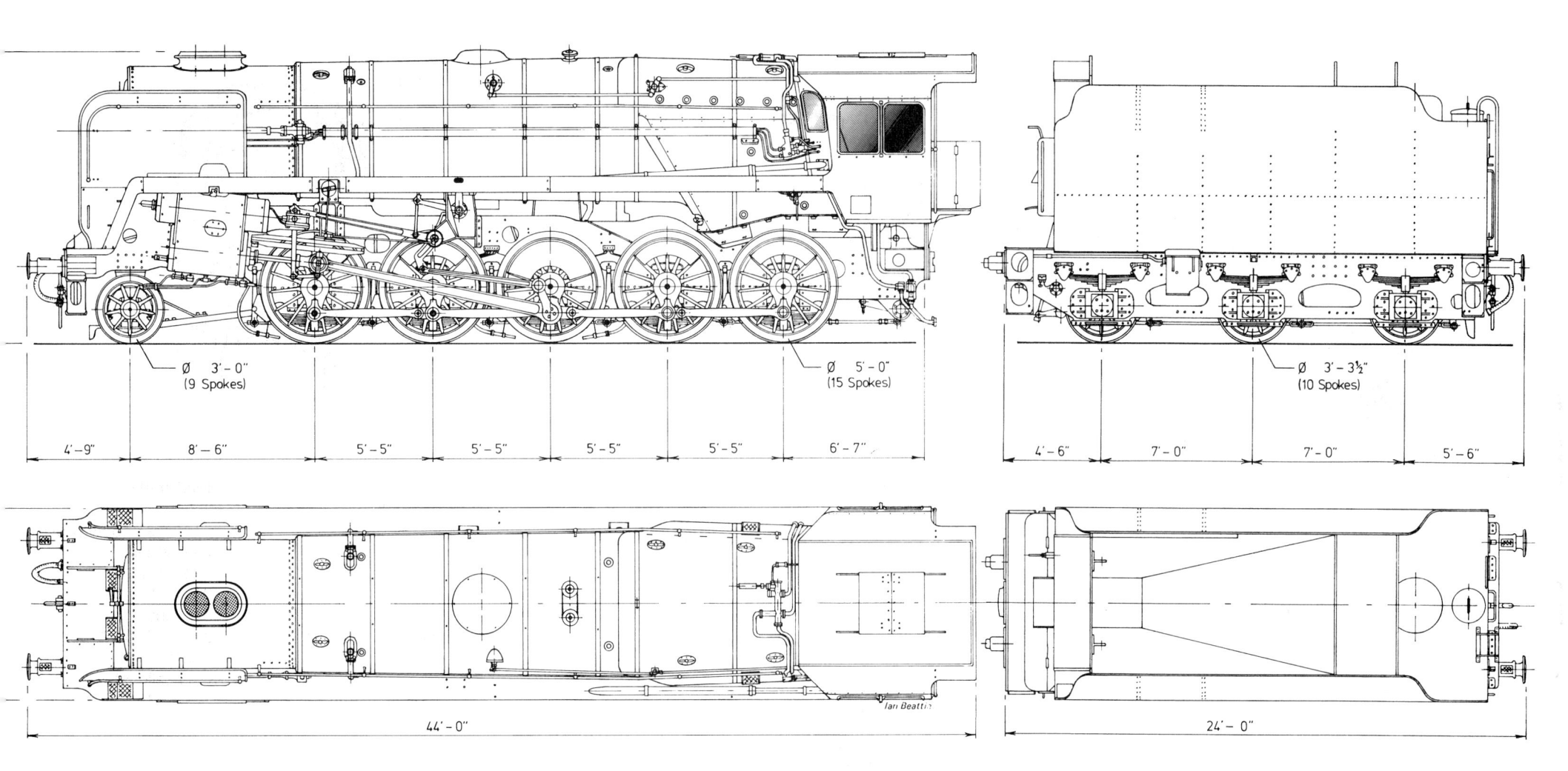

Note the flangeless centre-coupled wheels, and the sandbox fillers on the right-hand running plate (there is a third filler, at the junction of smokebox and boiler, hidden in the plan view by the boiler and in the front view by the steam pipe).

Of the comparatively large number built no fewer than nine 9Fs survived beyond withdrawal, which took place between 1964 and 1968 and thus making these immensely capable engines some of the most short-lived of all British motive power. Survivals include (at the time of writing) two 2-10-0s lying in Barry scrapyard which without doubt will eventually join their classmates on preserved railways.

[Editor's note. The last two 9Fs to leave Barry were No.92207, in October 1986, and 92245, in February 1988. Sister 'resident' No.92085 was not so lucky, being famously one of two locomotives – the other was ex-GW 'Large Prairie' No.4156 – cut up by Woodham's in 1980.]

Overall length:	66'2"
Cylinders:	2, 20" x 28" bore/stroke
Boiler Pressure:	250 lbs/sq in
Heating Surface:	2549 sq ft
Grate Area:	40.2 sq ft
Tractive Effort:	39667 lbs
Mean Weight in Working Order:	141 tons 15 cwt*
Coal Capacity:	9 tons*
Water Capacity:	4725 gallons*
Number Built:	251, 1954-60
Preserved:	9

*Type BR1C Tender

One of the named Southern Region engines, 1954-vintage Class 5 No 73082 *Camelot* (now preserved) plus BR1B tender is caught on the boil at Nine Elms, the principal shed serving Waterloo terminus, on 19th September 1959.

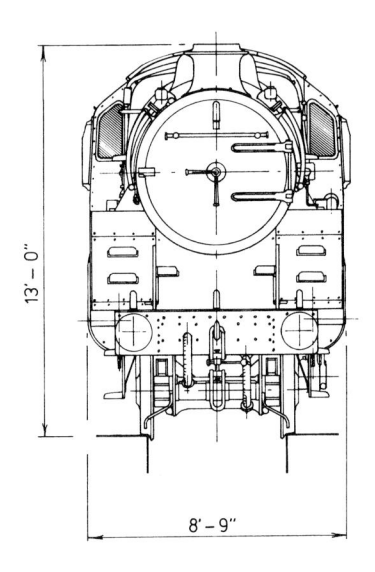

Type:	Mixed-Traffic
Overall Length:	62'7"
Cylinders:	2, 19" x 28" bore/stroke
Boiler Pressure:	225 lbs/sq in
Heating Surface:	2,008 sq ft
Grate Area:	28.7 sq ft
Tractive Effort:	26120 lbs
Mean Weight in Working Order:	125 tons 3 cwt*
Coal Capacity:	7 tons*
Water Capacity:	4,250 gallons*
Number Built:	172, 1951-7
Preserved:	5

*Type BR1 Tender

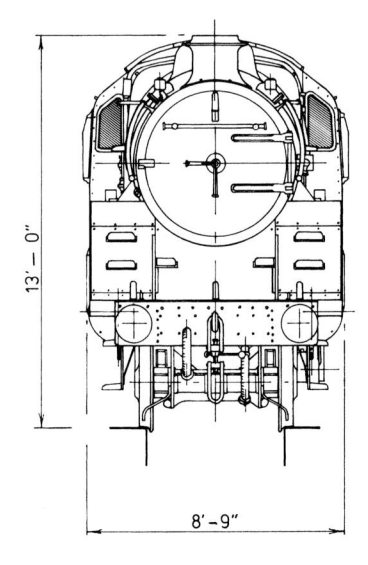

Standard Class 5 4-6-0 (and Caprotti gear locos)

PLANNED originally as a 4-6-2 complete with, interestingly, bar frames, the British Railways Standard equivalent to the GWR 'Hall', LNER B1 and LMS 'Black Five' mixed-traffic fleets proved *inter alia* a highly versatile design, indicated by the numbers outshopped: 172 between 1951 and 1957, the majority emanating from the ex-LMS Derby workshops – as befitted engines based largely on Stanier's ubiquitous 'Black Fives' – plus 42 built at Doncaster in 1955-7.

Numbered 73000-73171 inclusive, the Class 5s were distributed widely to all Regions of BR where they displayed rousing performance, exceptional reliability and - most importantly – popularity with locomotive crews. Employed on all manner of services from top link express passenger work (normally of course the preserve of Pacifics but which the powerful 4-6-0s were eminently capable of handling to similar effect) to the humblest of pickup goods duties, their qualities vindicated BR's decision to build these machines rather than to perpetuate the parent LMS blueprint. In any event the firm decision to instigate and utilise standard fittings throughout the BR fleet pre-empted such lines of thought. Although the boiler was descended directly from that installed on Stanier 2-8-0s and 'Black Fives', many other parts were common to the contemporaneously-erected BR Pacifics, such as the wheels, cylinders (linered down) and Walschaert's valve motion.

Successive batches of Class 5s varied somewhat in fittings and fixtures such as provision of dual air/vacuum braking systems on selected locomotives – and particularly in tenders which varied widely in water and, to a lesser extent, coal capacities, supply of which type depended on the area allocated and conditions of use. For instance, the Southern Region being devoid of water troughs, those Class 5s so allotted were attached to tenders capable of carrying a generous amount of water. Also, the only named BR Class 5 engines ran on that Region: 20 names were transferred from withdrawn 'King Arthur' 4-6-0s: the plates *[replicas, without the 'King Arthur Class' suffix – Ed.]* were mounted on running plate valances over the driving wheels.

Withdrawals began in 1964, the last engines being decommissioned during the final days of steam in 1968. Fortunately no fewer than five examples escaped ultimate dismemberment and are now preserved in sympathetic hands.

91

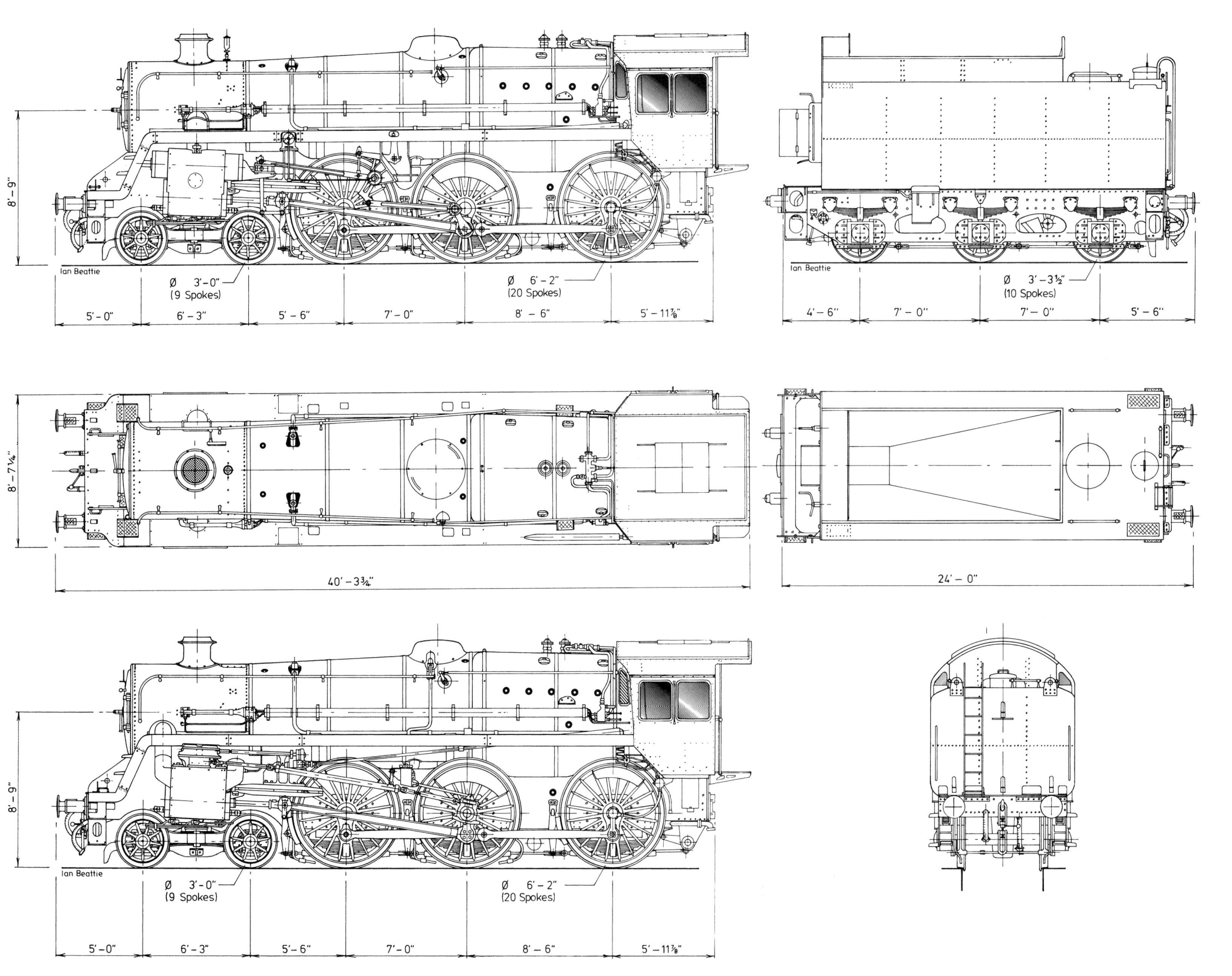

Notes on the drawings

The drawings show an early Class 5 engine featuring a chime whistle surmounting the smokebox, which was replaced in most cases by a conventional whistle atop the firebox: many later-built engines however ran throughout their lives with conventional whistles behind the chimney. The cab is modified from the original, following crew complaints of excessive draughts, and conforms with the layout used by all Class 5s beyond the initial and thus experimental handful. The tender illustrated is the Type BR1 attached to 60 engines of the class (others used were types BR1A, G, H and BR2, 2A, differing in carrying capacities but all sharing an identical underframe layout), and sports doors, fallplate and tanktop footsteps as adaptations in the light of experience.

BR Class 5 4-6-0, Caprotti valve gear

As a result of outshopping the unique 3-cylinder BR Standard 4-6-2 No.71000 *Duke of Gloucester* (see RM July 1987) with British Caprotti valve gear, a decision was made to widen experience with this relatively novel form of motion by so equipping a series of 30 Standard Class 5 4-6-0s, Nos.73125-54: these locomotives were erected at Derby in 1956-7 and took to the rails toting large-capacity tenders, types BR1B and C (for BR1C drawings see RM April '88, p.177 *[and elsewhere in this section – Ed.]*). Whilst compared with the simple and thoroughly proven Walschaert's motion the Caprotti mechanism was expensive, precision-made, and required regular and above all careful maintenance; the engines thus fitted gained a perceptible power advantage over their orthodox classmates without loss of reliability. They represented a further step forward in steam technology, progress of which of course ceased in the wake of dieselisation. A single example of the Caprotti Class 5 4-6-0 is fortunately preserved, at the Midland Railway Centre, Butterley.

Notes on the drawings (Caprotti)

Beyond the valve gear there is little evident dissimilarity with the Walschaert-controlled Class 5: a conventional whistle mounted on the firebox (using the spare union on the steam manifold, see plan view of Walschaert Class 5), the running plate set slightly further forward in relation to the smokebox and twin lubricators mounted beneath the right hand running plate. The right-hand Caprotti valve gear was a mirror-image of the left-hand one shown, reversing of which was achieved via a transverse shaft beneath the boiler.

73031 is seen at Sheffield Midland with steam feathering from the safety valves on 21 August 1960, as it comes off an express from Bristol. The well-oiled machine sports lined green livery. PHOTOGRAPH: DOUGLAS DOHERTY.

LEFT: the low winter sun highlights the Caprotti valve gear on No.73137, pictured with one of the early 'Peak' diesels (later Class 44) on Derby shed on 12 December 1961. The 5 was built at the ex-MR works a short distance away in December 1956.

English Electric 'Deltic'/BR Class 55 Co-Co

OWING to their high-profile career as top link passenger hauliers over the East Coast Main line – coupled with a distinctive growl from power units under acceleration that bespoke immense power and aped by no other railborne prime mover – the 22 'Deltics' are arguably the best known and most revered of all British Railways' diesel-electric locomotives. Even now, 17 years and more since their disappearance from main line service, the 6 surviving Co-Cos still elicit what almost amounts to hero worship.

The story began in early 1955 on the emergence of a prototype Co-Co by the English Electric Group from its Dick Kerr works in Preston. This unique engine, outrigged with aluminium side 'lozenges' and appliqué end 'whiskers' atop powder blue overall (a shade seemingly delicate for so large and powerful a machine), featured two 1650hp 2-stroke diesel power units of a most unusual configuration. Developed by Napier – a member company of the English Electric consortium – these were initially designed for use in naval motor gun boats, in which application they provided reliability and extraordinarily high speed: such boats were sold to navies throughout the world in the years following World War 2.

In rail terms these powerplants appeared ideal, given their high yet smoothly rendered power and light weight through extensive use of alloy castings. Each sported 3 crankshafts disposed at the corners of an upturned triangle, with mutually opposed pistons moving along the sides of the triangle in 3 groups of 6 pistons. Power was centralised into a single driveshaft and this in turn was mated to an electrical generator. With much light-alloy body and frame componentry the upshot was 3300 horsepower in a 100-ton 'box', a worldbeating combination at the time. Since Napier had named the power unit 'Deltic', from the Greek letter Delta (written as a triangle, ∆), the resulting locomotive was likewise christened *Deltic*.

Entering regular service with BR in December 1955 after numerous trials, the singleton experimental machine was allotted to numerous localities in the London Midland and Eastern Regions until 1959, when the big Co-Co began the final phase of its career on passenger duties over the ECML. Stored from spring 1961 following severe engine failure, *Deltic* was refurbished by its sponsors and presented in April 1963 to the Science Museum at Kensington. For some thirty years its imposing presence enraptured children of all ages, until reorganization of the Land Transport Gallery prompted the locomotive's removal and conveyance to the National Railway Museum in York in October 1993.

Given the success of this very powerful one-off machine and in line with the diminution of steam traction provided for in the BR Modernisation Plan of 1955, a fleet of 22 facsimiles was ordered by BR in 1958 specifically to replace top link steam on the ECML. Deliveries commenced in January 1961 from English Electric's subsidiary the Vulcan Foundry at Newton-le-Willows and the 22nd example was completed in April 1962. Chronologically numbered D9000-21, all were named eventually, several in the LNER tradition of racehorses and the remainder for regiments of the Regular Army.

For 20 years the 'Deltics' dominated express passenger timetables over the ECML, deploying very high speeds (they were geared to 105 mph and often held this maximum for long stretches) with relatively good reliability although maintenance was apparently very costly. The initial Brunswick green livery gave way to Rail blue in the later 1960s and the onset of TOPS brought number changes. Nos.D9001-21 became 55 001-21 whilst D9000 was assigned No.55 022 as TOPS could not accept engine numbers ending in three zeroes.

The introduction to the ECML of IC125 High Speed Trains in the mid-1970s ended the 'Deltics'' ubiquity and withdrawals of Co-Cos began in January 1980. The final 'Deltic'-powered BR service took place in January 1982 yet that characteristic 'Deltic' roar (accompanied it must

ABOVE: an interested bystander takes a good look at *Deltic*, in charge of the 8.20am from Kings Cross at Peterborough North on 23 February 1959. The wisp of steam betrays the heating boiler, in operation on this late winter's day. PHOTOGRAPH: PHILIP J. KELLEY.

BELOW: one of the engines within D9005 *The Prince of Wales's Own Regiment of Yorkshire* erupts with the characteristic smoke plume. D9001 *St.Paddy* and the gas holders at St.Pancras look on in this late 1960s scene at Kings Cross. PHOTOGRAPH: PHIL CALEY.

ABOVE: D9015 *Tulyar* poses on the stabling point at Kings Cross on 28 December 1971. Named after the winner of the 1952 Derby, St.Leger and King George VI & Queen Elizabeth stakes, 'No.15' is one of the six production machines to survive into preservation.

BELOW: 'Deltic' renaissance - a Virgin Cross Country service with resplendent D9000 *Royal Scots Grey* at the head, thunders through Chatham on 5 June 1999. PHOTOGRAPH: PHIL CALEY.

be said by vast plumes of exhaust sometimes the equal of a steam locomotive) emitted by these majestic hauliers may thankfully still be witnessed on preserved railways and once again on the national network thanks to frequent hirings of D9000 *Royal Scots Grey*. *[Several others are now main line certified – Ed.]*

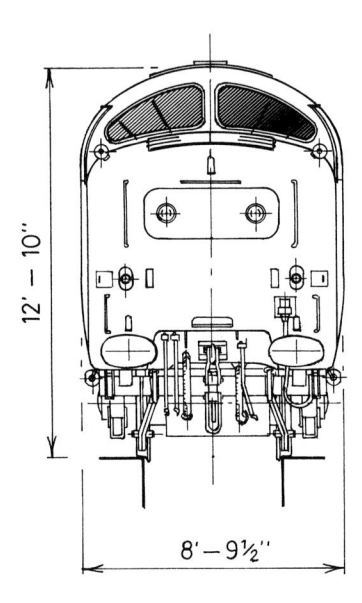

Type:	Express Passenger Diesel-Electric
Engines:	2, Napier Deltic D18-25 18-cyl
Tractive Effort:	50000 lbs
Power Rating:	3300 hp
Mean Weight in Working Order:	100 tons
Number Built:	22, 1961-2
Building Company:	English Electric
Preserved:	6 plus Prototype

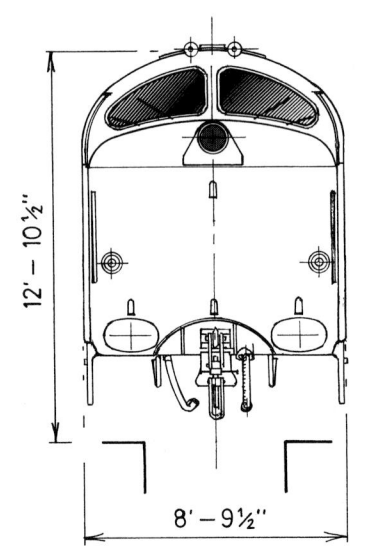

Notes on the drawings
Very few external changes were made to the 'Deltics' appearance over their lives. however such have been incorporated in my renderings (which include *inter alia*

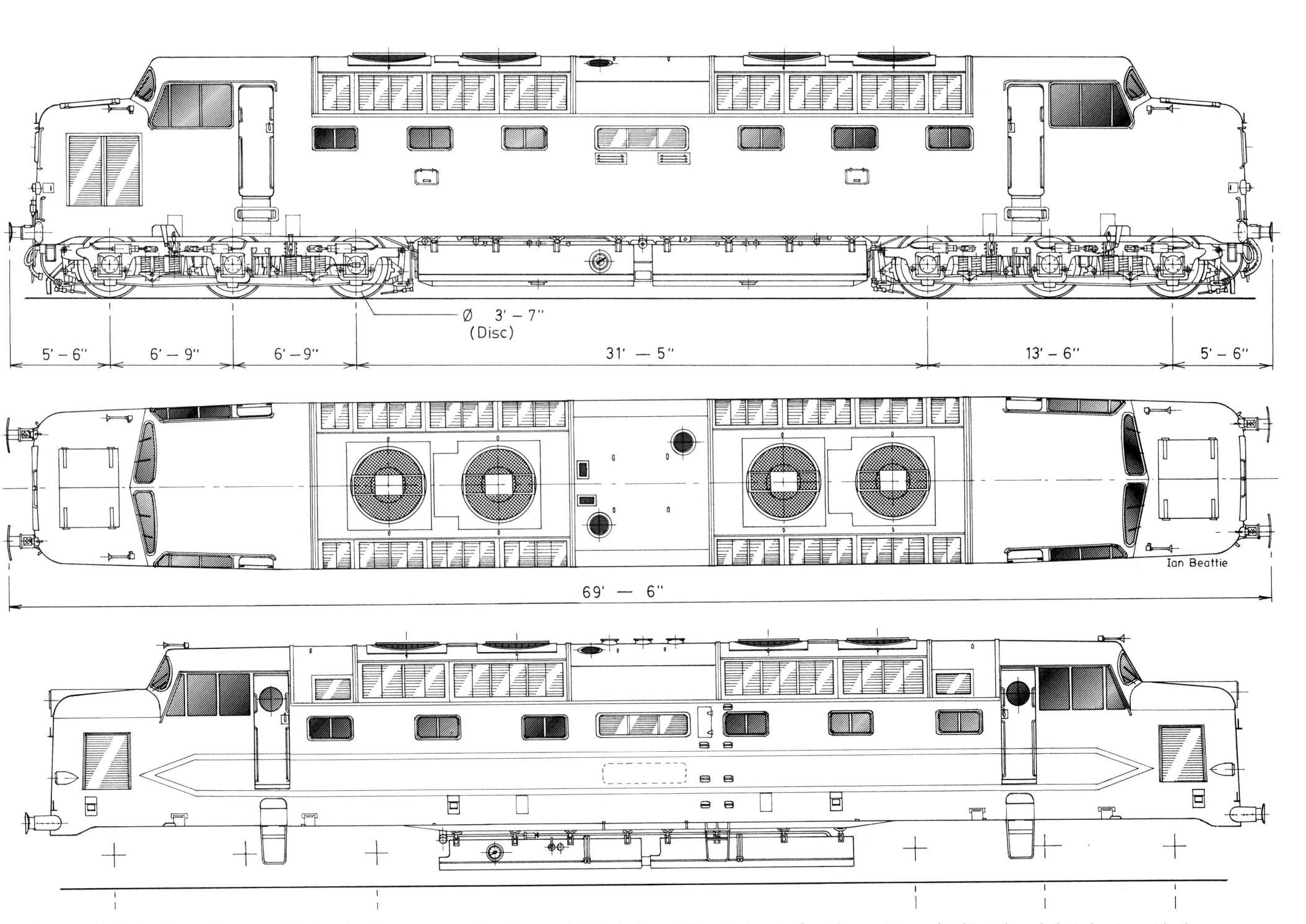

horns resited atop the end noses and twin sets of louvres beneath the central bodyside grille). Note that although mooted at the design stage end gangway doors were never provided, thus precluding non-stop London-Edinburgh expresses habitual in steam days. Marker lamps occupy the former route indicators and several engines ended their days with a single set of screen wipers per end.

The prototype 'Deltic' is superficially similar but becomes more different the longer it's studied! Firstly the production engines were 21" longer overall and the bogies, while much the same, were slightly stretched on the prototype ('Deltics' shared their bogies with the English Electric Type 3 or Class 37 Co-Cos, which see RM March 1997). The dashed outline on the side view denotes the nameplate. Note that the protuberant headlamp nacelle either end remained unfilled; the resultant hole was at first blanked off.

95

English Electric Classes 08 and 13

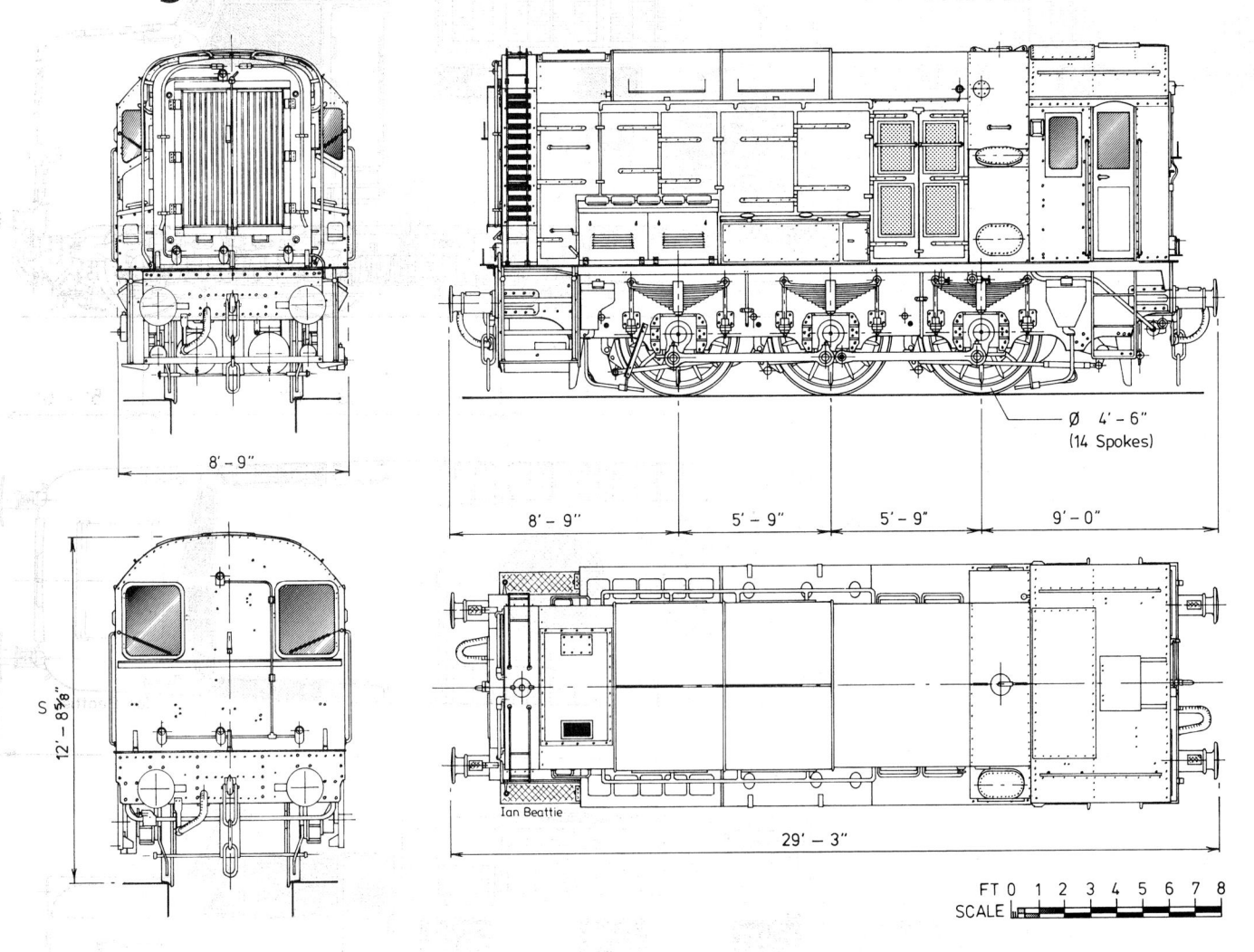

WITH ITS design stretching back to the 1930s through experimentation by the largest of the Groups, the ubiquitous, all-purpose and omnipresent BR standard Class 08 0-6-0 diesel shunter has been around for a very long time, and seems set fair to remain with us for a considerable while to come.

Before World War II the LMS, impressed by the instant availability and relative operational economy promised via diesel power, invoked a number of diesel shunting prototypes from several British private locomotive manufacturers and featuring differing methods of power transmission to the wheels. Amongst the more successful designs was that submitted by the English Electric Company, whereby the six-coupled wheels were driven by a six-cylinder 350 horsepower engine via two nose-suspended electric motors and reduction gearing to the fore and aft axles. A series of 100 such shunters was authorised, but before this could come to fruition war was declared and the LMS, together with its three co-Groups, was placed under centralised control: the order was rescinded, or more accurately rechannelled for the products to be operated under War Department auspices.

By the time Nationalisation was enacted the LMS possessed just 24 of these shunting engines, of which 14 were WD machines built in 1944/5 for specific use on the LMS system; all 24 had been erected by the ex-Midland Railway shops at Derby. In common with many useful Grouping loco designs the infant BR sanctioned further building of such shunters. By the time production ended in 1952, 120 engines were in service (including the ex-LMS units), of which all but the final batch of 36 had been outshopped by Derby – the final three dozen emerged from Darlington.

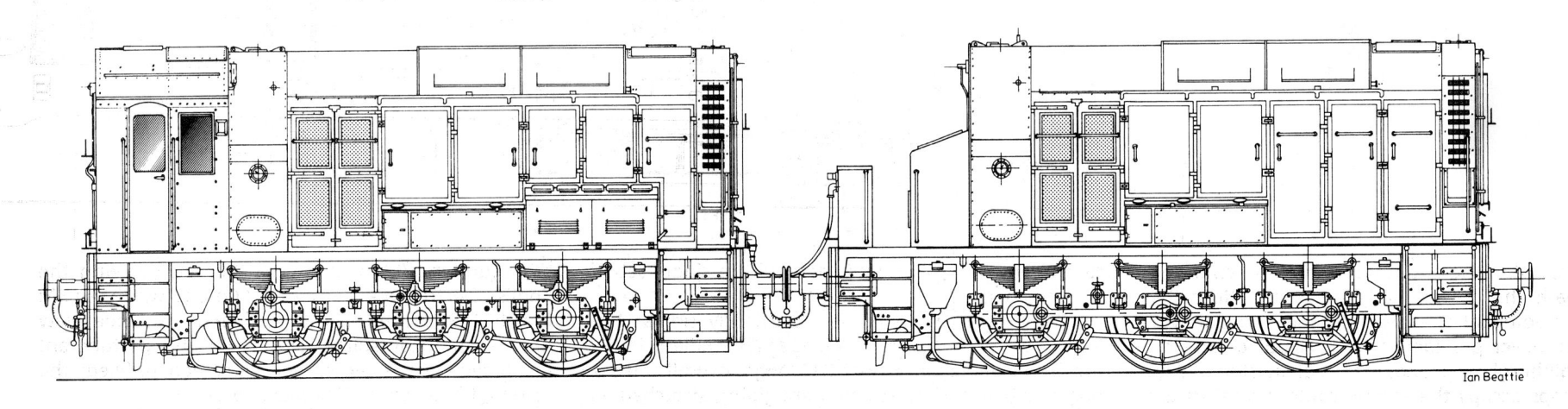

During this production period BR requirements vis-à-vis diesel shunters within this 350hp power range had crystallised; the English Electric design had proved eminently suitable for BR's countrywide shunting, short-distance and branch goods duties, so that with minor modifications a further span of production was approved, which in the event lasted more than 10 years and almost 1,000 units.

All but identical to their LMS and early-BR antecedents (and exceptionally difficult to differentiate visually), the post-October 1952 machines, which we now, under the TOPS scheme, identify as Class 08, sported taller wheels – at 4'6" diameter against 4'0½" – that rendered a tractive effort figure enhanced by 5,000 lbs. As before, English Electric supplied the power units and electrical necessities whilst BR supplied the rolling chassis and assembled the vehicles. Derby bore much of the brunt in the assembly stakes, aided by Darlington, Doncaster, Horwich and Crewe in achieving the huge numbers required. In addition a set of 27 shunters having higher final gearing (for a maximum of 27 mph, as opposed to the standard 20 mph) was built specifically for the Southern Region and was eventually classified 09. To all other intents and purposes they were/are identical to the 08s.

An exception to the 100% English Electric involvement was attempted for an early, mid-1950s batch for which Blackstone power plants were used and GEC provided the electrical equipment, however this wayward departure was not repeated and the resulting 'non-standard' locos were sold comparatively quickly out of BR service. The Dutch Railways (NS), however, purchased what transpired to be a highly useful fleet of 08 shunters that continues in wide service throughout the Netherlands.

Over the years many minor modifications have been applied to the 08s, both to enhance their utility and to prolong their lives, and the liveries worn have reflected general BR trends over the years: today the gaudy Network SouthEast and even InterCity liveries may be witnessed, and several 08 station pilots sport pre-Grouping colours.

The particular needs of the hump marshalling yard at Tinsley evolved the extraordinary Class 13 locomotives, which were no more nor less than two Class 08 shunters coupled together. Each 08's weight was augmented for extra adhesion by deep and heavily weighted buffer beams – the all-up weight scaled 120 tons, for an overall length of approximately 60' – and the combination was controlled, pneumatically, from a single cab, the cab of the 'leading' unit being removed and thus becoming a 'cow and calf'. Three such adaptations were used at Tinsley from 1965 until hump shunting ceased there in the mid-1980s.

Smartly attired in EWS maroon, 09 008 marshals postal vans at Plymouth on 27 April 1999. Photograph: Alan Pike.

Class 13 No.D4500 (a combination of the former Nos.D4188 and 3695) work Tinsley's hump yard on 26 September 1971.

Notes on the drawings

The Class 08 loco is shown much as built, including ladders flanking the radiator, vacuum braking apparatus only and 3-link couplings. Successive batches differed marginally in small fittings, indicated for example by access door hinge straps (compare with the Class 13 08s). Note electric lamps plus steam-age lamp irons front and rear – the central lamps and brackets have now been removed.

Note the somewhat updated versions used for the Class 13 combination: radiator ladders supplanted by handrails and the radiator side ducts partially blanked off *inter alia*. Note that the 'calf' has no battery box over the right-hand front wheel.

Type:	6-coupled D/E shunter
Engine:	6-cyl English Electric 6KT
Tractive Effort:	35000 lbs
Power Rating:	350 hp
Mean Weight in Working Order:	49 tons
Number Built:	996, 1952-62
Building Company:	BR/English Electric
Preserved:	62 (at time of writing)

Class 25 Bo-Bo

THE TYPE 2 diesel specification as envisaged and ordained as a result of British Railways' Modernisation Plan of 1955, whereby steam locomotion was to be supplanted by diesel or electric traction, covered the power range 1001-1500hp with a mixed-traffic capability. The fleet of such machines built from 1958 into 1967 comprising Classes 24 and 25 was not only the second largest on BR but met the design and operating criteria with considerable élan.

Virtually identical to the preceding 151-strong Class 24 Bo-Bos, which had been outshopped from 1958 and equipped with 1160-horsepower Sulzer engines (although introduced several years after the combined classes were complete, the TOPS-related category numbers are most convenient to be used hereinafter for identification purposes), the Class 25 variation arose through the uprating of Sulzer's 6LDA28-type power units to 1250 hp, which units were incorporated in the ensuing 327 locomotives. BR undertook the great bulk of production 'in house', divided between Darlington and Derby, and outshopping took place from spring 1961; however at a time of intense production pressures on BR a batch of 54 locos was allotted to the Beyer Peacock Company of Manchester. Unfortunately by the time building of the 25s commenced at Gorton (mid-1965) the long established private manufacturing plant was plagued by serious financial problems; these deepened to the point – indeed terminally – where the company had to be released from BR's contract. Thus on emergence of the 36th Bo-Bo in July 1966, production lines were disbanded and the historic firm closed down; the 18 locos outstanding on the order were subsumed by the BR erecting shops.

Proving excellent and reliable performers equally on passenger and freight duties, moreover thoroughly appreciated by crews, the Class 25s were divided into four basic sub-groups:

25/0 the initial 25 outshopped from Darlington shared BTH-sourced electrical equipment with the generic Class 24 Bo-Bos; number ranges were D5151-75, latterly 25 001-25.

25/1 57 locos built in 1963 with improved generators and driving motors; numbers allocated were D5176-232, subsequently 25 026-82.

25/2 as 25/1 but having slightly revised body styling; 165 built 1963-66 and numbered D5233-7597, later 25 083-247.

25/3 outshopped 1965-67, these locos sported differing generator installations and enhanced overall performance. Body design was quite radically altered, with cantrail outlets in place of side louvres and end gangways omitted permitting full-depth centre windows to be utilised. 80 were erected, initially numbered D7598-677 and thereafter 25 248-327.

A further subdivision was inaugurated in 1986. Twelve Class 25/3 engines were adapted for specialised Railfreight use; classified 25/9, these were renumbered 25 901-12.

Allocated in their time to all BR regions bar the Southern, the 25s were most prominently found on the LMR. With freight traffic in decline and the overall BR motive power roster undergoing much rationalisation, these 'first generation' Bo-Bos were early candidates for withdrawal, which was duly enacted between 1978 and 1987. No fewer than 20 have been preserved, a remarkable figure.

Notes on the drawings
The illustrations herewith specifically relate to the 25/3 subclass, the final production variant of the Class 25 fleet assembled at Derby and by Beyer Peacock. Note that the body sides are virtually mirror images, bar the window locations and sundry minor items. The underframe details do however differ considerably.

Holiday time! Taking a break from their normal freight duties are a couple of 25/3s, skirting the sand on the famous sea wall section of the former Great Western main line at Dawlish, with a Nottingham-Paignton extra. Pairs of non-heat Type 2s on summer Saturday additional services were also frequent sights on the ex-Cambrian system amongst others. PHOTOGRAPH: JOHN CHALCRAFT.

Type:	Diesel-Electric
Engine:	1, Sulzer 6LDA28-B
Tractive Effort:	45000 lbs
Power Rating:	1250 hp
Mean Weight in Working Order:	74 tons 8 cwt
Number Built:	327, 1961-7
Building Companies:	BR, Beyer Peacock
Preserved:	20

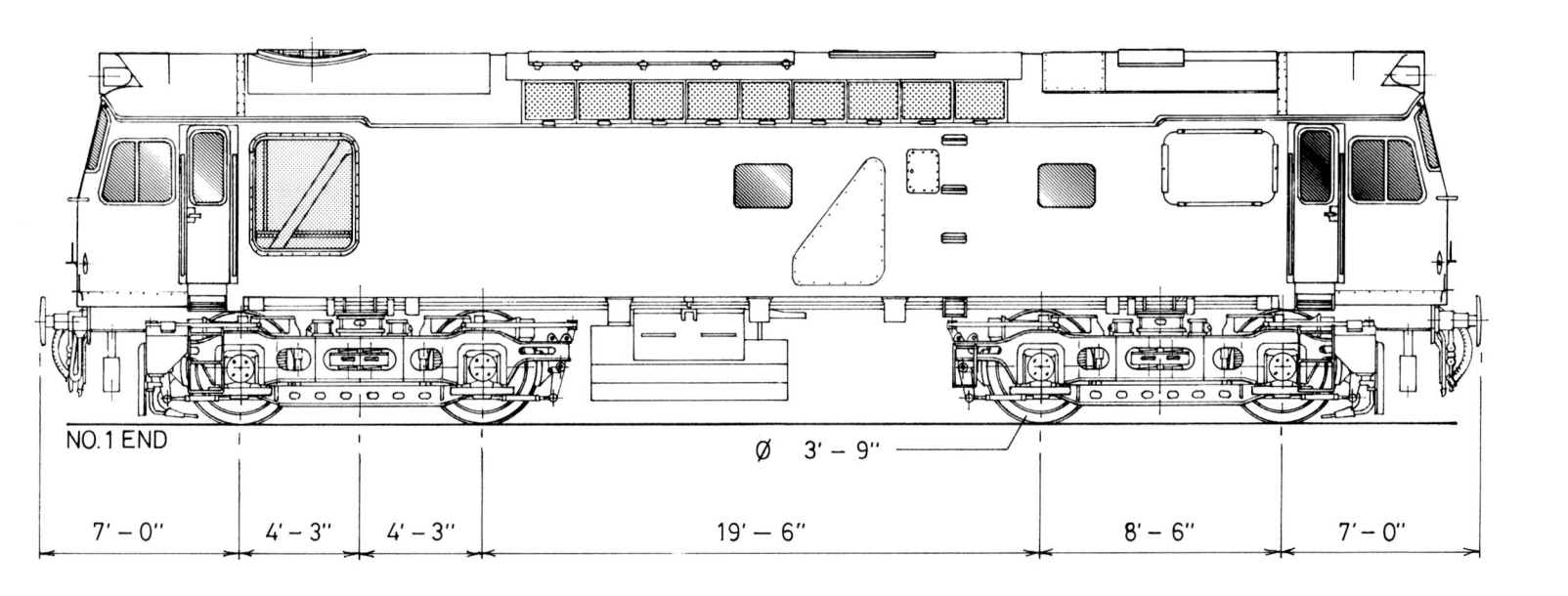

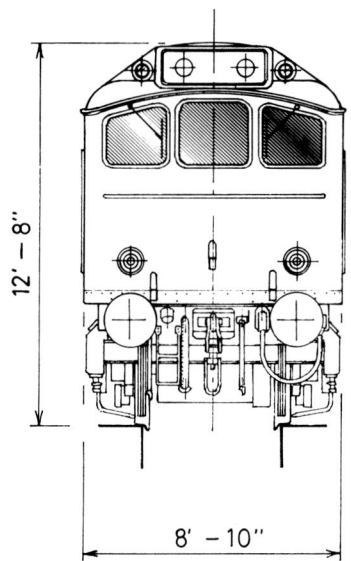

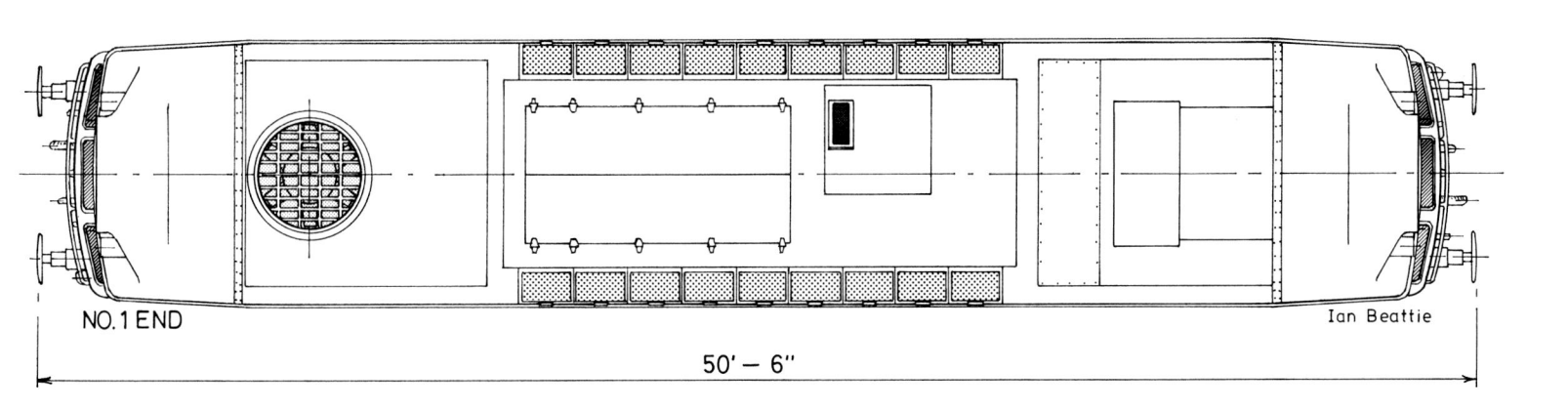

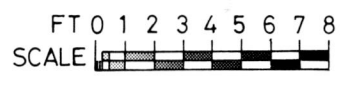

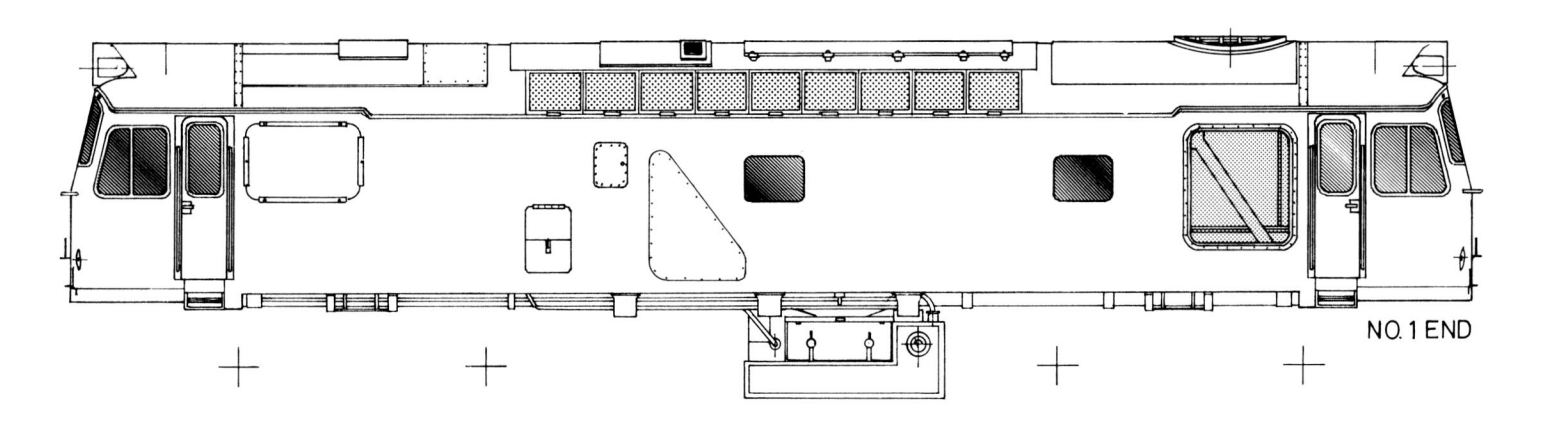

NO.1 END   Ø 3' - 9"

7' - 0" | 4' - 3" | 4' - 3" | 19' - 6" | 8' - 6" | 7' - 0"

12' - 8"

8' - 10"

NO.1 END   Ian Beattie

50' - 6"

FT 0 1 2 3 4 5 6 7 8
SCALE

NO.1 END

Class AL1/81 Bo-Bo

THE PROVISIONS of the celebrated BR Modernisation Plan of 1955 called for *inter alia* the electrification to the overhead 25kV alternating current format of the West Coast Main Line. Work began on this massive undertaking during the late 1950s with the first stage, between Manchester and Crewe, opening to traffic in September 1960; Rugby was reached by the end of 1964 (following a politically-inspired hiatus) and eventually the route throughout from London (Euston) to Manchester and Liverpool was completed in March 1967. *[The route to Glasgow went live in 1974 – Ed.]*

Specifications were despatched in the late 1950s to five individual manufacturers for the supply of 100 suitable locomotives for the route, since it was considered that such a radical form of long-distance traction power (for BR) required five prototype solutions in the first instance in order to arrive at the optimum specification for second-generation engines. Thus these five sets of machines, classified (pre-TOPS) AL1-5 inclusive, constituted the 'first-generation' electrics.

Given an insistence on Bo-Bo wheel/drive arrangement, performance parameters, certain established items of equipment and – most importantly – driving controls in common, the classes were allowed to differ in their electrical and mechanical make-up in order to assess and develop the said optimum specification; numerous electrical and mechanical equipment manufacturing companies from Britain and Europe took part in this important exercise and those principally involved in the assembly of 25 Class AL1 locomotives were Associated Electrical Industries Ltd, who supplied much of the electrical gear and assembled the machines at its Rugby works, and the Birmingham Railway Carriage & Wagon Co. which was responsible for the mechanical componentry.

The initial engine was delivered in November 1959 and numbered E3001, superseded in 1973 under the TOPS system by 81 001 in accordance with the new and still current Class 81 identity. As the 'prototype of a prototype', No.E3001 was used for proving runs and driver familiarisation from December 1959 on the then short distance of electrified line completed. Of the ensuing 24 examples, two were outshopped with the lower gearing initially considered vital for freight working quickly shown to be superfluous; on re-gearing to standard these engines were renumbered to the basic AL1 sequence, but at the advent of TOPS these engines in concert with a number of AL1s withdrawn due to irreparable accident damage conspired to the TOPS renumbering by no means corresponding with the precursive E3xxx series.

The basic construction of the machine comprised a strongly built body braced and stress-loaded to support both the roof-mounted electrical gear, which at the outset included two Stone-Faiveley current collection pantographs per locomotive (one was subsequently removed as unnecessary) and to bring the overall weight to a very trim 80 tons, as specified by BR, aided in addition by glass-fibre cab roofs. Tap-change control and an ability to switch automatically between 6.25kV and 25kV power sources were design features, however when the 25kV system was standardised on the LMR the dual-voltage selection installation was abandoned.

For their first 5-10 years or so of what has emerged as a highly successful career as express hauliers over the WCML, the Class 81 engines sported a distinctive 'electric blue' livery complemented by cast aluminium identity numbers and BR motifs; this gave way to the all-pervasive (until comparatively recently) and deeper shade of Rail Blue complete with the standard format of decal applique. A programme of overhaul in the mid to late 1970s altered the locomotives' overall specification to a degree: outwardly most evident were three air brake reservoirs mounted in place of the second pantograph, the route indicator panel at either cab end was blanked-in by a black panel surmounted with white marker discs, and modified types of smoothing choke were suspended between the bogies beneath the 'corridor' side (see below).

E3005, in allover 'electric blue' livery with white cab surrounds, officiates at Nuneaton on inauguration day of WCML electric services to this point, 2 March 1964. An inspector is on hand to ensure all is well. PHOTOGRAPH: BRITISH RAILWAYS LONDON MIDLAND REGION.

Notes on the drawings

A typical Class 81 Bo-Bo is shown as current from the late 1970s to date. The partial side view depicts the four glazed windows that light the corridor for access between cabs and body-mounted control gear (the corresponding 'main' side view sports a series of ventilation grilles for this gear in lieu), and in this view the pantograph is in running mode. *[This article's appearance coincided with the end of the 81s' careers on BR; one, E3003/81 003, enjoys preservation at the Barrow Hill Roundhouse at the time of writing – Ed.]*

Type:	Express traffic
Tractive Effort:	48000 lbs
Power Rating:	3200 hp
Mean Weight in Working Order:	79 tons 6 cwt
Number Built:	25, 1959-60
Building Company:	AEI Ltd.
Preserved:	1

101

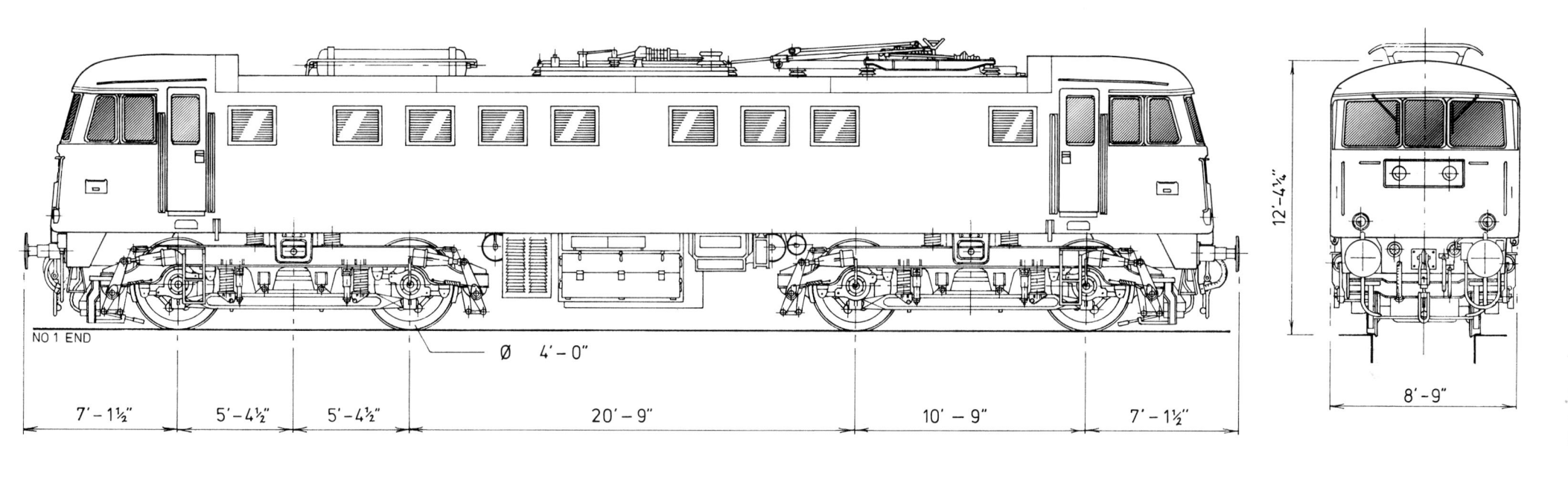

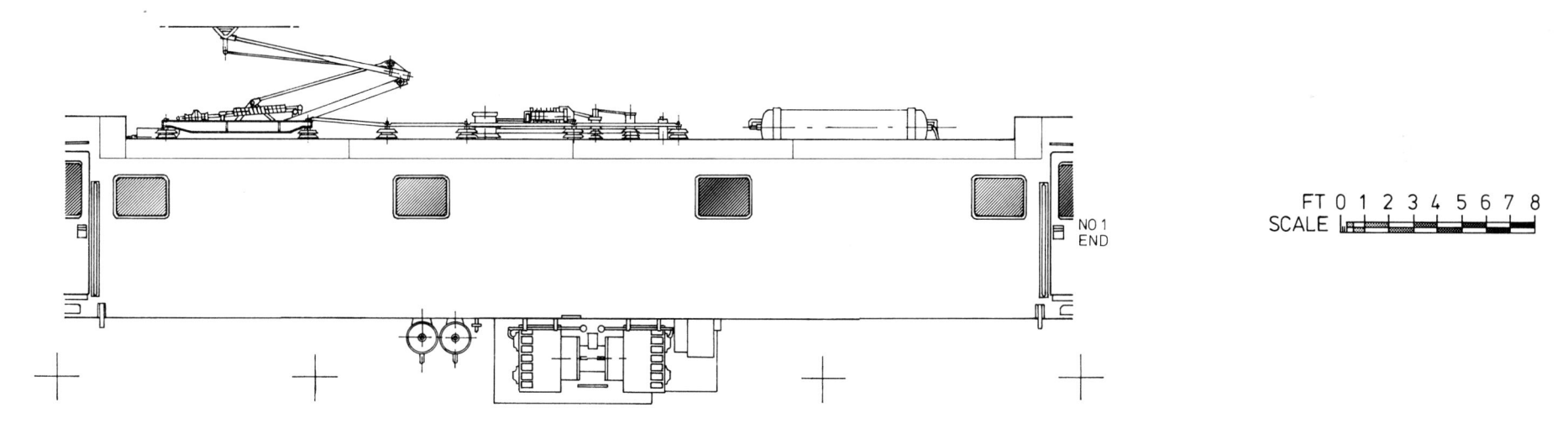

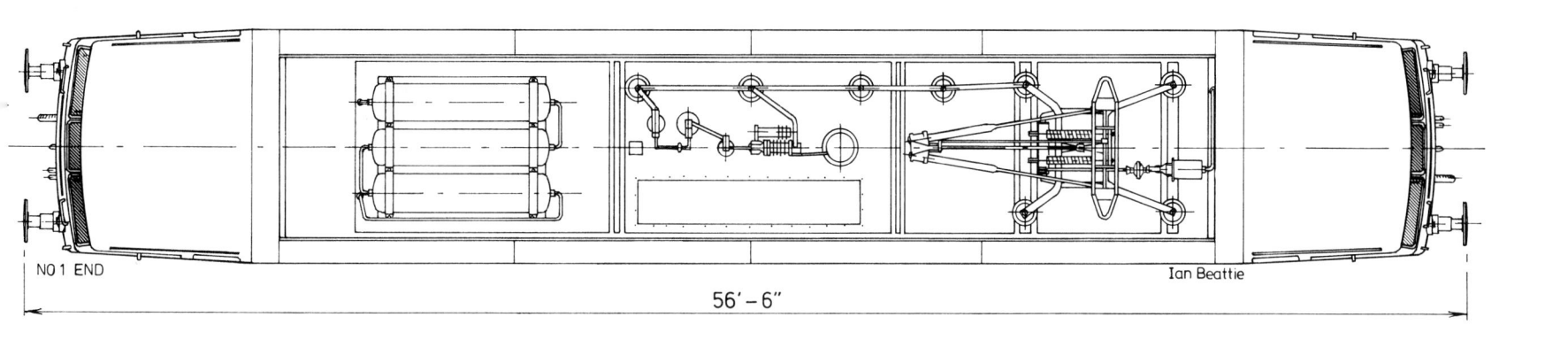

ABOVE: from this superb vantage point above Ranelagh Bridge servicing point, just outside Paddington, we witness doyen D1000 *Western Enterprise* on the turntable as D1011 waits behind. The offset roof fan grilles can be seen clearly. PHOTOGRAPH: PHIL CALEY.

RIGHT: D1003 *Western Pioneer* heels to the curve at Hatton North Junction on 20 July 1962, with an express for Birkenhead. Pictured wearing maroon livery, the locomotive was taken out of service in January 1975. PHOTOGRAPH: DOUGLAS DOHERTY.

Class 52 'Western' C-C

FOLLOWING the pioneering tradition established by the Great Western Railway and maintained over more than a century, the Western Region of British Railways instigated a concept of indigenous motive power under the provisions of the 1955 Modernisation Plan (whereby steam haulage was to be abandoned in favour of diesel and electric traction) quite disparate to the diesel-electric formula adopted by all other BR Regions.

During the 1950s the West German railways, Deutsche Bundesbahn or DB, had developed a large and highly successful fleet of diesel-hydraulic locomotives, in which all axles were driven directly by hydraulic transmission powered in turn by high-revving diesel engines. First fruit of the liaison between BR (WR), DB and various German engineering concerns involved was the 'Warship' B-B Class *[see RM August 1996 – Ed.]*, based on the DB's V200 design, of which building began in 1958; however the need for a more powerful haulier for top link passenger work, replacing the 'King' and 'Castle' 4-6-0s, was quickly identified. While similar in overall concept to the precursive 'Warships' the larger, heavier machines necessitated 3-axle bogies. As before, two engines were installed in each locomotive – 12-cylinder diesels built by Bristol Siddeley under licence from Maybach, but of uprated power compared with those fitted to 'Warships' – linked to Voith hydraulic gearboxes which again drove all axles, classifying the 74 new engines as C-Cs.

Of the total built, 35 were allotted to the ex-GWR works at Swindon, plus a further 39 ordered from the old LNWR/LMS Crewe shops; ostensibly this seems a curious decision, but it was taken as Swindon had not the capacity to construct so many locos in the period stipulated, and as it transpired Crewe eventually built 44 machines, the additional five being those from the WR allocation that Swindon simply could not accommodate.

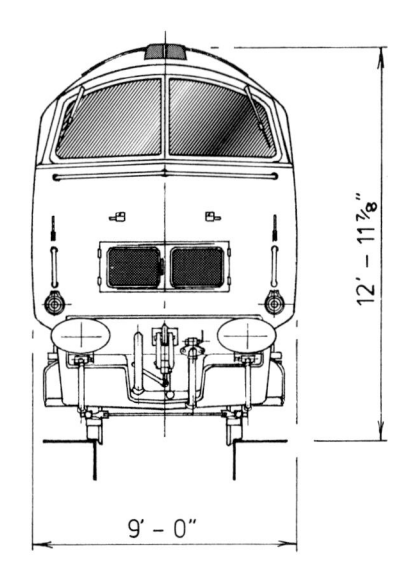

The first engines were outrigged in experimental paint schemes: desert sand, Brunswick green and maroon. The unique sand livery was if nothing else distinctive but was rapidly dropped as impractical; a number of locos were outshopped in green although maroon was the ultimate choice of livery and prevailed until the era of uniform Rail blue was imposed. Part of the acknowledged charisma of these excellent machines was invoked by the use of vivid individual names, all prefixed by 'Western' and hence the class title by which they remain collectively celebrated as arguably the most famous British diesel design yet built. Though best known for exploits on premier passenger services in the west of England, the 'Westerns' were equally at home on fast freight haulage – the stone trains from Merehead currently handled by the immensely able American Class 59 Co-Cos were the domain of 'Westerns', indeed quarry owners Foster Yeoman preserve one of the seven surviving 'Western' locomotives as a memento of days past. *[For the 59, see RM October 1986. The 52 then at Foster Yeoman carried the identity D1035* Western Yeoman: *it now resides on the West Somerset Railway under its proper guise, D1010* Western Campaigner *– Ed.]*

Allotted classification 52 under the TOPS scheme, new numbers were never carried (Nos. D1000-1073

102

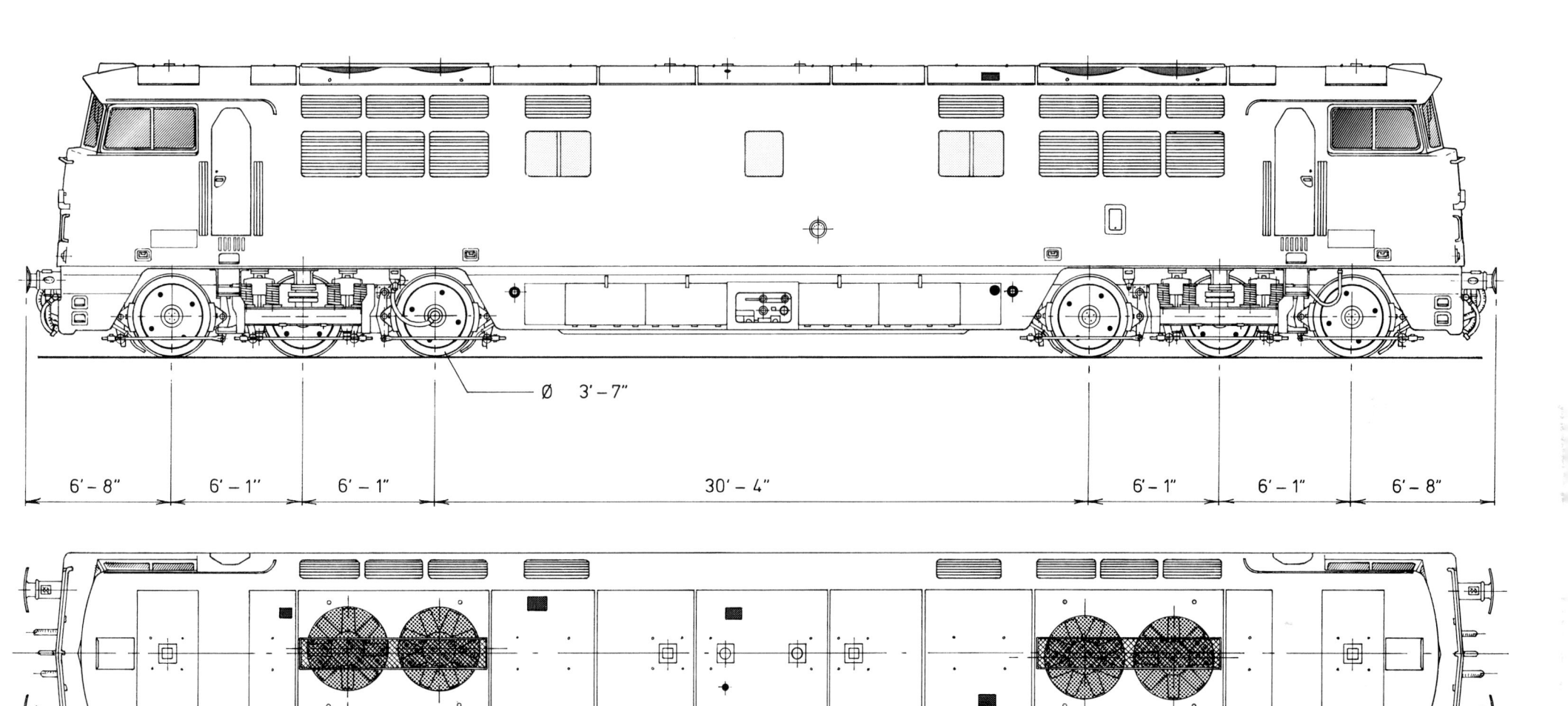

were retained to the end) since the fleet was withdrawn years, even decades before natural obsolescence had set in. Certainly the 'Westerns' suffered their fair share of teething troubles – for a short time the entire class was taken out of service for essential modification – and some aspects of the basic design were by hindsight less than ideal, but their non-standard format in the overall picture of BR motive power dominated by the diesel-electric configuration spelled their premature demise. Advances in technology had also caught up with the 'Westerns': for instance they were not fitted for multiple operation, and lack of electric train heating prevented seasonal haulage of the latest coaching stock (and which equipment was deemed too dear to install retrospectively). Withdrawals commenced in 1973 with the final engine removed from revenue service in 1977, however as already stated no fewer than seven representatives have been saved for posterity so 'Westerns' remain a familiar sight – and their characteristic drone when under way a nostalgic sound – albeit on preserved lines.

Notes on the drawings
Both sides of the locomotive are identical to all intents and purposes (one or two access hatches vary), and hence the illustration of one side only which serves for both. Note that the cooling fan vents are slightly offset from the locomotive centreline as seen in the plan view.

Type:	Diesel-Hydraulic
Engines:	2, 12-cylinder Maybach MD655
Tractive Effort:	70,000 lbs
Power Rating:	2700 hp
Mean Weight in Working Order:	108 tons
Number Built:	74, 1961-4
Building Company:	BR, Swindon & Crewe
Preserved:	7

Section 6
Experimental and narrow gauge locomotives

Locomotive | Page
Hawker Siddeley experimental diesel-electric *Kestrel* | 104-105
Leek & Manifold Valley Light Railway Kitson 2-6-4T | 106-107
Fell diesel mechanical 4-8-4 | 107-108
Manx Northern Railway Dübs 0-6-0T *Caledonia* | 109
Festiniog Railway 2-4-0ST+T/Penrhyn Railway 0-4-0ST | 110-111
Lynton & Barnstaple Railway Baldwin 2-4-2T *Lyn* | 112

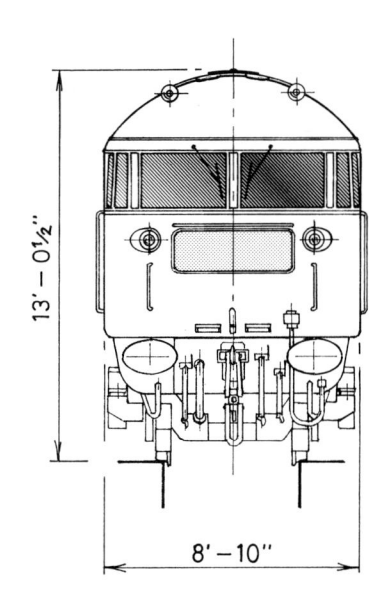

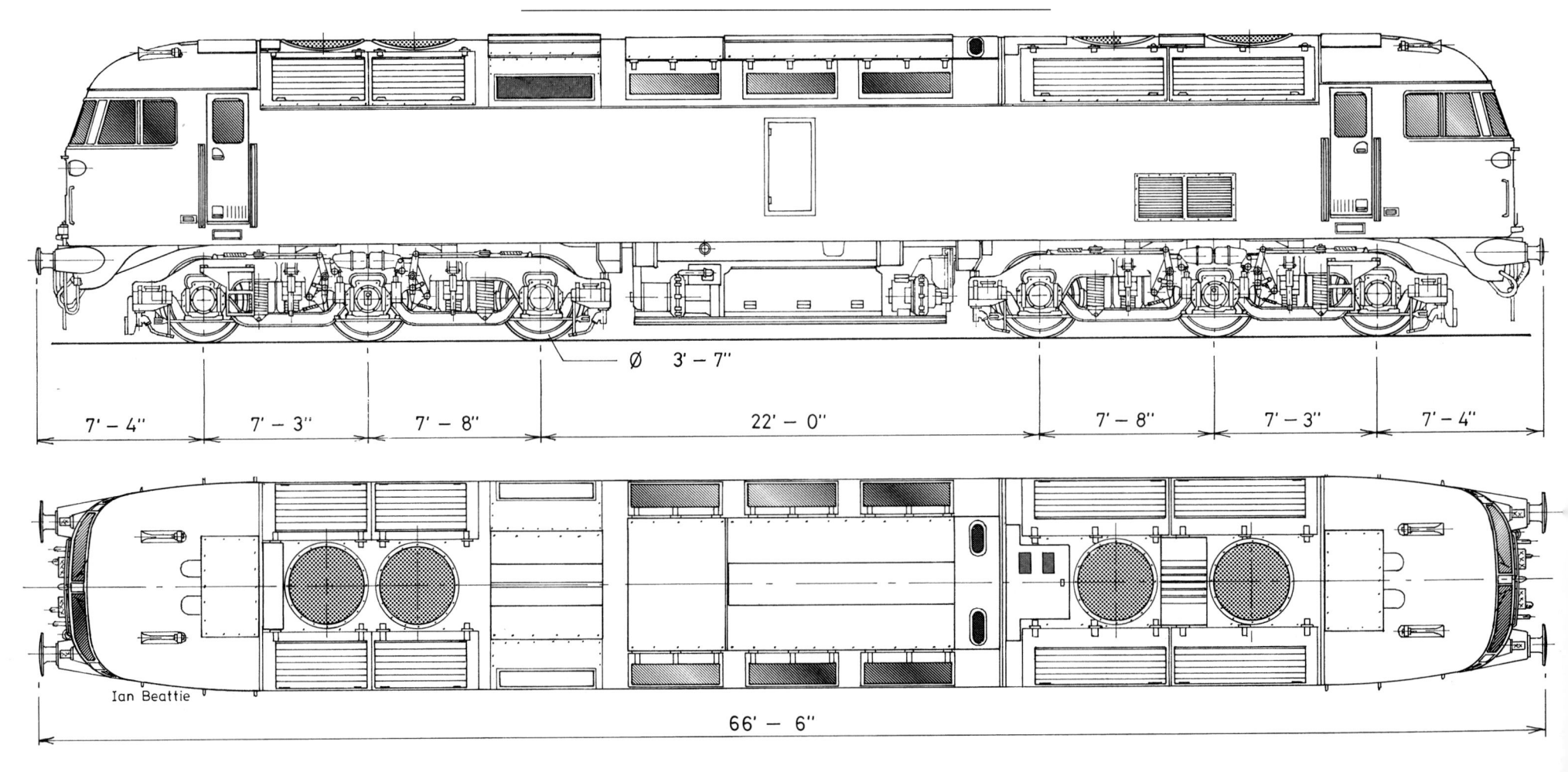

Brush *Kestrel* Co-Co

PROMPTED by the widely publicised success of the Type 5 'Deltic' Co-Cos *[see RM May 1999 and elsewhere in this volume – Ed.]* on East Coast Main Line express passenger traffic during the 1960s, with the consequent notion that future locomotives of this nature should sport a massive 4400 horsepower rating, the celebrated manufacturers Messrs Brush elected to produce an experimental machine to demonstrate the company's prowess in this particular field, with an eye to export markets as well as hoped-for sales to British Railways.

Construction commenced at Brush's Loughborough plant in 1966 and the end result emerged in late 1967; public launch followed in January 1968 at Marylebone Station in London, when BR accepted the engine for running trials.

The locomotive's livery alone – golden yellow over chocolate brown – ensured her distinctiveness. Named *Kestrel* and numbered HS4000 (denoting the Hawker Siddeley Group, of which Brush was a subsidiary, and the nominal 4000hp rating) with the Group logo beneath the side windows, the adventurous newcomer was an amazing spectacle. Within the unique, part-streamlined yet lightweight bodywork sat a single power unit, a 16-cylinder Sulzer diesel very similar to those used in the highly successful Brush/Sulzer Type 4 Co-Cos first assembled at Loughborough in 1962 and nowadays known best as Class 47s, connected to Brush electrical machinery that included, for the first time, brushless main and auxiliary generators (apologies for the unavoidable pun!). The whole sat on massive three-axle bogies of unequal wheelbase – ie the outer axles differed in distance from the central axle – comprising single-piece cast frames with coil-and-beam suspension systems plus three immensely powerful traction motors per bogie. Designed for continuous running at 110mph, the maximum for *Kestrel* was 125mph which, however, was never attained on BR metals. At the time of her introduction *Kestrel* was allegedly the most powerful single-engined diesel-electric loco in existence.

While pleased to accept the locomotive on a trial basis, ownership remaining with Hawker Siddeley, BR quickly identified a fundamental problem that instantly undermined her passenger-hauling utility: the axle-loading exceeded that allowed by BR for this method of construction (in particular, the method by which the traction motors were suspended on the bogies) allied to the very high speed potential.

Trials began on various freight routines early in 1968, on which HS4000 demonstrated considerable prowess, however May that year witnessed the remarkable level of performance of which the machine was capable, on hauling a special train loaded to 20 coaches over the steeply-graded WCML in North-West England. Thence the Co-Co was assigned to Shirebrook depot on the Eastern Region, for working heavy coal trains from colliery to marshalling yard, interspersed with a prolonged session of scientific tests at Derby in autumn 1968. In order to overcome the excess weight Brush replaced early in 1969 her original bogies with those used for Class 47 Co-Cos, which effectively reduced not only the weight to required limits but also the horsepower at the wheels and thus the tractive effort, due to the lower rated Class 47 traction motors. Now acceptable for passenger operation under BR rules, the distinctive Co-Co was allocated to the ECML and thereafter enjoyed an enviable reputation for superb performance on crack King's Cross-Newcastle express services.

Although *Kestrel* was a conspicuous success in her designed role, at least in re-bogied guise, the *raison d'être* as far as Britain was concerned had long evaporated: BR had been developing express passenger multiple units for the ECML and other principal routes culminating in the world-famous HST 125s (and hence the figure for this machine's top speed). Thus with the benefit of hindsight it can be seen that Brush's magnificent design was an anachronism from the very outset.

Since by then the fact that its creation was not going to be replicated for BR was obvious, when *Kestrel* was taken into shops at Barrow in mid-1970 for engine overhaul Brush entertained negotiations for the locomotive's purchase by the (then) Soviet railway network. Accordingly, upon HS4000's eventual withdrawal from Shirebrook early in 1971 the Co-Co entered Crewe Works for sundry alterations – principally adaptation to the Russian 5' gauge – and thence exported from Cardiff Docks. On arrival in the Soviet Union *Kestrel* was placed on display at a railway exhibition at Scherbinka during summer 1971, but from that time onwards her fate went unrecorded.

With the opening up of the former Soviet Union attempts have been made to discover the whereabouts of *Kestrel*, but – according to a note in the magazine *Traction* – it would appear that this powerful machine, believed dismantled for study by engineering students, was scrapped as recently as 1993.

Notes on the drawings
As befitted her experimental status sundry detail modifications were made to *Kestrel* during her life with BR; the drawings depict the vehicle in typical guise complete with original bogies.

Note that (1) the opposite bodyside, not illustrated, is basically a mirror image of the profile shown, excepting that the central opening panel is 1'5" shorter and without the twin low-set grilles shown here (part of the dynamic brake resistance cooling system); and (2) that the shutters either side of the two sets of fans opened and closed under thermostatic operation: they are displayed here in closed mode.

A photo unidentified as to both location and photographer: displaying its inimitable livery and running on original bogies, Kestrel is seen hauling a massive coal train with apparent ease during its Shirebrook days in summer 1968.

Type:	Experimental D/E
Engine:	1, Sulzer 16LVA24
Tractive Effort:	70000 lbs
Power Rating:	4000hp
Mean Weight in Working Order:	126 tons
Number Built:	1, 1968
Building Company:	Brush
Preserved:	No

Leek & Manifold 2-6-4T

HAD IT SURVIVED just a few more years this famous little outfit in the depths of the glorious Peak District could well have joined the ranks of preserved narrow gauge systems. It was certainly different to anything we now enjoy.

Frequently marketed, rather disparagingly to modern eyes, as a "toy railway" in addressing its main source of income, tourists, the Leek & Manifold Valley Light Railway Company (hereinafter called the LMVR in deference to prolixity) was formed as a result of the Light Railways Act of Parliament, wherein allowance was made for less stringent standards of passenger carriage than that rightly insisted upon for main line working.

Leading light of the company was the local MP Colonel Charles Bill, and the first sod was ceremonially cut by the 8th Duke of Devonshire in 1899. Whilst the gauge of 2'6" had already been decided upon, a *contretemps* concerning the work necessary to construct the undertaking was resolved by appointment of a celebrated consulting engineer. Born in 1857 and thoroughly versed in railway matters, Everard Calthrop had recently completed the 2'6" gauge Barsi Light Railway in India, a highly successful network that eventually comprised some 200 route miles: the 9¼ miles of the Leek & Manifold seemingly stood little comparison.

Opened in 1904 and running from Hulme End southwards beside the Rivers Manifold and Hamps to Waterhouses in north-eastern Staffordshire, the LMVR was operated from the outset by its standard gauge neighbour, the North Stafford Railway for an emolument of 55% of the gross receipts. To connect the LMVR with its station at Leek the NSR built a spur to nearby Waterhouses, causing the LMVR to supply transfer wagons that carried standard-gauge NSR trucks piggyback-fashion rather than employ the time-consuming procedure of trans-shipment at the terminus.

Just two locomotives were needed to work the line; for these Calthrop drew on his Indian experience and in 1903 approached Kitson & Company the celebrated locomotive manufacturers. Having supplied the Barsi Railway with 4-8-4 tanks, to Calthrop's specifications, the company adapted this proven blueprint, allowing for an axle loading no greater than 5 tons, and delivered in 1904 two 2-6-4 tasks to the LMVR. The 'colonial' influence was obvious: lifting jacks on the running plates (uncommon in Britain but mandatory overseas where the art of tracklaying was perforce less rigorous), double-roofed tropical cabs, fittings ready for cowcatchers, and those immense carbide headlamps that became very much a trademark of the Leek & Manifold, which however were probably never lit. Elaborate coaches accompanied these exotic power units.

Given numbers and names encapsulated in large cast plates on the side tasks, the engines – No.1 *E.R.Calthrop* and No.2 *J.B.Earle* – worked the line on the 'one engine in steam' principle, necessitating minimal signalling. Incidentally John B. Earle was first resident engineer for the line. Initially livery was lined 'milk chocolate', changed before World War 1 to the distinctive NSR madder lake (following a particularly acute financial crisis, vicissitudes that perennially beset the LMVR, the NSR becoming virtual owner of the line); on Grouping the LMS, into which the NSR was absorbed, applied crimson lake livery to the two engines, the final change being to plain black in the late 1920s.

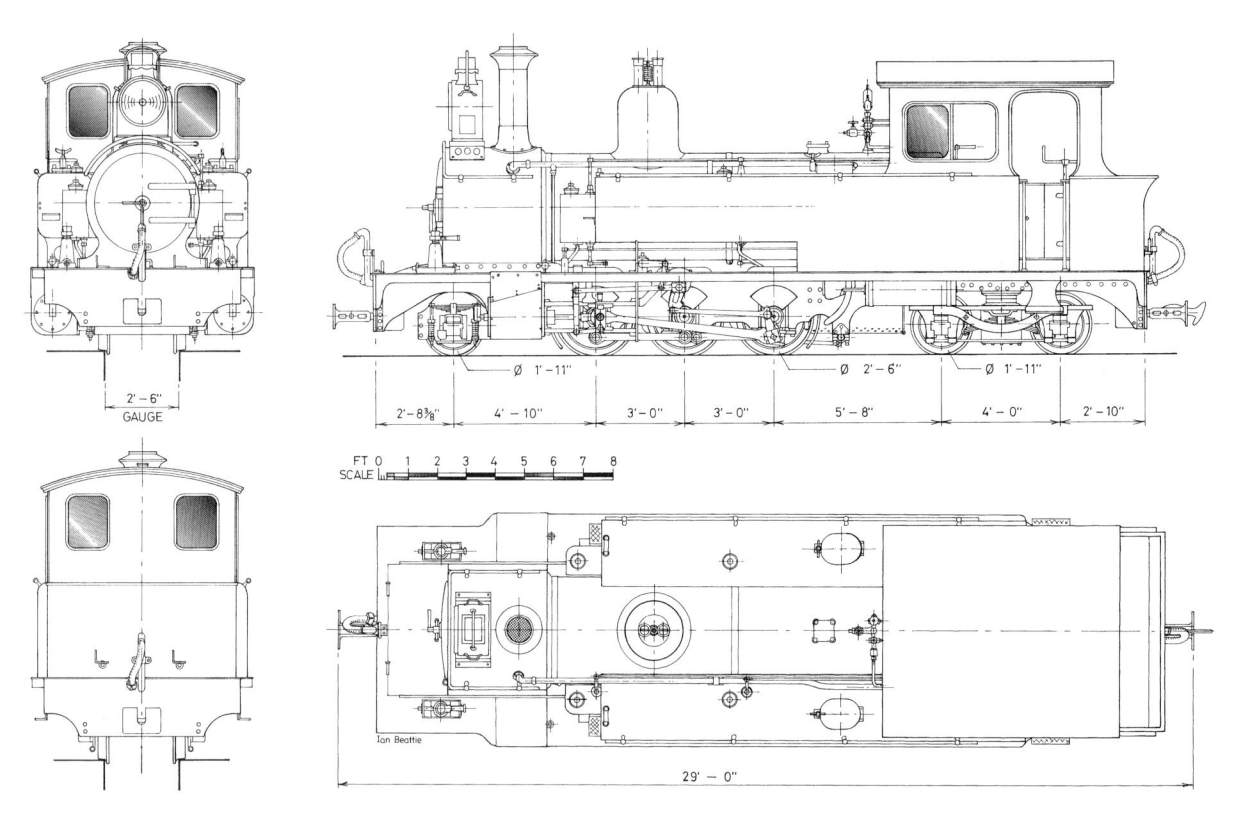

An evocative period shot of 26-4T No.2 *J.B. Earle* captured at the head of a passenger train at Hulme End in the early years of the Leek & Manifold Valley line; note the ornate coaches (In light yellow livery) complete with steps due to the low platform surface. Behind the sparklingly clean engine can be seen the carriage shed. PHOTOGRAPH: B. MATTHEWS COLLECTION, c/o FRANK HORNBY.

106

Very little in the way of modifications was made to the sturdy little machines; in 1914 overhaul to both engines at the NSR Stoke-on-Trent Works (the engines' base at Hulme End, effectively the LMVR headquarters, was adequate for everyday and light maintenance demands) changed their appearance somewhat: a single Ross 'pop' supplanted the Ramsbottom safety valves atop the dome, the bunker sides and back were raised to increase coal capacity and – most fascinatingly – piping forward of the leading wheels was installed for jetting water onto the rails to alleviate flange squeal consequent upon the many tight curves. Surprisingly effective overall, this equipment could obviously cause more problems than it solved in cold weather!

Final and, as it turned out, irrevocable closure of the delightful but loss-making Leek & Manifold took place in 1934; engine No.2 was officially withdrawn in 1935 at Crewe and scrapped in 1937, however No.1, although withdrawn officially in 1936, remained under wraps at Waterhouses and was used to haul the rail-removing train in early 1937. It was cut up in October that year.

Notes on the drawings

Shown here is the Kitson 2-6-4T in original condition, as delivered to the Leek & Manifold. It is known that a plate for mounting the vast headlamp on the rear spectacle panel was provided when new; but was removed early on as a superfluity. Delivered with hooters, these were replaced by whistles before the line opened to the public; likewise valve motion covers were supplied, in the manner of tram engines, but these did not survive long. Exposed rivetting appeared eventually at the smokebox rear edges and on the running plate between and forward of the visible frames (probably during the NSR overhaul aforementioned). Note that the cab side windows were in fact fully glazed, however the rear portion was habitually slid forward and thus 'open' as shown here in illustration and photo alike.

The advice and assistance during production of these notes and drawings of Leek & Manifold experts Bob Gratton and Robert Cartwright are gratefully acknowledged.

Type:	Mixed-traffic Tank
Cylinders:	2, 11½" x 16" bore/stroke
Boiler Pressure:	150 lbs/sq in
Heating Surface:	405 sq ft
Grate Area:	10 sq ft
Tractive Effort:	8993 lbs
Mean Weight in Working Order:	26 tons 16 cwt
Coal Capacity:	1 ton
Water Capacity:	600 gallons
Number Built:	2, 1904
Preserved:	Neither

Found by Frank Hornby in the scrap sidings at Derby Works on 12 April 1959, the Fell experimental No.10100 in 4-4-4-4 guise stood abandoned here for a further 15 months before its final *dénouement*.

Fell experimental 4-8-4 diesel mechanical

THE UNIQUE Fell locomotive was a synthesis of inputs from several proponents of diesel rail propulsion, of whom H.G.Ivatt, last CME of the LMS, was the most famous and Lt-Col L.F.R.Fell the most influential. That the machine was a 'lost cause' was more a function of the era in which it was constructed rather than any mechanical complexity or oddity, since alongside the contemporaneous LMS diesel-electric locomotives Nos.10000 and 10001 it was truly a pioneer of alternative British main line traction.

Formerly an employee of the LNER at Doncaster, Lt-Col Fell had invented a system of power transmission via fluid couplings, for the exploitation of which he had founded his own company, aptly titled Fell Developments Ltd. His system interested Ivatt who, in early 1948 at the very outset of the nationalised British Railways, contrived to obtain permission for building an experimental locomotive incorporating Fell's patents, together with the engine development firm of Ricardo. This latter association rapidly broke up and subsequently used were Paxman Type 12RPH 12-cylinder, 500hp power units.

The unique Fell layout employed four engines, two at each end set side by side and disposed 'north/south' under the cuboid 'snouts' of the bulbous, rather ugly body. The engines were linked to fluid couplings and drove the two innermost of the four coupled axles via differential gears, quill shafts and a common gearbox; this method of transmission was designed to emulate the smoothness and flexible performance typical of a steam locomotive, qualities unattainable from early electrical transmissions as applied to pioneering diesel locomotives. Two further engines, AEC units of 150hp apiece and housed within the main body of the vehicle, were utilised to power pressure chargers for the main engines, and two train heating boilers were installed too for No.10100's intended role as express passenger haulier.

The theoretical reasoning behind the fitment of four engines in lieu of a single unit of equivalent total horsepower became logical in respect of fuel consumption and smooth progression of power. The fluid couplings attached to all four engines were empty of oil when the latter were idling, however on acceleration from standstill the coupling of No.1 engine was filled under pressure, the engine opened up and drove the locomotive; thereafter the remaining three engines were brought into action sequentially at predetermined velocities until, from 25mph up to the maximum of around 80mph, all engines provided the requisite power. For those interested in statistics, No.1 unit alone was in action from 0 to 6mph; Nos.1 and 2 engines from 7 to 17mph; Nos.1, 2 and 3 from 18 to 24mph; and from 25mph upwards the locomotive was powered by the full set.

Constructed in the ex-LMS workshops at Derby, the Fell 4-8-4 emerged in summer 1950 in black livery with silver lining and numbered 10100; following a prolonged period of adjustment and development within the works confines the unique machine was publicly launched at Marylebone station in May 1951. A lengthy series of trials was then embarked upon, principally on the ex-MR St.Pancras-Manchester route and including the old Cheshire Lines Committee trackage, interspersed with use on revenue-earning traffic on which the 4-8-4 entered formally in January 1952. A 12-month period of inactivity elapsed in 1954, caused by a major and extremely expensive breakdown, before re-emergence from Derby during 1955 in unlined BR green livery and onto tests over the Settle-Carlisle route, which apparently were very successful. Thereafter the Fell returned to intermittent duties on the St.Pancras line, during which time the only really obvious external modification in its lifespan was enacted – the central coupling rods were removed, thereby producing in effect a 4-4-4-4 wheel arrangement: quite why this was done is lost in the mists of time.

The end came in October 1958, at Manchester Central station. Whilst awaiting departure at the head of the 12.25pm to Derby a debilitating fire broke out in one of the Fell's train heating boilers; the hulk was ingloriously towed to Derby. The locomotive was officially withdrawn in December 1958 and eventually cut up for scrap in July 1960. Thus ended a courageous and quite successful experiment; however with a huge improvement in design and reliability of electrical transmissions for rail use during the 1950s Lt-Col Fell's innovatory mechanical system was clearly an engineering cul-de-sac and his eponymous locomotive met the fate of many such brave ideas.

Type:	Diesel-mechanical
Engines:	4, 12-cyl. Paxman 12RPH
HP Rating:	2000 hp
Tractive Effort:	29400 lbs
Mean Weight in Working Order:	120 tons
Number Built:	1, 1950
Withdrawn:	1958
Preserved:	No

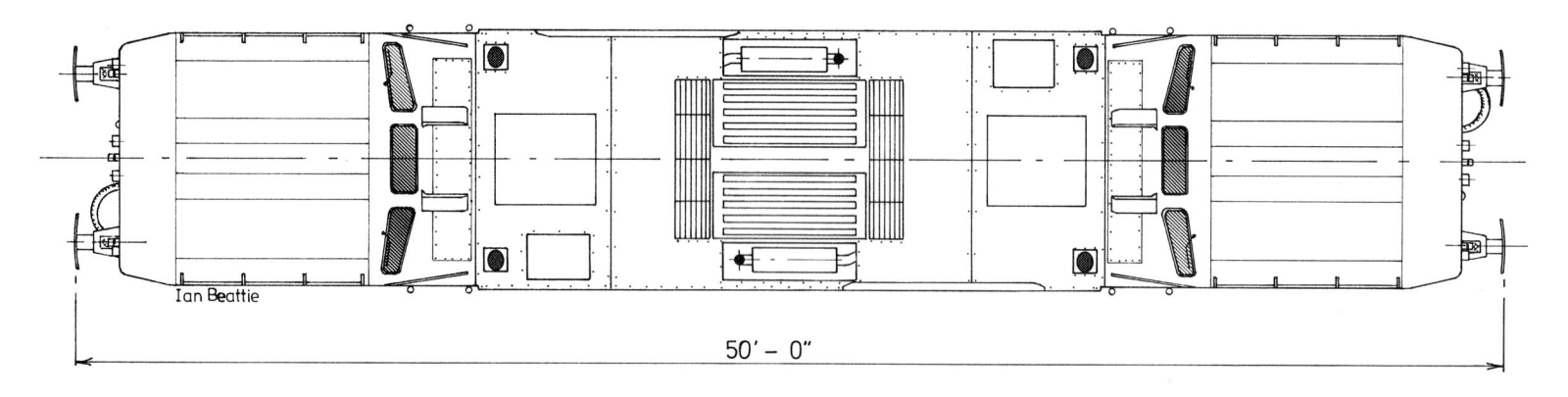

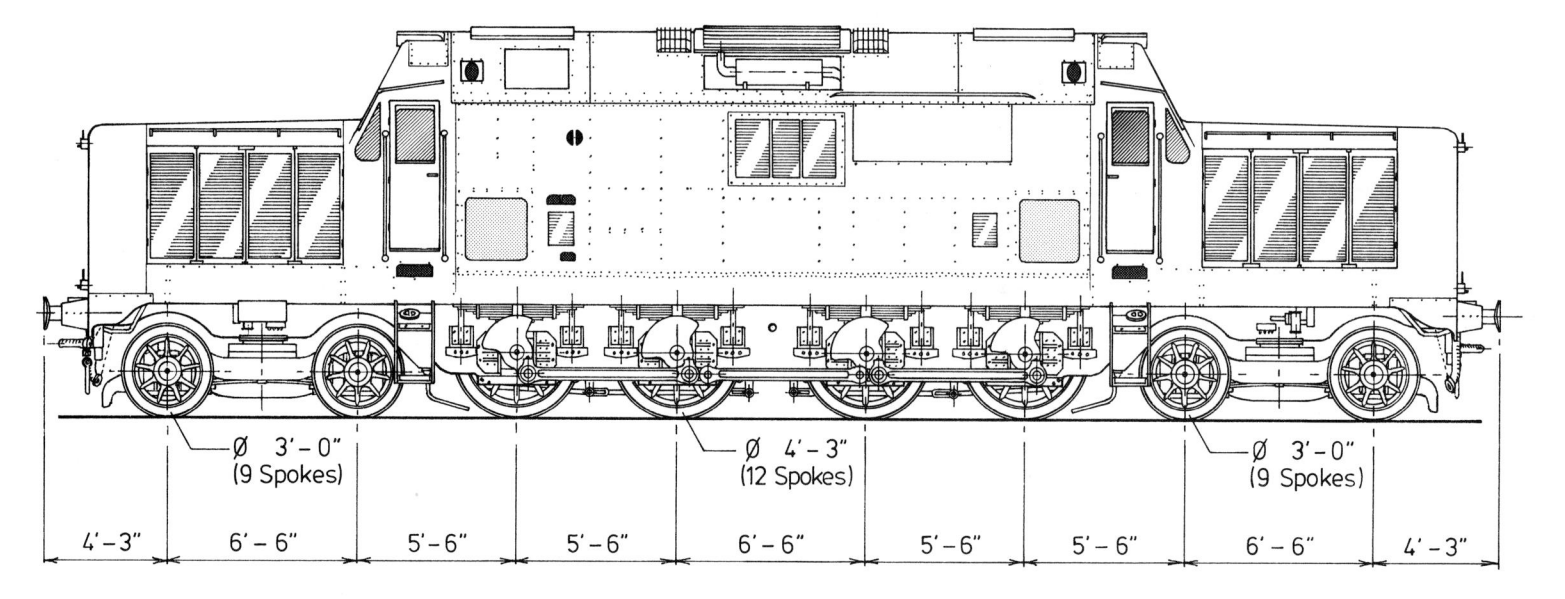

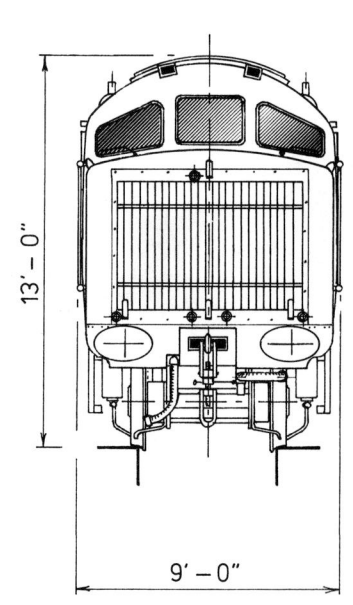

Manx Northern 0-6-0T

ENTIRELY independent of the original Isle of Man Railway, the Manx Northern Railway company was established in 1877 to link St.Johns, on the IoMR Douglas-Peel route, with Ramsey via a 16-mile, north-eastwards-curving line.

Two 2-4-0 tank engines were acquired from Sharp Stewart & Co of Manchester during 1879 in time for the line's opening, with a third 2-4-0T delivered by Messrs Beyer Peacock in 1880 to the same design as that employed on the IoMR (see RAILWAY MODELLER May 1993 for drawings).

Just south of St Johns is Foxdale village and the site of once profitable lead mines: in 1882 a company was founded to construct a branch thereto, the completed line was leased to the MNR and, in order to conquer the heavy inclines on the branch, a single, more powerful 0-6-0T was specifically erected by Henry Dübs & Co of Glasgow, to works number 2178. Given the logical number 4 by the MNR and christened *Caledonia* (the Latin name for Scotland, land of its origin), the engine hauled both freight and passenger traffic over the branch.

After many vicissitudes, financial and otherwise, the MNR was purchased by the IoMR in 1904 and the unique 0-6-0T acquired the number 15 under new ownership. The Foxdale mines closed in 1914 and the branch remained open for passenger business for only a short while thereafter, however as much the most powerful locomotive on the island *Caledonia* performed useful work during the First World War ferrying personnel to and from prisoner-of-war camps.

Following the Armistice however *Caledonia* was but seldom used, its power outweighed by the propensity for its relatively long coupled wheelbase to spread the track alarmingly. Fitted with snowploughs front and back on an almost permanent basis, its weight and surefooted qualities lending themselves well to such activity, No.15 spent decades lying dormant on shed, being steamed on merely a handful of occasions for snow clearance duties.

In latter years *Caledonia* resided as a static exhibit in the IoMR Museum at Port Erin however the centenary of the Snaefell Mountain Railway this year *[1995 – Ed.]* has prompted a thorough restoration and return to steam for the 6-coupled tank – then as now unique on the island – since it played a significant part in construction of the SMR in 1895.

Notes on the drawings
These are somewhat composite drawings, depicting sundry details present on the locomotive at one time or another: the well-oiled caveat of choosing a particular time and adhering to it for accurate modelling holds as true here as anywhere.

Note that the bufferbeam-mounted safety chains are shown on the side view only, for clarity's sake. The water tank(s) here are not the originals – the rivet pattern differs and bufferbeam lower corners were initially cut diagonally but rapidly altered to the curved cut-aways shown, certainly during MNR days. Ross 'pop' safety valves displaced the Ramsbottom variety and chimney styles vary (marginally anyway) according to period.

Caledonia waits in the servicing siding laid halfway up Snaefell at the Bungalow in October 1995. PHOTOGRAPH: ALAN PIKE.

Type:	6-Coupled Tank
Cylinders:	2, 13" x 20" bore/stroke
Mean Weight in Working Order:	27 tons
Number Built:	1, 1885
Preserved:	Yes

109

Penrhyn/Festiniog Railway Hunslet 0-4-0ST

INAUGURATED as long ago as 1801 and steam-worked from 1876, the narrow gauge Penrhyn Railway linked a series of slate quarries south of Bethesda in Caernarvonshire with Port Penrhyn, just east of Bangor on the coast of North Wales, a distance of some 6 miles. A privately owned concern never open to the general public, the railway existed solely for the transport of slate and thus, beyond staff trains, passenger traffic was not a factor in the line's management.

Latterly in its history the railway's locomotive fleet comprised some 30 engines, of which all but three were used inside or within a short distance of the quarries. The three 'outsiders' handled trains on the overland haul to and from Port Penrhyn and were small but powerful 4-coupled saddle tanks supplied (as were the majority of later Penrhyn hauliers) by Messrs Hunslet of Leeds. The first of these, *Charles* of 1882 is preserved as a static exhibit in the Penrhyn Castle Museum; the remaining two are *Blanche* and *Linda* which, having been outshopped in 1893 (Hunslet works numbers 589 and 590 respectively), are currently celebrating their centenary, in full working trim under the aegis of the Festiniog Railway. *[This article dates from the April 1993 issue – Ed.]* The heyday of the Welsh slate railways was undoubtedly the Edwardian era; thereafter workings were gradually run down in scale to the point where the owners of the Penrhyn Quarries deemed a switch to road transport was merited. The rail system was accordingly closed throughout in 1963.

During 1962 however, the two Penrhyn 'Ladies', surplus to requirements, were transferred on loan to the thriving, tourist-orientated and enthusiast-run Festiniog Railway. Outright purchase was completed in 1963, since when the two sturdy little engines have become such an integral part of the Festiniog operation that their initial 70-year sojourn on the Penrhyn lines tends to be overlooked; perhaps equally responsible for this attitude is the considerable variety of modifications borne by the engines over the past 30 years.

ABOVE: an historic photograph from Penrhyn Railway days, *Blanche* is caught in full steam at Port Penrhyn in July 1954, accompanied by another Hunslet 0-4-0ST, the cableless *Winifred* of 1885 vintage, in the background.

LEFT: captured on a lengthy stone embankment above Minffordd, *Linda*, resplendent in lined black, runs light past the camera. This view into the cab will be of great use to modellers.

RIGHT: *Blanche* eases a train off the Cob and into Portmadoc. Both these modern views date from 1997.
TWO PHOTOGRAPHS: ANDREW BURNHAM.

Among the major alterations in that time have been provision of tenders early in FR ownership; superheaters were added to the boilers, oil firing was installed in 1970/71 and around the same time both engines were rebuilt with leading carrying axles to become 2-4-0STs (with tenders perhaps this should read 2-4-0STT or even 2-4-0ST+T: take your pick, there are no hard-and-fast rules to cover this eventuality). In addition the original cylinder slide valves on *Blanche* have been relaced by piston valves and the same locomotive sports a permanent tender cab, whereas *Linda* now carries a removable version of the latter. (It should perhaps be emphasised that in view of the ongoing programme of modifications applied to both engines this is the situation that obtains at the time of writing.) In addition *Linda* experimentally has been reworked to burn coal on the gas producer principle, which essentially utilises fuel much more efficiently than hitherto.

Interestingly, in Penrhyn days the engines were driven from the right, however the FR preferred otherwise and both tanks were speedily adapted for driving on the left-hand side of the cab.

Notes on the drawings
These attempt to cover the chief alterations in the tanks' general appearance to date. The principal drawings show the tanks comparatively early in FR ownership, as 0-4-0STs complete with tender, which beyond carrying fuel also holds additional water.

Subsidiary drawings 'A' and 'B' depict the cab side, rear and roofline of the tanks in their Penrhyn incarnation, ie as pure saddle tank engines. Note that although not drawn here the chimney equalled the height of the cab - the former was subsequently increased to the height shown in the main illustrations. Note also the original style of buffing equipment.

The conversion to 2-4-0ST guise is the purpose behind drawing 'C', which also shows the stovepipe chimney recently worn by *Linda*, the slightly extended smokebox given to both engines, and the piston-valve-controlled cylinders applied to *Blanche*.

Since 1962 the Festiniog Railway has also fitted to both 'Ladies' *inter alia* vacuum brake apparatus and much enlarged sandboxes flanking the chimney (the original Hunslet equipment comprised small cylindrical 'boxes, in the same position using identical control cranks and rods).

Cylinders:	2, 10½" x 12" bore/stroke
Boiler Pressure:	140 lbs/sq in
Heating Surface:	307 sq ft
Grate Area:	5.2 sq ft
Tractive Effort:	6,320 lbs
Weight in Working Order:	12 tons 5 cwt (as built)

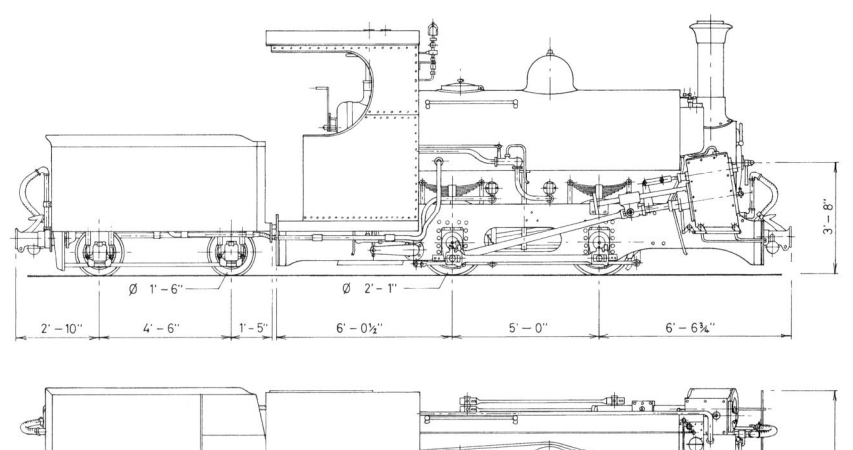

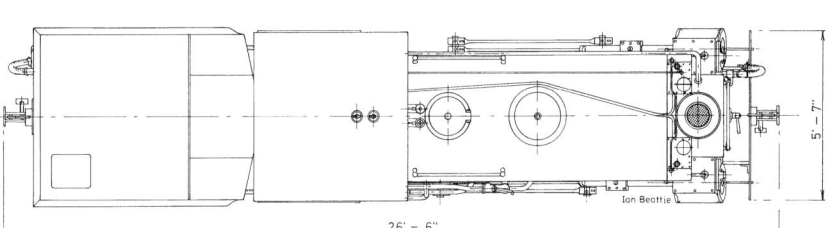

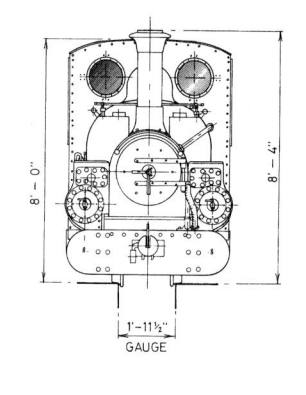

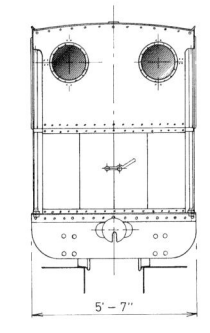

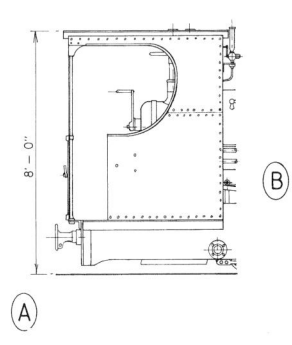

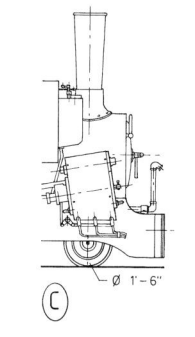

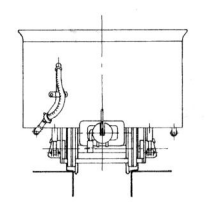

Lynton & Barnstaple Baldwin 2-4-2T *Lyn*

HAD THE delightfully picturesque Lynton & Barnstaple Railway survived beyond the Second World War it would proably still be in operation today, albeit as a preserved line, in the manner of its paradigm the Festiniog Railway, whose quaint 1'11½" gauge it shared.

In the 19th Century the North Devon resort of Lynmouth, with its associated town of Lynton separated by 500' in height and connected via a funicular railway within the dizzily steep Lyn gorge, was a popular upmarket holiday resort. Getting there however was fraught with difficulties (the area was quite reasonably advertised as the English Switzerland) given the narrow and inadequate lanes thereabouts before the advent of road motor transport; the nearest rail approach served Barnstaple, the principal town of the region.

To cut short a rather convoluted story, a narrow gauge connection between Lynton and Barnstaple was undertaken – the sponsorship for which was unusual in being entirely local – under the dynamic chairmanship of publisher Sir George Newnes, a prominent resident and generous benefactor of Lynton (his company was celebrated for publishing *inter alia* Conan Doyle's inimitable 'Sherlock Holmes' stories).

The little railway opened in May 1898 having over-

Undergoing maintenance in the surprisingly bright and clean interior of the Shops at Pilton Yard on 29 September 1933, just 2 years before scrapping, is the unique 2-4-2T *Lyn*.
PHOTOGRAPH: THE LATE W.G.BOYDEN, FRANK HORNBY COLLECTION.

come many problems during construction, caused chiefly by the exceptionally hilly terrain it traversed: although perched some distance – and altitude – from the town, the neat and attractive little terminus at Lynton was a prelude to 19¼ miles of writhing trackwork encompassing 7 intermediate stations or halts through some of the most glorious scenery England has to offer. By contrast the Barnstaple terminus was simply a bay platform alongside the standard gauge LSWR Town station.

To work the railway, 3 distinctive little 2-6-2Ts were purchased from Messrs Manning Wardle of Leeds: these were named after Devon rivers. However the desirability of a fourth locomotive was keenly felt within weeks of opening and, because at the time no British manufacturer could offer speedy delivery, the L&B authorities turned to the USA and specifically the vast Baldwin Locomotive Works in Philadelphia. The outcome was a delicious 2-4-2T of archetypally American appearance and construction, including bar frames, boiler-mounted 'dome' sandboxes and a commodious wooden cab.

Whilst passenger traffic was always vital to its well-being, goods haulage (especially coal) assumed considerable and eventually equal importance to the L&BR, all duties being performed by the stalwart little tank engines. Due to its 'foreign' nature not so popular with enginemen as the 2-6-2Ts (of which a fourth joined the fleet in 1925), the 2-4-2T, named *Lyn*, nevertheless competently held its own and worked consistently without major failure over more than 35 years.

Under the act of Grouping, the L&BR was absorbed

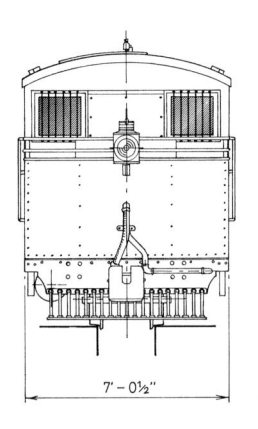

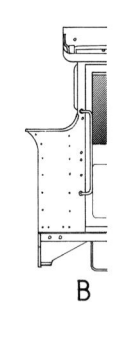

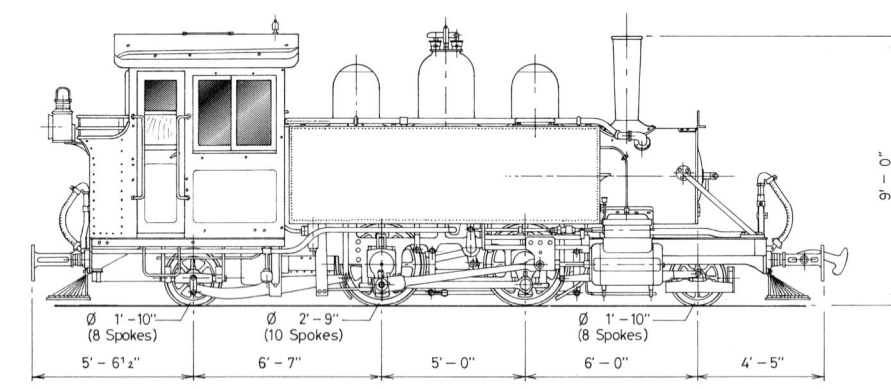

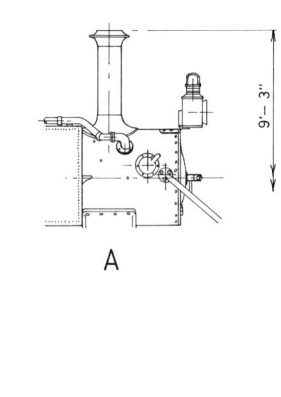

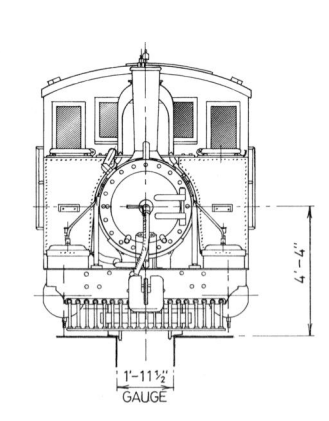

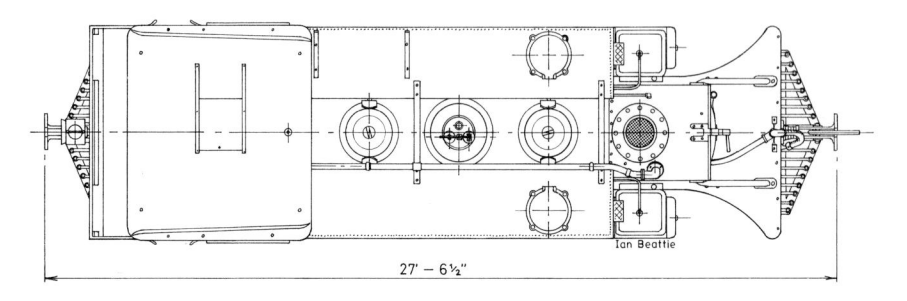

112

by the newly formed Southern Railway in 1923; the little railway took on a somewhat more professional air under SR guidance and amongst other changes was the application of SR lined green engine livery, in place of L&B deep green bordered in black with orange lining (*Lyn* was thus caparisoned at Eastleigh Works, whence it had been transported for overhaul in 1929: everyday servicing was carried out by the L&BR at Pilton Yard in Barnstaple). The locomotives were assigned numbers – never an L&B practice but retained their distinctive names; the American tank was identified as No.762.

For all the money and effort spent in upgrading the L&BR under its hegemony, the return in terms of overall custom fell dramatically in the face of increasing road transport competition and the SR felt compelled to close the line. Thus the L&BR passed into history in September 1935. In the subsequent, sad little auction of effects *Lyn* fetched just £50 and was scrapped forthwith.

Notes on the drawings
The principal views here depict *Lyn* in its post-First World War state, without the steam heating apparatus (but visible in the photo) that was a late fitment.

Scrap view 'A' shows the original smokebox (the boiler was renewed in 1907 with an all but identical replacement) complete with copper-capped chimney – retained on boiler renewal until displaced by the Urie style stovepipe version shortly after World War One – and access door for ash removal. This latter feature was operated by air blast accompanied by hand raking (hence the door) but was not transferred on boiler renewal. Scrap view 'B' displays the original, unrailed coal bunker and its associated rivetwork.

Note that the original door differed from the later configuration illustrated in the full side view. Lamps were not permanently affixed but slotted onto brackets – note that in the main views *Lyn* is set to proceed bunker first, whereas in view 'A' chimney-first is the order. The original whistle, an American 'hooter', was mounted on the dome alongside the safety valves (a blanking plate marks its position in the plan view), supplanted by a smaller, roof-mounted version.

Type:	Mixed-Traffic Side Tank
Cylinders:	2, 10" x 16" bore/stroke
Boiler Pressure:	180 lbs/sq in
Heating Surface:	379.2 sq ft
Grate Area:	7.7 sq ft
Tractive Effort:	7418 lbs
Mean Weight In Working Order:	22 tons 1 cwt
Coal Capacity:	15 cwt
Water Capacity:	800 gallons
Number Built:	1, 1898
Preserved:	No

Index, and date of first publication in RAILWAY MODELLER

08 & 13 0-6-0	96	July 1990
14xx 0-4-2T	4	January 1997
15xx 0-6-0PT	22	April 1985
2251 0-6-0	16	November 1989
25 Bo-Bo	98	March 1995
47xx 2-8-0	18	February 1986
4F 0-6-0 and 7F 0-8-0	29	December 1987
52 'Western' C-C	102	December 1989
55 'Deltic' Co-Co	93	May 1999
56xx 0-6-2T	20	May 1984
81 Bo-Bo	100	December 1991
A1 4-6-2	62	November 1985
B1 4-6-0	60	June 1986
Barry B1 0-6-2T	6	November 1987
'Black 5' 4-6-0	26	December 1998
Bulleid Light 4-6-2, unrebuilt	69	April 1989
Diesel railcars No.19-38	12	August 2000
Fell experimental 4-8-4 diesel	108	August 1991
Great Central Railway 'Director' 4-4-0	46	February 1991
Great Eastern Railway 'Claud Hamilton' 4-4-0	48	August 1989
Great Northern Railway N2 0-6-2T	44	September 1982
Hawker Siddeley *Kestrel*	104	June 1995
Highland Railway 'Jones Goods' 4-6-0	32	May 1986
Ivatt Class 2 2-6-2T	36	July 1995
J39 0-6-0	52	January 1995
K3 2-6-0	58	October 1993
Lancashire & Yorkshire Railway 'Dreadnought' 4-6-0	38	February 1987
'Large Prairie' 2-6-2T	14	August 1993
'Leader' experimental 0-6-6-0T	78	March 1992
Leek & Manifold Kitson 2-6-4T	106	April 1996
London & North Western Railway 'Super D' 0-8-0	34	July 1993
London & South Western Railway Beattie 2-4-0WT	82	September 1985
London & South Western Railway M7 0-4-4T	74	June 1982
London, Brighton & South Coast Railway Class L 4-6-4T	64	November 1993
London, Brighton & South Coast Railway 'Terrier' 0-6-0T	68	December 1981
London, Tilbury & Southend 4-4-2T	40	August 1982
Lynton & Barnstaple Railway *Lyn*	112	April 1994
Manx Northern Railway *Caledonia*	109	May 1995
N Class 2-6-0	80	March 1996
N15x 4-6-0	66	October 1998
North British Railway 4-4-2	54	February 1999
North Eastern Railway Raven Class A2 4-6-2	50	January 1985
Pehrnyn/Festiniog Railway 0-4-0ST	110	April 1993
'Princess Royal' 4-6-2	42	May 1990
'Schools' 4-4-0	76	August 1999
South Eastern & Chatham Railway H Class 0-4-4T	72	January 1989
Standard Class 3 2-6-2T	84	April 1999
Standard Class 4 2-6-4T	86	July 1991
Standard Class 5 4-6-0	90	September 1989
Standard Class 9 2-10-0	88	April 1988
Stanier 2-6-0	40	March 1986
'Star' 4-6-0	9	May 1998
Taff Vale A 0-6-2ST	8	June 1987
V2 2-6-2	56	February 1992

ON THE BACK COVER: V2 *Green Arrow* at Marylebone (PHIL CALEY); D1015 at Old Oak Common (ALAN PIKE); FfR *Linda* at Boston Lodge.